THE KNOCK

WHY MOST BELIEVERS STOP ONE PRAYER AWAY FROM THEIR MIRACLE

APOSTLE DR. IVON L. VALERIE

SAPIENTIAL PUBLISHING | WE PUBLISH THE WISE

THE KNOCK
Why Most Believers Stop One Prayer Away From Their Miracle

Copyright © 2026 by Apostle Dr. Ivon L. Valerie

All rights reserved. No portion of this book may be reproduced, stored in a retrieval system, or transmitted in any form or by any means—electronic, mechanical, photocopy, recording, scanning, or other—except for brief quotations in critical reviews or articles, without the prior written permission of the publisher.

Published by Sapiential Publishing House
https://sapientialpublishing.com

Unless otherwise noted, Scripture quotations are taken from the ESV® Bible (The Holy Bible, English Standard Version®), copyright © 2001 by Crossway, a publishing ministry of Good News Publishers. Used by permission. All rights reserved.
Scripture quotations marked (NIV) are taken from the Holy Bible, New International Version®, NIV®. Copyright © 1973, 1978, 1984, 2011 by Biblica, Inc.™ Used by permission of Zondervan. All rights reserved worldwide. www.zondervan.com. The "NIV" and "New International Version" are trademarks registered in the United States Patent and Trademark Office by Biblica, Inc.™
Scripture quotations marked (NKJV) are taken from the New King James Version®. Copyright © 1982 by Thomas Nelson. Used by permission. All rights reserved.

Some names and identifying details have been changed to protect the privacy of individuals.

ISBN: 979-8-9928490-8-0 (hardcover)
ISBN: 979-8-9928490-7-3 (paperback)
ISBN: 979-8-9928490-6-6 (ebook)

Cover and Interior design by Ivon Valerie

10 9 8 7 6 5 4 3 2 1 0

First Edition

Contents

DEDICATION	V
ACKNOWLEDGEMENTS	VII
AUTHOR'S NOTE	XI
The Door I Almost Walked Away From	
HOW TO USE THIS BOOK	XV
THE PRAYER THAT CHANGED EVERYTHING	1
Introduction	
1. THE ANATOMY OF UNANSWERED PRAYER	9
2. THE FIRST DIMENSION	33
Asking and the Death of Self-sufficiency	
3. THE SECOND DIMENSION	57
Seeking: When Faith Gets Feet	
4. THE GEOGRAPHY OF BREAKTHROUGH	77
Positioning Yourself Where Miracles Happen	
5. THE WILDERNESS OF SEEKING	97
When You're Doing Everything Right But Seeing No Results	
6. THE THIRD DIMENSION	119
Knocking and the Crisis of Proximity	

7. THE SOUND OF FOOTSTEPS — 135
Recognizing When Breakthrough is Imminent

8. WHEN THE DOOR OPENS — 149
Stewarding the Blessing You Fought For

9. THE EVERYONE PROMISE — 165
Why This Works for Ordinary Believers

10. THE FATHER'S HEART — 179
Understanding Who's on the Other Side of the Door

11. THE LIFE OF THE KNOCKER — 193
Becoming A Person of Relentless Faith

APPENDIX A — 207
Thirty-One Days of Knocking

APPENDIX B — 231
The Knocker's Creed

APPENDIX C — 235
Testimony Collection Template

STUDY GUIDE — 239

SCRIPTURE INDEX — 255

NOTES — 263

ABOUT THE AUTHOR — 283

DEDICATION

To my wife Jeanetta, my partner in every knock, every wilderness, every breakthrough. This book exists because you never let me give up, even when I wanted to. Your faith lifted me when mine was at its lowest. I love you.

To our daughters, I hope you always remember that breakthrough belongs to you, and that the God we serve always keeps His promises to those who keep asking, seeking, and knocking.

To Faith & Works Ministries, your breakthroughs gave me the confidence to share with others that this truly works.

And to every believer who has ever faced a closed door, wondering if God heard your prayers, if your faith was enough, or if breakthrough would ever come; this book is for you. Keep knocking. The door will open soon.

ACKNOWLEDGEMENTS

This book was born in a wilderness I didn't ask for and couldn't escape. But I didn't walk through it alone, and the words on these pages exist because certain people refused to let me quit knocking.

To my wife: You stood with me when the door stayed closed. When I wanted to walk away, you reminded me who God is. Your faith held steady when mine wavered. You didn't just believe in this message; you lived it beside me, often carrying more than your share while I wrestled with God. This book exists because you refused to let me give up on God. All we built, every breakthrough, started with your unwavering belief that the door would open. It did. Thank you for knocking with me.

To my daughters: You've watched your parents live as knockers, and I pray that shapes how you see closed doors for the rest of your lives. You've seen us wait, press, and believe when nothing seemed to be moving. You've celebrated breakthroughs with us and learned that delay isn't the same as denial. May you grow up knowing that breakthrough is your inheritance, that God hears every prayer, and that the door always opens for those who refuse to quit knocking. This is your legacy.

To the Faith & Works Ministries congregation: You knocked when your own doors stayed closed. You shared your breakthroughs, your setbacks, your moments of doubt, and your stories of sudden opening. There are testimonies in this book that exist because you believed God's Word enough to act on it. You are living proof that this works, that breakthrough isn't reserved for special believers, and that everyone who knocks really does see the door open. Thank you for trusting a man who is still learning to knock himself.

To Pastor Marcus J. Raymond: My Bible School friend, my brother in the wilderness. Your book "THE WILDERNESS SEASON" met me in a moment when I needed understanding for what I was experiencing. Our conversations about wilderness theology, the purposes of delay, and what God does in the dark shaped my understanding of the space between prayer and breakthrough. Some of the insights in Chapter 5 came directly from our discussions. You helped me see that the wilderness wasn't where I got lost but where God was doing something I couldn't yet see. Like a lone traveler in a vast desert, navigating the terrain taught me that God's light guides even when shadows threaten to obscure. Through your guidance, you modeled a leadership principle that every aspiring mentor can follow: supporting others by sharing wisdom and walking the journey ahead of them. Thanks for helping me edit this massive undertaking. Your insights and knowledge remain pillars for this book. Thank you for walking this road ahead of me and leaving breadcrumbs.

To my mentors and my spiritual father: You saw potential in me before I saw it in myself. You spoke life when I felt dead. You corrected me when I needed it and championed me when I doubted. The theology in these pages was tested in your presence, sharpened by your wisdom, and released with your blessing. Thank you for modeling what it looks like to knock for a lifetime and never lose faith that God is good.

To those who stood by us during the COVID wilderness: When the world shut down, and our finances were shaken, you didn't just pray for us. You provided. When the help we expected didn't materialize, and we wondered how we'd survive, you showed up. Some of you will never know how your provision, your encouragement, your refusal to let us fall, sustained us in months when we couldn't see a way forward. God used you to keep us knocking when everything in us wanted to quit. We made it to breakthrough because you wouldn't let us stop.

To the larger organization that partnered with us: You believed in the vision God gave us when it was still just a seed. Your support accelerated what God was building through Faith & Works Ministries. Thank you for seeing what this could become and investing in the breakthrough that was still on the other side of the door.

To the knockers: Every believer standing at a closed door right now, wondering if God hears, questioning if breakthrough is really for you, fighting the urge to walk away one prayer before your miracle. This book is for you. I wrote it because I almost quit knocking right before my door opened, and I don't want you to make that mistake. The principles here aren't theory. They're tested. They work. And if they worked for me, I am confident they can work for you. Remember that even Jesus experienced moments of waiting, as when He spent forty days in the wilderness and waited for the right time to fulfill His purpose. These moments were powerful parts of the greater redemption narrative, reminding us that every delay has a divine purpose. Keep knocking and trust that each step is intertwined with God's story, where every closed door is a chapter in the redemption God is weaving. When the time is right, the door will open. "Every delay serves a divine purpose." Let this be your daily declaration, a reminder that perseverance in faith is always met with a response.

Finally, to my Lord and King: The One who taught us to ask, seek, and knock in the first place. Thank You for not letting me walk away. Thank You for answering a dangerous prayer with patient revelation. Thank You for proving that Your Word is true, that breakthrough is real, and that You really do open doors for everyone who keeps knocking. This message was Yours before it was mine. I'm just grateful You trusted me to carry it.

AUTHOR'S NOTE

The Door I Almost Walked Away From

I nearly gave up knocking eighteen months before the door finally opened.

The wilderness began quietly, like it often does. I faced questions I couldn't answer and prayers that seemed to vanish into silence. I noticed a growing gap between what I read in Scripture and what I saw in believers' lives. The Bible promised breakthroughs, but reality brought delays. In that space, my faith began to crack.

For over eighteen months, I struggled with God. It wasn't a gentle or polite struggle, but the kind where you hold on until you get an answer, even if it leaves you changed. As a pastor who preached about faith and breakthrough, I couldn't align what I taught with what I lived. People prayed, but God didn't seem to answer; or if He did, it didn't look like the promises we believed in.

One question kept bothering me: If Matthew 7:7-8 is true, if everyone who asks receives, everyone who seeks finds, and everyone who knocks sees the door open, why are so many of us left standing at closed doors, feeling worn out and discouraged?

So I prayed a bold prayer, the kind you only pray if you're serious, because it risks everything. I asked God to prove His Word was true by showing me how to live it, or I would stop believing. Looking back, I know this was wrong. You can't give God ultimatums. But it was honest, and I've found God responds more to my real desperation than to perfect words.

Then COVID-19 arrived.

I was supposed to preach at a conference in Trinidad. I flew out in early 2020, and while I was there, the world shut down. I barely made it back to Sint Maarten before the borders closed, and suddenly, everything changed. Churches closed, and travel stopped. For someone who preached across the region, this was more than inconvenient; it was devastating. My savings dwindled, relationships became strained, and the help I expected never came. The difficult season I was already in became even harder.

Each morning, I faced the same closed door. Every night, I wondered if God was listening. The silence felt overwhelming, and the loneliness was hard to bear. I was close to giving up on everything I had believed since I was young.

But in that dark time, something changed. God began to answer, not with a sudden breakthrough, but by revealing things to me step by step. Matthew 7:7-8 took on new meaning. I realized that asking, seeking, and knocking aren't just different words for the same thing. They are stages of pursuit, each requiring a different kind of faith.

The insights came gradually, like the slow arrival of morning after a long night. I wrote down everything God was teaching me: why some prayers go unanswered, how we need to let go of self-reliance before we can truly ask, how seeking means putting faith into action, and how breakthroughs can happen in unexpected places. I learned about the reasons for difficult seasons, the struggle of being close to a breakthrough but not seeing it yet, how to notice when change is near, and what to do when the door finally opens.

After eighteen months in the dark, I received divine revelation I couldn't have gained any other way.

In 2021, during the global pandemic, my wife and I started Faith & Works Ministries. We did this not in spite of the hard times, but because of them. Suddenly, doors that had been closed for a year and a half began to open quickly. New opportunities came, our needs were met, and relationships came together. The breakthrough I had been waiting for finally arrived.

But what still troubles me is that I almost gave up just a month, or maybe even two weeks, before it happened. I was that close to quitting, thinking God's Word worked for others but not for me, and nearly walked away from a door that was about to open.

How many believers do the same? How many stop knocking in the seventeenth month of an eighteen-month wilderness? How many walk away from doors that were about to open? How many stop praying just before the breakthrough they've been seeking for years finally comes?

That's why I wrote this book. It's not because I have all the answers, but because I nearly made the biggest mistake of my life, and I don't want you to do the same. What God taught me during that hard time wasn't just for me. It's for every believer standing at a closed door, wondering if God hears them and if breakthroughs are really for everyone or just for a few special people.

This message is for those who are tired. For those who have been knocking so long their hands ache. For those who have prayed until they had no words left. For those who are one bad day away from giving up on everything they've believed. For those standing at doors that should have opened long ago, wondering what they might be doing wrong.

You're not doing anything wrong. You just haven't finished knocking yet.

The principles in this book have been tested. I tried them myself before sharing them with anyone. The people at Faith & Works Ministries lived them too, and I've seen doors open for those who didn't give up. This isn't just theory or empty motivation. It's a practical guide for moving from unanswered prayers to breakthroughs, from closed doors to new opportunities, and from hard times to God's promises.

But before you start reading the first chapter, I want you to know something. This book will challenge you. It will make you think about your beliefs on prayer, God's character, and what you expect from Him. It will encourage you to act when you'd rather wait, and it will ask you to keep knocking even when you feel like quitting. At some point, maybe in the middle when things get tough, you might want to stop reading and give up.

Don't give up. The door will open, but only if you keep knocking.

What you're holding is the message God gave me after I came through the hardest season of my life. It's the answer to the bold prayer I prayed eighteen months before my breakthrough. It's proof that God's Word is true, that breakthroughs are real, and that the door really does open for anyone who doesn't give up.

I'm still knocking. There are always new doors, new breakthroughs, and new challenges that need the same determination. The journey never really ends, because the Christian life is about always seeking, always pressing forward, and always believing that God's promises are worth holding onto. But now I know how to keep knocking, what to do when the door stays closed, and how to get through hard times without losing faith. I am sure now that the door will open.

Let me show you how.

Your brother in both hard times and breakthroughs,
The Knocker

HOW TO USE THIS BOOK

This book offers more than just information. It aims to help you make real changes. How much you benefit depends on how you use it. You might read it quickly and feel inspired, or take your time and discover real breakthroughs. The decision is up to you.

For Individual Reading

If you're reading this on your own and treating it as a personal journey, here are some ways to get the most out of it. Keep your Bible close whenever you read this book. Use the Notes section at the back to write down your thoughts, prayers, and track your breakthroughs as you go through each chapter. You'll need both. The Bible shows that every principle here comes from Scripture, so you can see these are God's promises, not just my ideas. The journal helps you notice what God is doing, what you're learning, and how things are changing as you move through asking, seeking, and knocking.

Take your time with each chapter. Every chapter builds on the one before it, so if you skip ahead or skim, you might miss something important for what comes next. Try to spend at least a day with each chapter before moving on. Give yourself time to think, work through anything that challenges you, and try out the action steps. Unhurried reading nurtures lasting transformation by allowing habits in Christ to form deeply and meaningfully. Remember, this is not about finishing fast. The goal is to finish changed, not just to finish quickly. If you missed a day? Simply return and continue your journey. Grace awaits everyone, including you.

At the end of Chapter 2, you'll be asked to write down three specific things you're asking God for. Make sure to do this. Write them in the Notes section at the back of the book and add the date. These three requests will help you put what you learn into practice. As you go through the chapters, you'll see how your approach to these requests changes from asking to seeking to knocking. Pay attention to when things get harder, when you feel unexpected peace, or when you notice small changes. Write all of it down.

Use the Testimony Collection Template in Appendix C to record your breakthroughs as they happen. Don't skip this step. When your breakthrough comes, make sure to write down the story while it's still fresh. Note what you prayed for, how long you kept going, what challenges you faced, how God responded, and what you learned. Your breakthrough is not just for you. It can encourage someone else who is in the same place you are now, wondering if things will ever change.

For Small Group Study

If you're reading this book with a group, you're experiencing it as intended. This gathering is about creating impactful change in our lives, a chance to connect deeply and support one another in our journeys. Breakthroughs often happen in community, and having people around you who won't let you give up is one of the best supports you can have on this journey.

Plan to study one chapter each week for eleven weeks. This pace lets everyone read, think, and try things out before meeting to talk. Use the Study Guide questions at the back of the book to guide your discussions. These questions help you move from noticing what's in the chapter to understanding it, to applying it. To mark the transition from everyday life to study time, consider starting each session with a simple rule. This could be a reflective question about a personal experience that ties into the week's chapter, or a shared minute of silence to focus attention. Don't just discuss what the chapter said, talk about how it's changing your beliefs and actions.

Share stories of breakthroughs as they happen. When someone in your group experiences a new opportunity, celebrate together. Let their success encourage those who are still waiting. If someone is struggling or feels like giving up, help them stay committed. That's what community is for; we support each other when our faith feels weak.

I remember a time when I faced a similar crossroads. I was struggling with a project that seemed too daunting. I was on the verge of giving up. But sharing my doubts with the group led to an outpouring of support. Their encouragement gave me the strength to push through, and eventually, the project succeeded beyond my expectations. My experience taught me that vulnerability is not a weakness, but a bridge to deeper connections and resilience.

Make sure your group is a safe place to talk about struggles. Some chapters may reveal where people have given up, stopped asking because they doubt God will answer, or settled for closed doors instead of pushing forward. If your group isn't honest about these things, you'll miss the change this book aims to bring. Let people say when they're tired or have doubts. Then remind them why they started and why they shouldn't give up now. 'Honesty in the group is the foundation for lasting change.'

For Devotional Journey

Once you've finished the book, try using the 31-Day Devotional in Appendix A to make these principles part of your daily routine. This devotional guides you through a month, helping you remember what you learned and encouraging you to live out the knocker lifestyle. Each day, you'll find a Scripture, a reflection that gives a fresh look at the book's ideas, and a prayer to help you talk to God about the day's topic.

You can go through this devotional more than once, focusing on a new breakthrough each time. The principles stay the same, but how you use them will change based on your current situation. Some people complete it once and return to it every few months when they want to boost their determination. Others make it their main devotional routine, using it again and again as they work toward new goals.

Key Recommendations

Begin by choosing one breakthrough you want to pursue. Don't try to tackle everything at once. Start by defining your desired breakthrough as clearly and specifically as possible. What exactly do you want to change? Write down a single, concrete sentence that captures your goal. As you do this, make sure to listen to God's voice; it will guide you. His voice will bring both clarity and commitment, serving as a bridge between your inner calling and outward actions. Focus on what matters most to you right now, the thing that's been on your mind or in your prayers for a long time. Let that be your main focus as you read this book. Apply what you learn to that area first.

Don't feel like you have to do everything right away. Each chapter will offer steps to take, ideas to try, and ways to change how you think and pray. If you try to do it all at once, it can feel overwhelming, and you might give up. Focus on building one habit at a time. Learn to ask before you start seeking, and get used to seeking before you start knocking. Taking things in order is important.

Focus on building healthy routines instead of strict rules. The aim isn't to force yourself into a tough schedule, but to find a way of living that helps you keep going after God's promises without getting exhausted. Consider these routines as grace-filled practices, invitations to partner with grace rather than burdens of self-pressure. Train wisely instead of trying harder. Some days you might pray for a long time, and other days you might only manage a quick prayer. Both are important. What matters is that you keep going.

Look for or build a community of knockers, people who are also seeking breakthroughs. If you don't have friends who believe in this and are working toward it too, try to find them. Join a small group or connect with others online. Be around people who will encourage you to keep going, even when things take longer than you hoped. You don't have to do this by yourself.

Keep track of your progress and celebrate small victories. If you notice things getting harder, make a note of it. When you feel unexpected peace, write it down. Notice and appreciate even small changes. Breakthroughs usually happen step by step, not all at once, and if you're not watching, you might miss the signs that things are about to change. To aid in this process, consider reflective journaling with prompts such as, 'Where did I sense hope today?' These simple, daily questions can train your attention on the incremental work required to achieve breakthroughs. By doing this, you'll become more attuned to subtle shifts.

What to Expect

The first chapters will make you think differently about prayer. If you've thought God is reluctant to give, makes random decisions, or is strict with His requirements, you'll be asked to reconsider. Let yourself do that. What you believe about God shapes how persistent you are. If your view is off, you might give up before you see results.

The middle chapters will encourage you to act. Asking matters, but it's only the start. Faith needs to be put into practice. You'll be encouraged to seek wisdom, pursue new opportunities, and make changes in your life, relationships, and faith. Many people stop here; they pray but don't take steps. If you want real change, you need to move forward.

The last chapters will help you build endurance for the long journey. Some doors open fast, but others take months or even years of steady effort. It's important to consider what might be lost if you quit too soon. Imagine the missed opportunities, dreams unfulfilled, or personal growth that could have been achieved. Perhaps a moment of giving up is all that separates you from a significant breakthrough. You'll learn how to notice signs that your breakthrough is close, how to keep your faith strong during tough times, and how to keep going when you feel like giving up. This is where knockers are built.

By the end of this book, you'll notice a change in yourself. It's not just about learning new things, though you might. It's about how using these ideas changes your prayers, your actions, your mindset, and your view of God. Some breakthroughs will happen as you read. You might reach Chapter 7 and see your answer come. Others will take more time and effort after you finish. Both are normal and part of the process.

Before concluding the book, take a moment to reflect on what has already begun to change in your life. Ask yourself, what subtle transformations have I experienced in my thinking or behaviors? How has my understanding of prayer and persistence shifted? What new perspectives am I now considering about my journey and relationship with God? Reflecting on these questions can deepen your awareness of the growth already unfolding, priming you to sustain these changes as you move forward.

A Warning

This book isn't here just to motivate you. It's not meant to make you feel better about unanswered prayer. Instead, it calls for action. You'll need to look at your beliefs, face your doubts, and keep knocking even when you want to give up. Some chapters might challenge you. That's okay. Conviction is God's way of showing you where you've accepted less than what He promised. Consider the story of the persistent widow in Luke 18:1-8. She kept asking a judge who didn't fear God or care about people for justice, yet her persistence paid off. This narrative is a reminder of God's value for unwavering faith, encouraging us to keep knocking until the door opens.

You might feel like giving up. Perhaps by Chapter 5, you'll recognize that you are in a tough season that's lasting longer than you'd anticipated. In Chapter 6, knocking might feel like a battle, and you might be exhausted from trying. By Chapter 7, you could see signs that a breakthrough is close, but the door still isn't open. During these moments, it's natural to feel fear or even a sense of shame when prayers seem unanswered. Acknowledge those feelings; they are a part of the journey. Remember why you started reading this book. Think about what you're hoping for. And know that everyone who keeps knocking sees the door open. That includes you.

The door will open if you keep knocking. But consider the cost of turning away now: the lingering regret of never knowing what could have been if you had just persisted a little longer. This moment may be your call to keep the momentum, for the alternative is surrendering to what-ifs and letting resistance win over your aspirations.

Before we begin, let's focus on a simple first step to embark on this journey. Take a moment today to write down one doubt that has been on your mind. Reflect on it, and then spend five minutes praying about that specific concern. This small action marks the beginning of your path to knocking on the door of promise.

Let's get started.

THE PRAYER THAT CHANGED EVERYTHING

Introduction

TEN YEARS AGO, I found myself in a dark season, praying and asking God to show me He was real. Have you ever felt like the promises of faith are out of reach, with prayers left unanswered and hopes fading? Many believers feel this way when their spiritual lives don't match their hopes for an abundant life. I went through something similar over ten years ago. It wasn't a life-threatening problem, although at times it felt like it was. It wasn't a financial or marital issue, though my wife became increasingly concerned about how it affected me over time. The real culprit was a spiritual issue, the kind that shakes your foundation and leaves you with questions you can't answer.

I've been a Christian most of my life. I read the Bible, served in church, watched sermons, read Christian books, and prayed what I thought were good prayers. But one question kept coming back: If the Bible is true, why don't we live like it? Why don't we see the blessings it promises?

I want to be clear: I never doubted that God is real or that Jesus is who He says He is. I truly believed that. What bothered me was the gap between what the Bible promises and what I saw in the lives of faithful Christians. These were people who loved God, served, prayed, fasted, and gave generously. Yet many struggled with money, some were sick and didn't get better, and others felt stuck, even though the Bible talks about an abundant life. This struggle isn't new. The psalmists wrote about it, and early Christians faced hardship despite their faith. Realizing this is a common struggle helped me see I wasn't alone in my questions.

The more I noticed this gap, the more it bothered me. I'd read verses like Matthew 7:7, where Jesus says, "Ask, and it will be given to you; seek, and you will find; knock, and it will be opened to you," but then I'd see the same prayer requests on church prayer lists for months or even years. I'd read about faith in Hebrews 11, but then talk to believers who had prayed for years without answers. I'd preach about God's promises, then go home and wonder if I was offering something I hadn't experienced myself. Have you ever felt this way? Have you ever wondered why there's a gap between what the Bible promises and what you see in real life? This struggle is more common than we admit, and it's worth thinking about. Many people long for an abundant life with health, financial stability, and purpose, but still feel these blessings are out of reach. These shared struggles and unanswered prayers push us to look deeper.

This wasn't just a passing doubt; it was a real crisis. Like many crises, it took me to a place I'm not proud of. I did something that still makes me uncomfortable to recall. I put a fleece before God, but not like Gideon asking for confirmation. My heart cried out in a way that felt like the psalms, full of desperation and honesty. Alone in my prayer closet, I poured out my heart and said something like: "God, if Your Word is true, then prove it to me. Show me how to access this life You promised. Show me how to live in the reality of what Scripture says, not just the theory of it. Because if this isn't real, if Christianity is just a system that makes us feel better while we trudge through mediocre lives, then I'm not sure I can keep believing." This cry wasn't just an ultimatum; it was a plea for clarity and truth.

Even as I prayed, I knew I was taking a risk. You don't give ultimatums to God or put Him on trial. But I was frustrated and tired of pretending everything was fine. I needed to know if this was real. I needed to know if it was possible to actually live in what God promised, or if we were just reading words meant for another time and people. But the Bible shows us that God is patient with honest questions. Think of Job, who questioned God during his suffering and was still called faithful. The prophet Habakkuk also asked God hard questions, looking for understanding in tough times. These stories show that asking bold questions and seeking clarity are part of a faithful life.

What happened next is the reason I wrote this book. In what felt like silence, I experienced a breakthrough; one answered prayer that strengthened my faith and set me on a new path. My wife and I were able to buy our first home. It might seem small, but it happened while we were still recovering from the COVID-19 pandemic and dealing with health and money worries. Our finances looked bleak, and for years, buying a home seemed impossible. Our second child was only a year old. But God came through, and what we couldn't do for more than ten years happened during one of the hardest times. Seeing God's promise in action helped me through the months of searching and doubt that followed.

I'm still amazed that God didn't punish me for my attitude, even though He could have. He didn't scold me for my lack of faith, even if it displeased Him. Instead, He surprised me. He took me seriously and led me through a process that answered my question in ways I never expected.

But the answer didn't come right away. What followed was eighteen months that felt like the longest wilderness of my life. It wasn't just time passing; it felt like being in a desert where each day dragged on. As the months went by, the silence felt endless and heavy. By Month 3, my resolve had faded, and I started questioning everything I believed. By Month 6, I was deep in doubt, wondering if God was punishing me for being so bold. By Month 9, I worried I had gone too far by doubting Him. Yet by Month 12, in the middle of this silence, a deeper truth was forming; a lesson on persistence and working with God that would shape what was ahead. It was a process of moving from just asking to seeking and knocking with persistence, a journey that changed how I approach prayer and faith.

Looking back, I can see that God was answering my prayer the whole time. He just did it in the way that mattered most. He didn't give me a formula or a shortcut. Instead, He taught me something deeper. The problem wasn't that God didn't want to keep His promises. The problem was that many of us, myself included, approached prayer and faith in a way that kept us from real breakthroughs.

Most believers know how to ask, but many don't know how to seek, and even fewer keep knocking until the door opens. We've learned to pray, but not always to pursue what we've prayed for. In the gap between praying and taking action, many believers get stuck; not because God is holding back, but because we often give up too soon. This struggle can be summed up as 'Breakthroughs stall when prayer stops at asking.' We need to ask, seek, and knock. Each step is an action we must take with purpose and persistence if we want to see God's promises fulfilled in our lives.

One small moment made this shift clear to me. I remember when a long-overdue bill was finally paid. Without realizing it, I had used the principle of asking, seeking, and knocking. I called the service provider to look for options, asked for help, and kept praying until things worked out. This simple, everyday win reminded me of the deeper lessons God was teaching me. It wasn't just about the bill; it was about seeing God's promises come to life in quiet, faithful actions.

The breakthrough came in a way I didn't expect. After eighteen months in what felt like darkness, God started to show me new things. It wasn't one big moment, but a slow understanding that grew over time. He showed me patterns in Scripture I hadn't noticed before. I saw stories of people who got what they prayed for, and they all had something in common. They didn't just ask; they also sought. They didn't just knock once; they kept knocking until the door opened.

Then God brought me to Matthew 7:7-8, a passage I had known since I was a child but never really understood. "Ask, and it will be given to you; seek, and you will find; knock, and it will be opened to you. For everyone who asks receives, and the one who seeks finds, and to the one who knocks it will be opened." As I thought about these words, I began to see how deep they really are.

I used to think those were just three ways of saying the same thing, as if Jesus was repeating Himself for emphasis. But as I spent more time with those verses, my understanding changed. I saw that Jesus was showing us a progression, a sequence that grows in intensity and commitment with each step.

Asking is the first step. It means speaking up and admitting you need something you don't have. It's letting go of trying to do everything yourself and learning to depend on God. Most of us understand this part. We've been asking for things our whole Christian lives.

But seeking is different. Seeking is when prayer leads to action. It's when you leave your prayer closet and start actively going after what you're praying for. It's when you stop only talking to God about your need and start working with Him toward your breakthrough. Seeking means moving, searching, and being intentional. It's faith in action, not just faith in your mind.

Is there an area in your life where you've been waiting for change but haven't taken action? Where can you put your faith into action and take the next step? Think of one prayer request that has lingered, and decide how you can start moving forward with it today. To help you take this step, write down a specific action you will take in the next 48 hours. Share this commitment with a friend or family member who can help keep you accountable. These small, purposeful actions can build momentum and help create a sense of community as you work toward seeing God's promises in your life.

Then comes knocking. Knocking is the last step, and it's often where people give up. It means you're at the door of your answer, but it hasn't opened yet. You're close enough to sense something on the other side, but the door is still closed. Jesus uses strong language here. The Greek word for knock, krouo, means to strike or pound with urgency. It's not a gentle tap; it's persistent, expectant, and determined until you get a response. This persistence shapes our character, building patience and resilience, much as Paul describes in Romans 5:3-4: suffering produces perseverance; perseverance, character; and character, hope. There were times when the weight of unanswered prayers felt heavy, and I thought, 'I should quit right here.' But through knocking, we experience an inner change, learning to trust the process and developing strength that lasts beyond the answer. This journey not only brings us closer to what we want but also helps us grow spiritually, giving us a deeper reason for our persistence.

As God showed me these things over those eighteen months, I realized why so many prayers seemed unanswered. We stopped asking. We prayed passive prayers but expected active results. We waited for God to act, even while He waited for us to join in. When the breakthrough didn't come right away, we thought God wasn't listening or willing. But really, we just stopped too soon.

Everything changed for me when I realized Jesus doesn't say "if" you ask, seek, and knock. He says "everyone" who does these things. That means everyone, not just the super spiritual, the gifted, or the mature. This isn't just for a few people. It's for anyone willing to go through the process.

But here's the key, and it's why many believers feel stuck: you have to do all three. Asking alone isn't enough. Seeking without asking misses the starting point. Knocking without first asking and seeking means you're at the wrong door. But when you do all three: ask clearly, seek with purpose, and knock with persistence,

Jesus promises you will receive, you will find, and the door will open. To make this model easy to remember, I call it the ASK Pathway. By following the ASK Pathway, we bring together Asking, Seeking, and Knocking into a practical way of living out our faith.

It's not just a possibility. It's a sure thing, though it happens in God's timing.

When God brought me through those eighteen months and gave me this understanding, everything changed. It wasn't just my prayer life; it was my whole approach to faith. I stopped waiting for blessings to fall into my lap and started working with God for breakthroughs. I began using asking, seeking, and knocking in every area where I felt stuck. And doors started to open.

But the biggest change wasn't just for me. God brought something out of that season that reached beyond my own life. In 2021, my wife and I started Faith & Works Ministries in Sint Maarten. The name reflects what God showed me during that time: faith without works is dead, prayer without action is powerless, and asking without seeking and knocking leaves you stuck at the start of God's promises. We realized what we learned could help others, so we invite you to join us on this journey and become part of a shared mission. Whether it's through our virtual gatherings, prayer challenges, or sharing your stories in our community, we can build something together. This isn't just about us; it's about you and the power of faith and action. By joining the Faith & Works family, you can see the ASK Pathway at work in your own life and help make a bigger impact.

Our ministry helps believers learn how to access what God has already given, not through gimmicks or formulas, but by following the biblical pattern Jesus taught: ask, seek, knock, and keep going until the door opens.

I'm from Dominica, the Nature Isle of the Caribbean, and now my wife and I live in Sint Maarten. We have two daughters who watch us live this out every day. They see us asking God for specific things, seeking with purpose, and keep on knocking until breakthroughs come. They see that it works, not because we're special, but because God's Word is true and His promises hold when we follow His way.

This book is the result of a journey. It's the answer to the desperate prayer I prayed ten years ago. It's the insight that kept me from leaving my faith. And it's a framework that has changed not just my life, but the lives of many others who were stuck, praying prayers that felt unheard, and wondering if the Christian life was supposed to be so hard.

Before we go on, I want you to know this book isn't about positive thinking or self-help with a Christian label. It's about the real, biblical foundation of answered prayer, based on our reliance on God's grace and the active role of the Holy Spirit in our lives. While positive thinking depends only on human effort, the approach here is rooted in God's power and guidance, ensuring that He initiates and fulfills His promises. It's about seeing that God is ready to respond, but many of us come to Him in ways that keep us from receiving what He's already offered.

If you're frustrated with your prayer life, wondering if God has forgotten you, or seeing others move forward while you feel left behind, you're in the right place. If you've thought about giving up on your faith because the promises of the Bible don't seem to match your reality, you are definitely in the right place.

In the next eleven chapters, I'll show you what can change everything. You'll find out why your prayers may have stalled and what you can do about it. You'll learn the difference between asking, seeking, and knocking, and see where you might have stopped. You'll read Bible stories of ordinary people who saw impossible doors open, and you'll get practical steps you can use right away to move forward to where God has been waiting for you. As you start applying these principles, expect to see changes in your faith and life within the first 30 days. Are you ready to try the ASK Pathway this week and see the transformation it brings to your spiritual journey?

Chapter One

THE ANATOMY OF UNANSWERED PRAYER

It was a quiet evening, and the silence felt almost real enough to touch. I sat in the small church where I had served for years, surrounded by memories of past prayers. Each hope seemed to echo off the walls. I looked at the altar and remembered all the times I had knelt there, sharing my fears and dreams with God, hoping for a sign or comfort. But tonight, like many other nights, there was only silence. As the quiet filled the space between my prayers and heaven, I felt a familiar pain. That unique pain in praying and hearing nothing back. It's not like physical pain, which is obvious, or relational pain, which usually comes with some explanation. The pain of unanswered prayer is harder because it happens in silence. You pour out your heart, share your deepest needs, wait with hope, and then nothing. Just silence.

As I sat in the church chair and heard its legs creak, I pictured a single candle flickering in a dark room, its small light both weak and steady. That image reminded me of my own faith, struggling with questions that kept coming. Is there something in my life stopping my breakthrough? By breakthrough, I mean seeing my prayers answered clearly. Do I lack faith? Did I pray the wrong way? Should I have fasted longer or quoted more Scripture? Was I too specific, or not specific enough? Did God hear me? Does He care? Am I doing something wrong? Before long, it wasn't just about an unmet need. It became a crisis of faith. After years of silence, I realized something important: unanswered prayers don't mean God is absent. Instead, they invite us to trust Him more deeply and to grow while we wait.

If you've ever felt this way, you're not alone. And you're not wrong for feeling it. The frustration, confusion, or even anger you feel toward God when prayers seem to go unanswered isn't a sign of weak faith. It shows your faith is real and being tested. After all, you can't be disappointed in someone you never expected to help. Your disappointment means you believed God could and would answer. This is similar to what Habakkuk expressed when he questioned God while remaining committed, and to the Psalms, which show that faith and deep questions can coexist. The pain comes from the gap between what you hoped for and what you're experiencing. Even in these doubts, there's an invitation to trust God more deeply.

But unanswered prayer is more complicated than it seems. Often, when we say a prayer is unanswered, we simply mean it hasn't met our expectations for timing or outcome. However, this doesn't mean God isn't responding. A better way to approach this is to view 'unanswered' prayer as 'unrecognized' response. Most prayers receive answers that go unnoticed, happen on timelines we don't anticipate, or come in forms we're not expecting.

This difference matters because it changes how we think about prayer. Instead of asking, "Why isn't God answering me?" try asking, "How is God responding, and am I able to see it?" This shift may seem small, but it helps you move from feeling powerless to becoming an active part of God's process. Ask yourself if you've let a victim mindset shape your story. Think about how changing your perspective could change your prayers.

Let's start by facing a hard truth. There are prayers you have prayed with complete sincerity, pure motives, and strong faith that still haven't been answered the way you hoped. You've done everything you know to do: prayed with devotion, read the Scriptures, fasted, given your resources, and tried to remove any known sin from your life. Yet, despite all these efforts, nothing has changed. The diagnosis is still the same. The bank account is still empty. The relationship is still broken. The door is still closed.

If we're honest, this is where most Christian teaching falls short. When breakthroughs don't come quickly, we often hear one of two things from well-meaning believers. Either we're told we don't have enough faith, which adds shame to our pain. Or we're told that God's ways are mysterious and we just need to trust Him, which can feel like our pain is being dismissed. Neither response truly helps. One makes us feel broken. The other makes God seem random. Both leave us stuck, just with more guilt or confusion.

I remember a time when I thought I had figured out the formula for a breakthrough. I did everything I thought was needed: prayed hard, fasted, studied scripture, and stayed hopeful. But the answer didn't come, and I ended up feeling doubtful and frustrated. Through this, I learned how important it is to be honest and admit that sometimes we just don't understand, and it's okay to feel confused. Being honest helped me build a deeper relationship with God, one based on real trust, not just performance.

There were times when I questioned my own motives in prayer. One specific time was when I had been praying hard for a certain outcome, convinced it was what God wanted for me, but I was met with silence. During that time, I realized my motive was more about proving something to myself and others than truly seeking God's will. Facing this truth wasn't easy, but it helped me lower my guard and better understand what God was doing in my life. Being this honest can break down the walls we build around our pain and help us connect with God more openly.

It's only after this lesson that I realized there's another option. Maybe our prayers haven't been answered yet because there's a process to breakthroughs that many of us never learned. What if prayer isn't just a one-time request, but something we keep on doing, like tending to a garden? Just as a garden needs regular care, from planting the seeds to watering and watching them grow. In the same way, prayer needs ongoing effort and patience. The time between asking and receiving is meant for more than just waiting; it's about staying engaged, like watching an empty plot slowly become a thriving garden. As your faith and dedication to prayer develop, imagine this garden at different stages of growth; a reminder of how perseverance and faith can transform the seeds of your prayers into full, blossoming answers.

That's the revelation that changed how I see prayer, and it's what we'll explore throughout this book. But before we get to the solution, we need to understand the problem more deeply. The anatomy of unanswered prayer is complex, and if we misdiagnose the issue, we'll keep applying the wrong remedies. First, let's sharpen our tools for understanding. This will help us look more closely and better understand what's happening.

Let's take a closer look at the question of unanswered prayer and see what's really happening. Some of what we're about to explore might be uncomfortable. It could challenge beliefs you've held for years. It might even make you upset at first. But if you stick with me through the discomfort, you'll gain a clearer understanding of prayer that can change everything.

The first thing we need to understand is that not all prayers are created equal. That may sound wrong when you first hear it because we've been taught that God hears every prayer, and that's true. God does hear every prayer. But hearing a prayer and granting a request are two different things. God hears the prayer of the atheist cursing His name, but that doesn't mean He will give that person what they ask for. God hears the prayer of the believer asking for something that would ultimately harm them, but His love leads Him to withhold it.

So when we talk about prayers that seem unanswered, we have to start by asking an important question: What kind of prayer are we dealing with? Scripture reveals that some prayers are answered right away, others require ongoing effort, and some others receive a response different from what was requested.

Consider what James writes in his letter: "You do not have because you do not ask. You ask and do not receive because you ask with wrong motives, so that you may spend it on your pleasures." Here, James points out two reasons prayers aren't answered. The first is simple: we don't ask. We worry, complain, and talk about the problem with everyone except God, but we never actually bring it to Him in prayer. We'll talk more about this in the next chapter when we discuss the posture of asking. The second reason is more challenging: we ask, but with the wrong motives.

Before you get defensive and insist your motives are pure, let's look a little deeper. Motives can be tricky. What we think is a pure request often has layers we haven't noticed. You might be praying for financial breakthroughs, which seems reasonable. But if you look closer, are you asking for provision so you can honor God and help others? Or are you hoping for provision so you can finally afford the lifestyle you see other believers enjoying? Are you praying to glorify God or to prove something to yourself?

The same applies to almost any request. Praying for healing? Is it so you can serve God more effectively, or is it so you can avoid the discomfort and limitations of illness? Praying for a spouse? Is it so you can fulfill God's purpose together, or is it because you're lonely and think another person will complete you? Praying for a ministry opportunity? Is it so you can steward your gifts for God's glory, or is it because you want the platform and recognition that comes with ministry?

I'm not saying every prayer has to be completely selfless before God will answer. If that were the case, none of us would ever receive anything. We're human, so our motives are always mixed to some degree. But there's a difference between prayers that are mainly about God's kingdom and glory with some personal benefit, and prayers that are mostly about personal benefit with some spiritual words added.

God knows the difference. And while He's gracious with our mixed motives, there are some requests He simply won't grant because He loves us too much to give us things that would ultimately harm us or others. So when you're evaluating why a prayer hasn't been answered, ask yourself: If God gave me exactly what I'm asking for right now, would it actually be good for me? Would it draw me closer to Him or distract me from Him? Would it build His kingdom or just build my comfort?

These are hard questions, and answering them honestly takes self-awareness, which isn't always easy. But it's important because many prayers remain unanswered not because God is holding back for no reason, but because He sees things we don't. He knows that what we're asking for might not be good for us right now. He knows we might not be ready to handle what we're requesting. He knows the timing isn't right, even if the request itself is good.

This brings us to another category of seemingly unanswered prayer, perhaps the most common. These are prayers in which God's answer is 'not yet' rather than 'no,' but we interpret the delay as a denial. We ask for something legitimate. We ask with the right motives. We ask in faith. But the breakthrough doesn't come immediately, so we assume God won't answer at all. And this is where some believers get stuck, because waiting is one of the most difficult things we're ever asked to do.

Take a moment to think about your dreams and prayers that seem delayed or unfulfilled. What promises are you holding onto that feel stuck? As you keep reading, give yourself space to recognize these personal desires and bring them to God again, trusting that His timing is at work even when it feels far away.

Think about the story of Abraham and Sarah. God promised them a son. The promise was clear, specific, and it came directly from God Himself. But then nothing happened. Years passed. Then more years. Sarah's body aged past the point of natural childbearing. And in their frustration with the delay, they tried to help God out by having Abraham sleep with Hagar.

The lesson isn't that Abraham and Sarah lacked faith. The lesson is that even people of great faith struggle with divine delay. Even when you have a direct promise from God, the gap between promise and fulfillment can test you in ways that nothing else will. And in that gap, you'll be tempted to do one of two things. Either you'll try to force the breakthrough through your own effort, as Abraham and Sarah did. Or you'll give up and conclude that you heard wrong, that God changed His mind, that the promise wasn't really for you after all.

Both responses miss what God is doing in the waiting. Because delay is rarely just about the request itself. It's about what God is developing in you while you wait. It's about character formation that can only happen through sustained trust in the face of unfulfilled longing. It's about building a testimony that will help others who are standing where you're standing right now, wondering if they should keep believing or give up.

Scripture is full of examples where the delay was just as significant as the delivery. Joseph received dreams about leadership and authority when he was seventeen, but he didn't step into that role until he was thirty. That's thirteen years of slavery, false accusation, imprisonment, and being forgotten. Thirteen years where every circumstance seemed to contradict the promise God had given him. But those thirteen years weren't wasted time. They were essential preparation. The boy who had those dreams wouldn't have been ready to handle the responsibility of saving nations from famine. The man who emerged from prison was.

Moses spent forty years in the wilderness tending sheep before God called him to deliver Israel. David was anointed king as a teenager but spent years running for his life from Saul before he actually took the throne. Jesus Himself lived thirty years in relative obscurity before beginning His public ministry. If the Son of God needed three decades of preparation before launching into His purpose, what makes us think we should receive everything we ask for immediately?

To put this in a modern context, consider the story of a dedicated missionary working tirelessly to secure approval for a visa to serve in a new country. Despite meticulous preparation and fervent prayer, the process extended over several years. Initially, it seemed like an unnecessary delay. However, during that time, the missionaries improved their language skills, gained vital insights into the culture, and fostered crucial connections with local communities. When the visa finally came through, they were better prepared for the mission field. Or think about a startup founder tirelessly working to secure funding. After numerous rejections over the years, they finally secured the investment needed to launch. In that waiting period, they refined their business model and built a stronger, more resilient team. These modern examples show that delay often serves a purpose and prepares for what's to come.

The point isn't that God enjoys making us wait. The point is that God sees the whole picture while we only see the present moment. He knows what we need to become in order to steward what we're asking for. He knows when the timing will be optimal, not just for us, but for all the other lives connected to ours. He knows when provision will come in a way that will bring Him the most glory and us the most good.

But this is where things get tricky. While delay is different from denial, we can't always tell which one we're facing at the time. That uncertainty is part of what makes waiting so hard.

If God would just tell us, 'Yes, I'm going to give you this thing, but not for another five years,' we could handle that. We could plan. We could prepare. We could mark the calendar and count down. But God rarely gives us that kind of specific timeline, leaving us to trust in the dark. We're left to keep asking, keep seeking, keep knocking without knowing exactly when the door will open.

This is where faith becomes more than just agreeing with ideas. This is where faith becomes the substance of things hoped for, the evidence of things not seen. Faith that only believes when circumstances look good isn't really faith at all. That's just observation. Real faith is the ability to keep believing when everything you see tells you to give up.

This is what separates those who receive breakthroughs from those who don't. It's not because God loves some people more. It's not about having better theology or more spiritual gifts. The difference is perseverance. It's the willingness to keep going even when your excitement fades, when others stop encouraging you, and when you feel tired and ready to give up.

Now, before we go further, I need to address something that might be troubling some of you right now. Because there's a question underneath all of this that needs to be spoken out loud. What about the prayers that never get answered the way we hoped? What about the faithful believer who prayed for healing and died anyway? What about the couple who prayed for reconciliation and ended in divorce? What about the parent who prayed for a prodigal child who never came home?

These are the prayers that haunt us because they challenge everything we want to believe about God's goodness and faithfulness. They make us wonder if this whole framework of ask, seek, knock is just wishful thinking. Because if we're honest, we all know someone who asked, sought, knocked, and still didn't receive what they prayed for. They pursued God with everything in them, and the door never opened. Or it opened to something completely different than what they requested.

So let's deal with this head-on, because if we don't, it will undermine everything else in this book. The reality is that not every prayer gets answered with a yes in the way we envision. That's not a failure of faith or a flaw in the framework. That's part of living in a fallen world where we see through a glass dimly, where we don't have the full perspective God has.

But here's what's also true. God always answers. Always. Sometimes the answer is yes. Sometimes it's no. Sometimes it's not yet. And sometimes it's something better than what we asked for because God sees options we never considered. The key is learning to recognize God's response even when it doesn't match our request.

Think about what Jesus teaches in Matthew 7, right after He gives us the ask, seek, knock framework. He says, "Or which one of you, if his son asks him for bread, will give him a stone? Or if he asks for a fish, will give him a serpent? If you then, who are evil, know how to give good gifts to your children, how much more will your Father who is in heaven give good things to those who ask him!"

Notice what Jesus is doing here. He's establishing that God is a good Father who gives good gifts. But He's not saying that God will give you exactly what you ask for in exactly the way you ask for it. He's saying God will give you what's good. And sometimes what's good looks different than what we think we need.

A child might ask to play in the street. The loving parent says no, even though the child throws a fit, because the parent sees the danger the child doesn't see. The child might ask for something that seems harmless, but the parent knows will ultimately cause problems.

I know there's a risk in taking this analogy too far. We're not children asking for candy. We're adults praying for things like healing from cancer, provision for basic needs, and restoration of broken families. These are not trivial requests. They are desperate pleas born of real suffering. It can feel dismissive to compare them to a child wanting to play in the street.

But stay with me, because there's something important in this analogy. The point isn't that our requests are childish. The point is that our perspective is limited. We see what's happening right now. God sees the bigger picture. We see what we think we need at the moment. God sees what will truly help us in the long run. We see one life affected by this prayer. God sees how it will impact many lives over time.

I think about a conversation I had with a woman in our congregation several years ago. She had prayed for her marriage to be restored. She had asked, sought, knocked. She had done everything she knew to do. She had gone to counseling, changed her own behavior, interceded faithfully, and believed for breakthroughs. But her husband still left. The divorce went through. And she felt like God had betrayed her. She had done her part, and it felt like God didn't do His.

Years later, after she had walked through the grief and begun to rebuild her life, she told me something that shifted her entire perspective. She said, "I realize now that if God had given me what I prayed for back then, I would have spent the rest of my life in a relationship that was slowly killing me. I was praying to hold on to something that God was trying to free me from. I thought the answer was restoration. God knew the answer was release. And now, on the other side of it, I can see that His no was actually the most loving response He could have given me."

I'm not suggesting that's true for every divorce or every relationship that didn't work out the way we prayed. Sometimes relationships end because of human sin and hardness of heart, and that grieves God as much as it grieves us. But I am suggesting that God's perspective is bigger than ours, and sometimes what feels like an unanswered prayer is actually a different answer than we expected.

This is where trust becomes essential. If we're going to keep asking, seeking, and knocking, we have to trust that God is good. We have to believe that even when we don't understand His response, even when the door doesn't open as we hoped, God is still faithful. He's still working for our good. He's still committed to our well-being, even when the path looks different from what we expected.

But trust is hard when prayers go seemingly unanswered for extended periods. It's hard when you watch other believers receive breakthroughs while you're still waiting. It's hard when the person who barely prays gets the miracle while you, who have been faithful and fervent, are still standing at a closed door. This is where the theology of unanswered prayer gets messy, because we want formulas that work consistently. We want to believe that if we do X, Y, and Z, God will respond with A, B, and C. But God isn't a vending machine where you insert the right spiritual currency and get the product you selected.

He's a Father. And good fathers don't operate on a transactional basis with their children. They operate on relationship-based responses that take into account factors the child doesn't see or understand. Which means sometimes you'll pray and see an immediate breakthrough. Other times you'll pray and wait for years. Sometimes you'll pray and get exactly what you asked for. Other times, you'll pray and receive something completely different but ultimately better.

The unpredictability of this can be frustrating, especially in a culture that values certainty and control. We want to know the rules so we can follow them and succeed. We want a clear path from prayer to breakthrough. Some of us even want cheat codes. But the Christian life doesn't work that way. It works through relationships, which are always changing, personal, and often surprising. There are no cheat codes for breakthroughs.

This brings us to another critical piece of understanding unanswered prayer, and it's one that most teaching on this subject fails to address adequately. Sometimes prayers don't manifest because God is unwilling or because our faith is deficient, but because there's a spiritual battle we're unaware of.

In Daniel 10, we see Daniel has been praying and fasting for three weeks, seeking understanding about a vision God gave him. And during those three weeks, he hears nothing. No response. No breakthrough. Just silence. Then, finally, an angel appears to him and says something remarkable. "Do not be afraid, Daniel, for from the first day that you set your heart to understand and humbled yourself before your God, your words were heard, and I have come because of your words. But the prince of the kingdom of Persia withstood me twenty-one days."

Read that again slowly. From the first day Daniel prayed, God heard him. From the first day, the answer was dispatched. But a spiritual battle in the heavenly realms delayed the breakthrough for three weeks. Daniel had no idea this was happening. From his perspective, it looked like God wasn't answering. But the reality was that God had answered immediately, and the delay was caused by spiritual resistance, not divine reluctance.

This changes everything about how we understand unanswered prayer. Because it means there are times when the answer is already on the way, and we can't see it yet because there's warfare happening behind the scenes. It means that our prayers are accomplishing something in the spiritual realm even when nothing seems to be changing in the natural realm. It means that persistence in prayer isn't just about convincing God to respond, but about sustaining the spiritual breakthrough until it manifests in the physical.

Now, I want to be careful here because spiritual warfare language can be used to excuse lazy thinking or to blame demons for everything that goes wrong. Not every delay is caused by demonic interference. Sometimes the delay is caused by our own disobedience. Sometimes it's caused by natural consequences of past decisions. Sometimes it's simply God's timing working differently than ours. But we also can't ignore the biblical reality that there is a spiritual dimension to our lives, and sometimes breakthroughs are delayed because of resistance in that dimension.

The question then becomes, what do we do with this information? How does understanding spiritual warfare change the way we pray? For starters, it should give us patience when breakthroughs don't come immediately. If we know that God heard us from the first day, and that the answer has been dispatched but is slowed by resistance, then we can keep praying with confidence rather than giving up in discouragement. We can pray with the understanding that we're not trying to get God's attention. We already have it. We're simply sustaining spiritual momentum until the breakthrough manifests.

It also means we need to add a dimension to our prayers that many believers overlook. We need to pray not just for the thing we need, but also for the removal of any spiritual resistance blocking its arrival. We need to pray for angelic assistance, as Daniel's angel did. We need to pray for spiritual eyes to see what's happening in the realm we can't see naturally. We need to engage in prayer not just as a request but as warfare, understanding that there's an enemy who doesn't want us to receive what God has promised.

Many of us get stuck here because we've been taught a sanitized version of Christianity that doesn't account for spiritual opposition. They pray nice prayers, they believe nice things, and they expect breakthroughs to come easily. But Scripture paints a different picture. Jesus said that from the days of John the Baptist until now, the kingdom of heaven suffers violence, and the violent take it by force. Paul wrote that we wrestle not against flesh and blood but against principalities, against powers, against the rulers of the darkness of this age, against spiritual hosts of wickedness in the heavenly places.

This isn't meant to scare you. It's meant to prepare you. Because if you're going to pursue breakthroughs with the kind of tenacity Jesus describes in Matthew 7, you need to know that there will be resistance. The enemy of your soul doesn't want you to receive what God has promised. He will do everything in his power to discourage you from asking, to distract you from seeking, and to exhaust you before you finish knocking. And if we're not aware of his tactics, we'll attribute the resistance to God's unwillingness rather than recognizing it as spiritual warfare.

So when your prayers seem to hit a wall, when breakthrough feels blocked despite your faithfulness. Ask yourself: Is there spiritual resistance that needs to be addressed? Are there areas of unforgiveness, bitterness, or unconfessed sin that are giving the enemy legal ground in my life? Are there generational patterns or spiritual strongholds that need to be broken? Am I engaging in prayer as warfare or just as wishful thinking?

These questions aren't meant to give you another spiritual checklist. They're meant to help you see what's really happening when prayers aren't answered right away. Once you understand that unanswered prayer is complex and involves many factors beyond God's willingness and your faith, you can approach the process with more wisdom and patience.

Let's shift gears now and talk about another category of seemingly unanswered prayer. Fair warning, this one might be the most controversial. Sometimes prayers aren't answered because we're asking God to do something He's actually waiting for us to do. Let me say that again because it's important. Sometimes the reason we don't see breakthroughs is that we're praying for God to do something He's already empowered and equipped us to do ourselves.

This is where the difference between asking, seeking, and knocking becomes important. Asking means you admit you need something you don't have. Seeking means you start moving toward the answer. Knocking means you reach the door and keep trying until it opens. Notice the progression: it starts with recognizing your need, but it doesn't end with waiting. It leads to taking action.

Many believers don't experience breakthroughs because they pray and then do nothing. They ask God for provision but don't apply for jobs. They ask God for healing but don't make any lifestyle changes. Then they wonder why breakthroughs don't come.

This is the tension James addresses when he writes that faith without works is dead. It's the tension Jesus addresses in multiple parables where servants are expected to invest what the master gave them rather than just burying it and waiting for more. It's the tension we see throughout Scripture where God calls His people to partner with Him in bringing about the breakthrough they're praying for.

Think about the story of Joshua and the battle of Jericho. God promised to give them the city. That was the answer to their prayer for conquest. But they still had to march around the walls for seven days. They still had to blow the trumpets. They still had to shout. God could have just made the walls fall without their participation. But He didn't. He designed the breakthrough to require their engagement.

Or consider Elijah praying for rain after three years of drought. He prays seven times before his servant sees even a small cloud on the horizon. But Elijah doesn't just pray and sit still. He tells Ahab to prepare his chariot because rain is coming. He positions himself. He acts on what he's praying for before he sees full manifestation. That's the partnership between divine provision and human participation.

This idea of partnership between God's control and our responsibility is one of the great mysteries of Scripture, and it's often misunderstood. Some believers focus so much on God's control that they become passive, waiting for God to do everything while they do nothing. Others focus so much on their own responsibility that they wear themselves out trying to make breakthroughs happen on their own, leaving God out. But true faith holds both together. God is in control and will accomplish His purposes, and we are responsible for doing our part.

So when you're evaluating why a prayer hasn't been answered, one question to ask is: Is there something God has already told me to do that I haven't done yet? Is there an action step I'm waiting for God to take that He's actually waiting for me to take? Have I been praying for breakthroughs while sitting still, when God is waiting for me to start moving?

This doesn't mean you earn breakthroughs through effort. That would contradict the gospel of grace. But it does mean that faith expresses itself through action. Real faith doesn't just believe God can do something. Real faith believes God can do something and then moves in alignment with that belief. Abraham believed God would provide a son, but he still had to sleep with Sarah. Moses believed God would deliver Israel, but he still had to confront Pharaoh. David believed God would make him king, but he still had to fight Goliath, lead armies, and learn to govern. In every case, faith preceded breakthrough, but action bridged the gap between promise and fulfillment.

Now, here's where this gets practical for you. Think about the main thing you've been praying for. The thing that brought you to this book. The thing that feels stuck, blocked, or delayed. Have you only been asking, or have you also been seeking? Because asking is essential, but it's only the first step. And if you've stopped at asking without moving into seeking, then you're standing at the starting line, wondering why you haven't crossed the finish line.

We're going to dive much deeper into this in the next few chapters when we unpack asking, seeking, and knocking individually. But I want to plant this seed in your mind right now. Most prayers that feel unanswered aren't actually unanswered. They're just incomplete. God heard you. God responded. But His response is often an invitation to participate, not permission to sit back and wait passively. And until you recognize that invitation and accept it, the breakthrough you're praying for will remain just out of reach.

Let me give you another angle on this, because I think it will help bring some clarity. Consider the difference between prayers that ask God to do something for you and prayers that ask God to do something through you. Both are valid. Both are biblical. But they lead to very different approaches to engaging the waiting period.

When you pray for God to do something for you, like provide a job or heal a sickness or restore a relationship, there's often an element of waiting involved. You've done what you can do, and now you're trusting God to do what only He can do. That's appropriate. There are things only God can accomplish, and in those situations, our role is to trust, to persist in prayer, and to steward our hearts well while we wait.

But when you pray for God to do something through you, like use you to reach others or develop a gift or fulfill a calling, there's usually action required on your part. God isn't going to develop your gift while you're sitting on the couch. He isn't going to use you to reach others if you never leave your house. He isn't going to fulfill a calling you haven't prepared for or made yourself available for. In these situations, the breakthrough you're praying for often requires you to take steps of obedience even before you see the full picture.

Many believers blur these categories, which leaves them frustrated. They pray for God to do something through them, but they treat it like a prayer for God to do something for them. They wait passively for an opportunity to serve when God is waiting for them to create opportunities through faithful action. Or they pray for God to do something for them, but then try to force it through their own effort, essentially telling God they don't trust Him to come through, so they'll handle it themselves.

The key is discernment: knowing when to wait and when to act. It's about knowing when to trust God to do what only He can do, and when to step into what He's already given you to do. Some believers struggle here because discernment comes from being close to God. You can't sense His guidance if you're not spending time with Him. You can't know what He's asking if you're not listening. You can't see His invitations if you're not paying attention to the opportunities He gives you.

To illustrate, let me share a brief internal dialogue I often engage in when seeking God's timing: 'Lord, I feel uncertain about whether to proceed or to wait. If this is the right step, open the doors that need to be opened and close those that are not of You. Give me peace to move forward, or a gentle nudge if I should pause. Help me to see the opportunities You're presenting and give me the courage to act on them.' This internal prayer helps me to align with God's will, listening both in silence and through the circumstances He aligns in my path.

This is why prayer can never be just a formula. It's not a transaction; it's a relationship. Relationships need communication, presence, attention, and response.

God isn't a cosmic butler you call on when you need something. He's a Father who wants a real connection with you, who speaks, guides, and works with you to bring His kingdom to earth. When you see prayer this way, the question of unanswered prayer changes. You're not just asking God for things; you're looking for Him to transform you, work through you, and accomplish His purposes with you.

Let's look at one more dimension of unanswered prayer before we wrap up this chapter, and this one is perhaps the most difficult to grapple with. Sometimes prayers aren't answered in the way we hope because God is using the very thing we're praying to escape as the tool to form us into who He's called us to be. In other words, sometimes the trial itself is the answer, even though it doesn't feel like it from where we're standing.

Take a moment to recognize the emotion that comes with this realization. Think about the agony of praying over and over for relief, the tears shed in silence, and the sleepless nights filled with questions and doubt. These are moments when you wonder if God hears you at all. This pain is real and can feel genuinely overwhelming. Before we try to understand its purpose, I wanted to intentionally acknowledge that the hurt is real.

Paul deals with this in 2 Corinthians 12 when he writes about his thorn in the flesh. We don't know exactly what this thorn was. Scholars have debated it for centuries. Some think it was a physical ailment. Others think it was a persistent temptation, a relational conflict, or ongoing persecution. But whatever it was, it bothered Paul enough that he prayed three times for God to remove it.

I invite you to take a moment to connect with Paul's humanity. Pause for a few minutes and allow yourself to grieve unanswered prayers and recognize the deep cries that seem to go unheard. This time of lament helps us realize we're not alone in our struggles.

And yet, God told Paul no. Not 'not yet.' Not 'something better is coming.' Just no. But here's what God said when He further explained His answer: 'My grace is sufficient for you, for my power is made perfect in weakness.' In other words, God's response to Paul's prayer for deliverance was to say, 'I'm not removing this because I'm going to use it to display My strength through your weakness.'

That's a hard answer to receive. Because when we're suffering, when we're struggling, when we're dealing with something that feels unbearable, what we want is relief. We want God to remove the burden. We want the door of escape to open. We want deliverance. And sometimes God gives us exactly that. But other times, He gives us something different. He gives us grace to endure, strength to persevere, and a deeper revelation of His presence in the midst of pain.

This doesn't mean we should never pray for deliverance. We should absolutely bring our burdens to God and ask Him to remove them. But we also need to hold space for the possibility that God might answer that prayer by equipping us to carry the burden rather than removing it. And if that's His response, it's not because He doesn't care. It's because He sees something we don't. He sees that this very thing we're desperate to escape is actually the crucible in which He's forming something precious in us.

James writes about this in the first chapter of his letter. "Count it all joy, my brothers, when you meet trials of various kinds, for you know that the testing of your faith produces steadfastness. And let steadfastness have its full effect, that you may be perfect and complete, lacking in nothing." Notice that James doesn't say trials are joyful in themselves. He says to count them as joy, which is different. It's a choice to see them through the lens of what God is doing rather than just the lens of what we're feeling.

The testing of faith produces steadfastness. Steadfastness is the ability to keep going when everything in you wants to quit. It's spiritual stamina. It's endurance. And you can't develop it without trials. You can't build spiritual muscle without spiritual resistance. So sometimes God allows the very thing we're praying to escape because He knows that enduring it will produce something in us that we can't get any other way.

This is very hard to accept when you're suffering. When you're facing chronic illness, financial loss, betrayal, or any other trial that weighs on you, it doesn't feel like you're growing. It just feels painful. I don't want to make light of that or cover it up with easy answers. Pain is real. Suffering is real. And God doesn't expect us to pretend it doesn't hurt.

But what God does ask is that we trust Him even in the pain. That we believe He's working something good even when we can't see it yet. That we remain open to the possibility that the trial we're desperate to escape is actually the pathway to the breakthrough we've been praying for, just not in the way we expected.

I think about Job, who lost everything. His children, his wealth, his health, his reputation. And in the middle of that devastation, he prayed. He questioned. He demanded answers. He wrestled with God. But he never let go. And at the end of the story, after all the suffering, after all the unanswered questions, after all the well-meaning friends who gave terrible advice, Job says something remarkable. "I had heard of you by the hearing of the ear, but now my eye sees you."

Job's suffering led him to a revelation of God he never would have had otherwise. The trial that seemed to indicate God's absence actually became the means of experiencing God's presence more deeply. And while I would never suggest that Job's losses were worth it just so he could learn something about God, I do think Job himself would tell you that the intimacy with God he gained through the trial was more valuable than everything he lost.

This is the mystery of suffering that Scripture consistently points us to. God can use even the worst circumstances, even the things caused by human sin or spiritual warfare or natural disaster, and weave them into His redemptive purposes. That doesn't mean He causes those things. That doesn't mean He's pleased by our pain. But it does mean that nothing is wasted in His economy. Every trial, every unanswered prayer, every period of waiting has the potential to produce something of eternal value if we'll let it.

So when you're thinking about why a prayer hasn't been answered, sometimes the hard truth is that the answer is already coming, just not as deliverance. Sometimes the answer is grace to endure. Sometimes it's strength to keep going. Sometimes it's a deeper understanding of God's character. Sometimes it's building spiritual strength you'll need later. Each day, try writing down one thing you're grateful for, even in uncertainty. This small habit can help you put your trust into practice.

And sometimes, honestly, we just don't know why. There are answers to prayers that don't make sense from any angle we can see. There are situations where all the theological explanations feel hollow. There are seasons where the only honest thing to say is, "I don't understand what God is doing, but I'm choosing to trust Him anyway."

That's not an excuse. It's actually the heart of faith. If we could understand everything God was doing, if every prayer was answered just as we asked, and if the Christian life always followed a clear formula, we wouldn't need faith. Faith means trusting what we can't see, believing what we don't yet understand, and holding on to God's character even when His actions don't make sense to us.

As we finish this chapter, I want to give you some questions to help you think about the prayers in your life that seem unanswered. These questions aren't meant to make you feel guilty or condemned. They're meant to help you see things more clearly. Once you understand what's really happening with your prayers, you can respond more effectively, rather than just feeling helpless and frustrated.

First question: Have I actually asked, or have I just worried, complained, and discussed the problem with everyone except God? This might seem basic, but it's amazing how many prayers never get prayed because we're too busy talking about the problem to actually bring it to God. If you haven't asked, start there. Get specific. Get honest. Get desperate if you need to. But actually bring the request to God before you do anything else.

Second question: What are my motives for this request? Am I primarily seeking God's glory, or am I primarily seeking my own comfort or validation? Again, this isn't about having perfectly pure motives. That's an impossible standard. But there's a difference between prayers that are fundamentally about God's kingdom with personal benefit attached, and prayers that are fundamentally about personal benefit with spiritual language wrapped around them. Be honest about which category your request falls into.

Third question: Is there spiritual resistance blocking breakthroughs, and if so, what might be giving the enemy legal ground in my life? Are there areas of unforgiveness, unconfessed sin, generational patterns, or strongholds that need to be addressed? This isn't about being perfect before God will answer. It's about removing obstacles that hinder spiritual flow. Sometimes breakthroughs are blocked not because God is unwilling but because there's interference that needs to be cleared.

Fourth question: Is there an action God is waiting for me to take? Have I moved from asking to seeking, or am I still waiting passively for God to do everything? What would it look like to partner with God in bringing about the breakthrough I'm praying for? Where is He inviting me to step out in faith, to take risks, to position myself for the answer? Often, the reason breakthroughs feel delayed is that we're waiting on God to do something He's actually waiting on us to do.

Fifth question: Could this delay actually be divine timing rather than divine denial? Is God using this waiting period to develop something in me that I'll need when the breakthrough comes? What might He be forming in me through this trial that I couldn't get any other way? How might this delay actually be protecting me from receiving something I'm not ready to steward?

And finally: Am I willing to trust God even if the answer doesn't come in the way or timing I hope? Can I hold my request with open hands, surrendering the outcome to Him while still pursuing breakthroughs with everything in me? Can I believe that God is good even when His response doesn't match my request?

These questions aren't easy, and answering them honestly takes some real reflection. But they're important if you want to move past feeling abandoned with unanswered prayers and start seeing breakthroughs. Here's what I've learned over the past ten-plus years since God answered my desperate prayer in that difficult season: Most prayers that feel unanswered are actually still in process. God is working. The answer is coming. But there's a journey, and many of us give up before it's finished.

That journey is what this entire book is about. The progression from asking to seeking to knocking. The movement from passive prayer to active pursuit. The development of spiritual tenacity that outlasts discouragement, outworks opposition, and outlives every excuse that tries to keep you from breakthrough.

But before we can embrace that journey, we have to address the question of unanswered prayer. Because if you believe God isn't listening, if you think He's arbitrarily withholding from you, if you're convinced that breakthrough is only for other people, then you'll never have the motivation and discipline to keep pursuing. You'll ask once or twice, you'll seek halfheartedly, and you'll walk away from the door before it has a chance to open.

What I want you to understand as we move into the next chapter is this: God heard you. From the first moment you prayed, He heard you. Your prayers matter. Your requests are important to Him. He's not ignoring you, punishing you, or playing games with you. He's inviting you into a process that will not only bring breakthroughs but will transform you in ways you never imagined.

The reason we don't see more answered prayers isn't that God is stingy or reluctant. It's because most of us approach prayer as a single transaction rather than a sustained pursuit. We ask once and expect immediate results. We seek for a moment and then give up when the path isn't clear. We knock a few times and walk away when the door doesn't open right away. And then we wonder why we're not seeing the breakthrough that Jesus promised to those who ask, seek, and knock.

The word "everyone" in Matthew 7:8 should arrest your attention. Not some. Not the spiritually elite. Not those with great faith or perfect theology. Everyone. That means the promise is available to you regardless of your past, your present circumstances, or your spiritual resume. But the promise comes with a condition: you actually have to engage the process. You have to ask. You have to seek. You have to knock. And you have to keep doing all three until the answer manifests.

That's not legalism. That's partnership. God has already done His part by making provision available through Christ. He's already positioned Himself to respond to those who call on Him. He's already promised that everyone who pursues Him will find what they're looking for. But He's not going to override your free will or force breakthroughs on you while you sit passively. He's inviting you to partner with Him, to pursue with Him, to knock with Him until the door opens.

And here's what makes this different from works-based religion. You're not earning anything through your pursuit. You're not making yourself worthy of a blessing through your effort. You're simply positioning yourself to receive what God has already made available. Think of it this way: if someone offers you a gift but you never show up to receive it, whose fault is it that you don't have it? The gift was always yours. The giver was always willing. But you had to participate in the receiving.

That's what asking, seeking, and knocking is about. It's about actively receiving what God is actively giving. It's about showing up, staying engaged, and persisting until you possess what God has already promised. And when you understand it that way, the question of unanswered prayer shifts completely. Because the issue isn't God's unwillingness. The issue is our disengagement.

Most believers give up too soon. They pray with passion for a few days or weeks, then move on when breakthroughs don't come right away. They treat prayer like tossing wishes into a well, hoping something will happen, instead of seeing it as the main way to access what God has made available through Christ. Because they stop so quickly, they miss the breakthrough that was just on the other side of persistence.

I want to tell you something that might sound harsh, but I mean it with all the love and urgency I can muster. The reason you don't have what you've been praying for might not be because God hasn't answered. It might be because you quit too soon. You asked, but you didn't seek. You sought for a while, but you didn't knock. You knocked a few times, but you walked away before the door opened. And now you're living with unfulfilled promises, convinced that God let you down, when the reality is that you disengaged from the process before it was complete.

If that stings, good. Let it sting. Let it wake you up to the reality that breakthroughs are available, that the door will open, that everyone who asks receives, and that everyone who seeks finds and knocks sees doors open. But let it also ignite something in you. Let it spark a holy determination to return to the prayers you walked away from, to the doors you left standing at, to the promises you gave up on. Because it's not too late. God hasn't moved on. The invitation still stands. The promise still applies. And the door will still open if you start knocking again.

This is why it's so important to understand why prayers seem unanswered. When you realize that most prayers aren't really unanswered but just incomplete, and that delay isn't denial, and that God is working even when you can't see it, everything changes. Your frustration becomes hope. Your discouragement becomes determination. Your passive waiting becomes an active pursuit.

And that's when you start to see results. Not because God suddenly decided to start listening to you. He was listening all along. But because you finally aligned yourself with the process He designed for accessing breakthrough. You stopped treating prayer as a one-time request and started engaging it as a sustained pursuit. You stopped waiting for God to do everything and started partnering with Him in bringing about the answer. You stopped walking away from closed doors and started knocking with the kind of desperate, persistent, shameless audacity that refuses to quit until the door opens.

So as we close this chapter, I want you to do something. Take a few minutes right now and think about the main thing you've been praying for. The thing that feels impossible. The thing that brought you to this book. The thing you're tempted to give up on because it's been so long with no visible progress.

Got it in mind? Good. Now ask yourself honestly: Which level did I quit at? Did I ask a few times and then stop praying altogether? Did I seek for a while but then got discouraged when the path wasn't clear? Or did I make it all the way to the door but walk away because I was tired of knocking and nothing seemed to be happening?

Be ruthlessly honest with yourself here because this answer will determine your starting point for the rest of this book. If you never really asked, that's okay. I'm going to spend the next chapter teaching you how. If you asked but never sought, that's fine. I'm going to show you what seeking looks like in practical terms. If you sought but never knocked, or if you knocked but gave up too soon, I'm going to equip you with the stamina to return to that door and keep knocking until it opens.

The point isn't to condemn you for where you stopped. The point is to help you recognize where you are so you can move forward from there. Because here's the beautiful truth about God's grace: it doesn't matter how many times you've quit before. It doesn't matter how long it's been since you walked away from the door. It doesn't matter how much faith you lost or how discouraged you became. God's invitation still stands. The promise still applies. And if you'll engage the process starting right now, breakthroughs are still available.

Your prayers weren't unanswered. They're just not finished yet. In the next ten chapters, we'll work through them together. We'll move from asking to seeking to knocking. We'll build the kind of spiritual strength that lasts through every challenge. We'll learn to notice God's answers, even when they look different from what we expected. We'll build endurance, overcome spiritual resistance, and put ourselves in a place where miracles can happen. And we'll keep knocking until the door opens.

Because that's what Jesus promised. Everyone who asks receives. Everyone who seeks finds. Everyone who knocks sees doors open. Not might. Not maybe. Will. It's a guarantee. But you have to engage the process. You have to do all three. You have to keep going when everything in you wants to quit.

Are you ready? If so, go back to the door. It's time to stop making excuses and start pursuing breakthroughs with all your heart. Turn the page and begin the next chapter, where you'll learn about the first part of this journey: the posture of asking. Let go of self-sufficiency and accept the need to depend on God. Remember: ask, seek, knock. Your breakthrough starts now. Take the step and embrace it.

Chapter Two

THE FIRST DIMENSION

Asking and the Death of Self-sufficiency

"Growth Begins When Asking Starts Feeling Uncomfortable."
-*Apostle Dr. Ivon L. Valerie*

I knocked on the door, surprised by how loud it sounded. A friendly but careful voice invited me in. As I stood there, I felt that familiar awkwardness that comes with asking for help. I only needed a ride to church, but even this small request taught me something big about myself. Whether you're asking a friend for a ride to the airport or talking to your boss about time off, making a request can feel uncomfortable. It reminds us that we all need help sometimes, and that's not always easy to admit, especially if you grew up valuing independence.

That discomfort can feel even stronger when you ask God for help. Praying is more than admitting you need help from another person. It means coming to God, who has no needs or limits, and saying, "I can't do this. I need You." This shows our vulnerability and our willingness to accept help beyond ourselves. It's not easy, but it's exactly where God wants us.

Asking is not about convincing God to do something. It's the key that puts us in a place to receive what God already wants to give. Asking is what unlocks doors that we need to enter. One night, as I knelt in prayer, I felt that familiar tightness in my chest, a mix of hope and uncertainty. The room was quiet, but my thoughts were loud. I said to myself: "God already knows our needs; Jesus said, 'Your Father knows what you need before you ask him' (Matthew 6:8). So if God knows, why does He want us to ask?" As I pondered this question, I concluded that maybe it's in our vulnerability that we truly connect with God's heart and find the humility to receive all He wants to give.

Asking prepares us. It changes our attitude, our heart, and how we see our relationship with God. When we ask, we admit we need help and let go of the idea that we can do everything on our own. Being open in this way is the key to receiving what God wants to give.

Imagine you're at someone's house for dinner, and your host offers you food. If you say you're not hungry, even if you are, they probably won't insist. In the same way, God doesn't force His help on us if we don't admit we need it. That's why James says, "You do not have because you do not ask." It's easy to miss this, but it matters. You don't go without because God is stingy or because you're unworthy. You go without because you haven't asked. Maybe you've stressed, complained, or talked to others, but you haven't brought your need to God in a clear, expectant way.

Not all asking is the same. Think of prayer like the difference between a focused laser and a soft, unfocused light. A laser targets one spot, while regular light spreads out. In the same way, there's a big difference between casually mentioning something to God and asking with clear intention and expectation. For example, Tom faced financial struggles and prayed with focus: "God, by the end of this month, I need five hundred dollars for my rent, and I'm trusting You for this provision." Because his prayer was specific, he recognized God's help when an unexpected part-time job came just before his rent was due.

Persistent asking, shaped by grace, means treating prayer as a relationship, not just a task. It's about showing up regularly, trusting that God's grace helps you, and making sure your persistence comes from faith, not from trying to earn. The kind of asking Jesus talks about in Matthew 7:7 is different. The word He uses means to keep asking, not just ask once and move on. It's about being honest about your need and asking again and again, with clear requests and real expectations, until you see an answer. It's like tracking a package you ordered online. You know it's coming, so you keep checking the status, waiting for it to arrive. In the same way, keep asking God, expecting an answer, and with each prayer, bring yourself closer to seeing it fulfilled.

Imagine you're facing a financial crisis, with an eviction notice on your door, bills piling up, and no idea how to pay them. The stress is overwhelming. In this situation, a casual prayer might sound like, "God, please help me with my finances. You know my needs. I trust You. Amen."

There's nothing wrong with that prayer, but notice what's missing. It doesn't say what you actually need, how much, or by when. It's too general, so you can't really tell if or when God answers because there's nothing specific to look for.

Now let's look at a different option. "Father, I need two thousand dollars by the thirtieth of this month to cover my rent and utilities. I've done everything I know to do. I've cut unnecessary expenses. I've looked for extra income. I've been faithful with what You've given me. Now I'm asking You specifically to provide this exact amount by this exact date. I'm watching for Your provision. I'm expecting You to come through. I'll keep asking every day until I see this breakthrough. In Jesus's name, amen."

Do you see the difference? The second prayer is specific. It names the amount and the deadline. It takes responsibility and admits the need for God's help. It shows expectation, not just hope, and commits to asking more than once. That's the kind of asking that puts you in a place to receive breakthroughs, because it's focused, intentional, and gives you a clear way to recognize God's response.

But there are obstacles to our asking. I vividly remember a time when pride and unbelief were holding me back. I had just started life coaching, and a significant project wasn't going as planned. The stress was mounting, yet I resisted asking for help because I feared appearing incompetent. As I prayed about it, I felt a nudge to let go of that pride, but disbelief crept in, whispering that my concerns were trivial in the grand scheme of things. It took me some time to realize that this mindset was a barrier to experiencing God's provision. Three big barriers stand between us and the kind of real, persistent asking that Jesus teaches. If we don't recognize and deal with these barriers, we'll keep offering casual prayers and wonder why we're not seeing breakthroughs. These hindrances to asking are pride, unbelief, and false humility.

Let's pause for a moment. Take a little time to reflect. Think about a hidden fear you've never shared or a concern you've kept to yourself because of pride, unbelief, or false humility. Write it down, even if it's just for you. Admitting it is the first step to breaking down these barriers.

Asking yourself the following questions will help you spot your main barrier:

- **Pride:** Do you believe you should handle things on your own, feeling that asking for help makes you appear weak?

- **Unbelief:** Do you doubt that God will actually respond to your requests, allowing disappointments to lower your expectations?

- **False Humility:** Do you feel your needs are too small to bother God with, assuming they aren't significant enough for His attention?

Think about which one stands out to you right now. Take a moment to reflect, because chances are, at least one of these is affecting your life, maybe without you even noticing. Let's look at each one more closely.

The first barrier is pride. Pride, in this context, isn't about thinking you're better than other people. It's about the belief that you should be able to handle things on your own. It's that inner conviction that admits no vulnerability, whispering thoughts like 'I should be able to figure this out myself.' These thoughts perpetuate a mindset that views asking as weak or incompetent. However, in contrast to this notion, learned optimism holds that perceiving dependence as a strength can lead to greater resilience and positivity. Recognizing this, choosing humility over self-reliance not only allows you to seek support when truly needed but also enhances your overall well-being. Reframing dependence as a collaborative strength, as positive-psychology findings suggest, aligns with spiritual humility and boosts resilience, thereby transforming how we engage with challenges.

This kind of pride is especially common among people who have been fairly successful in life. If you've built a career, raised a family, solved problems, overcome obstacles, and generally managed life's challenges with some skill, there's a part of you that resists asking for help because it feels like admitting defeat. It feels like admitting you're not as capable as you thought. And that's tough to accept.

But here's where pride attempts to make us liars. Asking God for help isn't admitting defeat. It's just being honest about reality. The truth is, you've never really handled anything on your own. Every breath, every success, every problem you've solved happened because God gave you the ability. You've depended on Him all along. Asking doesn't make you dependent; it just helps you see what's always been true.

Think about a child learning to walk. At first, the child crawls everywhere because that's the only mode of transportation they know. But eventually, they start pulling themselves up on furniture, taking wobbly steps while clutching a parent's hand. And the parent is delighted by this, not offended. The parent doesn't say, "Why are you asking me for help? You should be able to walk on your own by now." No, the parent celebrates the child's willingness to reach out, to take risks, to ask for support while attempting something new.

That's how God views our asking. He's not disappointed that you need Him. He designed you to need Him. He created you for dependence, not independence. And when you finally acknowledge that need and bring your requests to Him, He's not thinking, "It's about time you admitted you can't do this alone." He's thinking, "Finally, my child is positioning themselves to receive what I've been wanting to give all along."

So if pride has kept you from asking, and you hear a voice in your head saying you should handle this yourself, know that this voice isn't telling you the truth. It keeps you stuck in self-sufficiency when God is inviting you to something greater. Pride says, 'I've got this.' Humility says, 'God, I need You.' The only way forward is to choose humility over pride, admit your dependence instead of pretending you're independent, and ask, even when it feels uncomfortable or makes you feel vulnerable.

The second barrier to real asking is unbelief. This one is trickier than pride because it often hides behind other things. It can look like resignation, lowered expectations, or just "being realistic." But beneath it all, there's a basic doubt that causes us to wonder, will God actually answer my request? You might not say it out loud or even realize you're thinking it, but deep down, you wonder if asking will make any difference, so you don't bother. What if we approached this doubt differently, as an invitation to explore rather than a discouraging obstacle? Imagine if unbelief were a chance to ask new questions rather than a reason to stop asking altogether. Instead of seeing doubt as a door closed, consider it a path to deeper curiosity, one that encourages you to engage more with your faith and explore fresh possibilities with a holy mind.

To transform this doubt into a stepping stone for healing, let's pause here. Take a moment to reflect on a specific past disappointment. What was one request you brought to God that didn't get answered as you hoped? Articulate this event directly to Him now, inviting Him into that narrative. Recognizing and accepting it creates a starting point for moving beyond abstract unbelief.

This kind of unbelief usually develops over time, often as a result of past disappointments. Maybe you asked for something years ago, and it didn't come through the way you hoped. Maybe you watched someone else ask and not get an answer. Maybe you've been taught, consciously or unconsciously, that God's promises are more symbolic than actual, more theoretical than practical. And over time, those experiences can lock up your heart like a padlock, hardening into a belief system that says, "Prayer is good for me psychologically and spiritually, but I shouldn't actually expect specific, measurable responses to specific requests."

If that's where you are right now, I want to be honest with you. I understand how you got here. Disappointment can make us lower our expectations, and after enough letdowns, it feels safer to expect less. But the truth is, unbelief doesn't protect you from disappointment. It just makes sure you never receive what you're asking for. Faith, according to Hebrews 11:6, is essential to pleasing God. "Without faith it is impossible to please him, for whoever would draw near to God must believe that he exists and that he rewards those who seek him." Take a moment and ask yourself: Do you really expect a reward when you pray? This question can reveal hidden doubts we often ignore.

Notice both parts of that requirement. You have to believe that God exists, and you have to believe that He rewards those who seek Him. The first part is easy for most believers. We believe God exists. We've built our entire worldview around that reality. But the second part is where many of us stumble. Do we really believe that God rewards those who seek Him? Do we truly expect that when we ask, seek, and knock, we'll receive, find, and see doors open? Or have we relegated those promises to the category of nice ideas that don't really apply to ordinary life?

Jesus addresses this directly when He says, "Therefore I tell you, whatever you ask in prayer, believe that you have received it, and it will be yours." That statement should either thrill you or trouble you, because it places a significant portion of the responsibility on the asker. It's not enough to just articulate the request. You have to believe you'll receive it. You have to pray with expectation, not just with hope or wishful thinking. You have to ask as though the answer is already on its way, even when you have no physical evidence to support that belief.

This is where many believers get stuck; they confuse belief with certainty. They think faith means knowing exactly how and when God will answer. But that's not faith; that's wanting control. Real faith is being sure of what you hope for, even when you can't see it yet. It's trusting that God heard you, that He's already working, and that breakthroughs are coming even if your situation says otherwise. It's asking while believing, not asking while doubting.

James writes about this tension when he says, "But let him ask in faith, with no doubting, for the one who doubts is like a wave of the sea that is driven and tossed by the wind. For that person must not suppose that he will receive anything from the Lord." Those are strong words. James is saying that doubt-filled asking doesn't just make you less likely to receive. It actually disqualifies you from receiving. Not because God is punishing you for doubt, but because doubt creates a posture that can't hold onto what God is giving.

So if unbelief has been your barrier, if you've been asking but doubting that God will answer, you need to deal with that first. Addressing it doesn't mean pretending to believe something you don't. It means going back to what you know is true about God's character, His promises in Scripture, and His track record in your life. Remember past breakthroughs, times when God came through, and moments when He provided in unexpected ways. Feed your faith and starve your doubt by focusing more on what God says than on what your circumstances show. My mother always taught me to trust God when I can't trace Him, and remember all He has done for me when it's hard to trust Him.

The third barrier to authentic asking is false humility, though it's really just pride wearing a religious disguise. This is the belief that your needs are too small or too insignificant to bother God with. It sounds humble on the surface. It sounds like you're being considerate of God's time and attention. But beneath this false humility lies an arrogant assumption that you can determine what's worthy of God's attention and what isn't.

When you say, "I don't want to bother God with this small thing," what you're really saying is, "I know better than God, I know what He should care about."

You're deciding on His behalf that your need isn't important enough for His involvement. But who are you to make that determination? Who are you to decide what matters to God and what doesn't?

Scripture paints a very different picture of what God cares about. Jesus says that not a single sparrow falls to the ground apart from the Father's knowledge. He says that the hairs on your head are all numbered. He says that God clothes the grass of the field, which is here today and thrown into the oven tomorrow. If God pays attention to sparrows and grass and individual hairs, what makes you think your needs are too small for Him?

There's no such thing as a need that's too small for God's attention. If it matters to you, it matters to Him. If it affects your life, He wants to be involved. The size of the need is irrelevant because God's capacity is infinite. He doesn't have a limited supply of concern that He has to ration out carefully. He can attend to the massive needs of nations and empires while simultaneously caring about whether you find a parking spot. That's what omniscience and omnipresence mean. Nothing is too big for His power, and nothing is too small for His care.

But here's the truth about false humility: it's not about protecting God's time or energy. It's about protecting yourself from disappointment. If you don't ask, you can't be let down if the answer doesn't come. If you call your need too small for God, you avoid the risk of asking and not receiving. It's a way to protect yourself that only appears to be a sign of spiritual maturity.

Real humility doesn't say, "My needs don't matter enough to ask." Real humility says, "I may not know what I need as well as God does, but I'll bring everything to Him and trust Him to respond with wisdom and love." Real humility admits total dependence without shame. It brings every need, big or small, trusting that God can handle it all without being overwhelmed or bothered.

So if false humility has been your barrier, if you've been holding back from asking because you didn't want to bother God with small things, I need you to hear me when I say God wants you to bother Him. He wants you to come to Him with everything. He wants to be involved in every area of your life, not just the big crises or major decisions. He wants to be your source for everything, from the monumental to the minute. And when you hold back because you think something is too small, you're actually robbing yourself of intimacy with Him and robbing Him of the opportunity to show His care for you in tangible ways.

These three barriers, pride, unbelief, and false humility, are the primary obstacles that keep believers from engaging in the kind of authentic, persistent asking that Jesus commands. And most of us are operating under the restrictions of at least one of them, often without even realizing it. So before you go any further in this book, before we move into the next dimension of seeking, you need to do an honest inventory. Which of these barriers is operating in your life? What's preventing you from bringing your needs to God with specificity, expectation, and vulnerability?

Take some time now to think about that question. Don't rush or assume you already know the answer. The foundation for everything that comes next is this first step of asking. If you can't ask well, you won't seek effectively, and you won't get to the point of knocking. Everything builds on this, so it's worth taking the time to break down any barriers holding you back from this important first step.

Now that we've identified the barriers, let's talk about what authentic asking actually looks like in practice. Because knowing what not to do is only half the equation. You also need to know what to do, how to engage this first dimension in a way that positions you for breakthroughs. And I want to give you a framework that's both biblical and practical, something you can start implementing immediately.

The first part of real asking is being specific. Vague prayers lead to vague results, if any at all. When you pray, 'God, bless my finances,' what does that mean? Are you asking for a raise, unexpected income, better money management, or more contentment? The request is so broad that even if God answers, you might not notice because you never defined what a breakthrough would look like.

But when you pray, "God, I need an extra five hundred dollars this month to cover unexpected medical expenses," now you have something specific. You can track that. You can recognize when it manifests. You can give testimony to God's faithfulness in concrete terms rather than vague generalities. Specificity creates accountability, both for you and for what you're believing God to do.

Some people hesitate to be specific because they think it's presumptuous, as if they're telling God what to do instead of surrendering to His will. But there's a big difference between demanding and having a conversation with God. When you bring a specific request, you're not insisting God do it your way. You're starting a conversation and giving God something clear to respond to. His answer might be yes, not yet, or something better. But at least you've made a clear request.

Think about how Jesus interacted with people who came to Him with needs. When blind Bartimaeus called out to Him, Jesus could have just assumed the man wanted healing. It was obvious. But instead, Jesus asked, "What do you want me to do for you?" He made Bartimaeus articulate the specific request. The same thing happened with James and John when they came to Jesus, saying they wanted Him to do something for them. Jesus asked, "What do you want me to do for you?" Even though He knew what they wanted, He required them to state it clearly.

Why? Because saying your request out loud does something for you. It makes your wants clear. It means you take ownership. It moves you from just hoping to actually asking. And it gives you something to look back on later if you start to doubt whether God heard you or if your prayers matter.

So the first practical step in learning to ask well is this: write down three specific requests. Not five or ten or twenty. Start with three. And make them as concrete and measurable as possible. Instead of "God, help my marriage," write "God, help my spouse and me have three meaningful conversations this week where we actually listen to each other." Instead of "God, provide for my needs," write "God, provide the twelve hundred dollars I need for car repairs by the fifteenth." Instead of "God, heal me," write "God, I'm asking for complete healing from this condition so that when I go to the doctor next month, the tests come back clear."

The difference is that these requests are clear and specific. You'll know if they've been answered or not. That kind of clarity is important because it lets you see God's faithfulness in real, concrete ways.

The second part of authentic asking is consistency. The Greek tense Jesus uses keeps asking. This isn't about praying once and moving on. It's about steady, repeated asking that keeps you aware of your need and expectation until the answer comes. Many people pray about something once or twice, and when nothing changes right away, they assume God isn't going to answer and move on. But Jesus teaches a different way. He says to keep asking, keep bringing it up, and keep standing before God with your need and your expectation. To help with this, try a daily habit: place three pebbles on your desk, and each time you pray, remove one. This simple action reminds you to keep asking, keep trusting, and keep tracking.

Now, some people hear this and think it sounds like nagging. They imagine God getting annoyed with repeated requests, like a parent tired of a child's constant pestering. But that completely misses the heart of what Jesus is teaching. In Luke 11, right after He gives the "ask, seek, knock" instruction, He tells a parable about a man who goes to his friend's house at midnight to borrow bread because unexpected guests have arrived and he has nothing to feed them. The friend initially refuses because his family is already in bed and he doesn't want to get up. But because of the man's persistence, his shameless audacity in continuing to knock and ask, the friend eventually gets up and gives him what he needs.

Jesus is using this parable to illustrate something profound about prayer. God isn't like the reluctant friend who needs to be pestered into responding. God is infinitely better than that friend. But the parable highlights the power of persistence, of refusing to take no for an answer, of knocking until the door opens. If persistence works on a reluctant human friend, how much more effective will it be with a loving Heavenly Father who wants to give good gifts to His children?

Consistent asking isn't about wearing God down. It's about several things. First, it keeps you engaged with the request. When you pray about something daily, you don't forget about it. You don't move on prematurely. You stay connected to the need and to your dependence on God to meet it. Second, consistent asking builds faith. Every time you pray, you're making a choice to believe that God hears you and will respond. That choice, repeated over time, strengthens your spiritual muscles. Third, consistently asking positions you to recognize the answer when it comes. If you prayed about something once six months ago and then forgot about it, you might not even notice when God provides. But if you've been praying daily, you'll be watching for breakthroughs with expectant eyes.

Take those three specific requests you wrote down, and commit to praying about them every single day for the next thirty days. Not long prayers. Not elaborate prayers. Just simple, direct, specific asking. "God, I need this. I'm trusting You to provide it. I'm watching for Your response. Thank You in advance for hearing me and answering." That's it. Thirty seconds, once a day, for thirty days. Can you do that?

Most people won't do this because it takes discipline and focus. It's easier to pray now and then when you feel like it, to ask God for help when you're desperate, and then forget about it when things calm down. But that approach doesn't lead to breakthroughs. It leads to forgetting what you even prayed for, so you never know if God answered.

Consistent asking gives you a way to share your story. When you pray daily for something specific, and it happens, you know for sure that God answered. You can point to the timeline and the details. This builds your faith and helps others when you share exactly what you asked for and how God came through. That's the power of being both consistent and specific.

The third part of authentic asking is expectation. This is closely tied to the unbelief barrier we discussed earlier, but it's important enough to focus on in its own right. When you ask, do it with real expectation that God will respond. Don't just hope He might answer or wish He would, but doubt it. Expect, with confidence, that an answer is on the way. To help with this, try a simple reminder: put a sticky note with the word 'Watch' on your laptop, or somewhere you'll see it often. Let it remind you to stay alert for God's response. You can also pause at noon each day and quietly say 'Watch.' This small habit helps make expectation a real part of your daily life.

It's also important to remember that waiting is a normal part of spiritual growth. Sometimes there are real delays in how our prayers are answered, and while we wait, our faith can still grow. Facing uncertainty doesn't mean God isn't responding or that you lack faith. It's a chance to trust and be patient. Remind yourself that God's timing is perfect, and your daily prayers keep your relationship with Him strong. Be patient with yourself and know that the process matters as much as the outcome.

This kind of expectation shapes how you pray and live while you wait for an answer. When you really expect God to answer, you pray with more energy and urgency. Your prayers feel like a partnership, not just a routine. You also start watching for God's response. You notice opportunities, unexpected help, and moments that could be answers. You're ready to see God at work because you're looking for it.

Jesus addresses this in the gospel of Mark when He's teaching about faith and prayer. He says, "Whatever you ask in prayer, believe that you have received it, and it will be yours." Notice the tense there. Believe that you have received it. Not that you will receive it someday in the distant future. That you have received it. Present tense. As though the answer already exists, even before you see a physical manifestation. That's expectation at its highest level, believing so completely that God has heard and responded that you thank Him for the answer before you see it.

This isn't about trying to hype yourself up or pretending something is true when it isn't. It's about understanding how things work spiritually. When you pray for something that matches God's will and promises, the answer is released right away in the spiritual realm. It's real, but it may take time to show up in your life. From God's point of view, it's already done. The moment you prayed in faith, the answer started moving toward you.

This is what Abraham understood when God promised him descendants as numerous as the stars. Scripture says that Abraham believed God, and it was counted to him as righteousness. Abraham didn't wait until Sarah got pregnant to believe. He didn't wait until Isaac was born to have faith. He believed God's promise before there was any physical evidence to support it. In fact, Romans 4 tells us that Abraham didn't weaken in faith when he considered his own body, which was as good as dead, or Sarah's barren womb. He faced the facts of the natural realm squarely, acknowledged their impossibility, and still believed God's promise. That's expectation. That's faith that sees past what is and envisions what God says.

So how do you build this kind of expectation in your prayers? It starts with knowing what God has promised. You can't expect something if you don't know it's available. That's why reading Scripture is so important for prayer. The more you know God's promises, the more confident you'll be in asking for things that match those promises. You're not just hoping God will be generous, you're asking for what He's already said He'll provide.

For example, Philippians 4:19 says, "My God will supply every need of yours according to his riches in glory in Christ Jesus." That's not a suggestion. That's not a maybe. That's a promise. So when you have a legitimate need, you can pray with the expectation that God will supply it because He said He would. You're not begging. You're not trying to convince Him. You're simply reminding yourself of what He's already promised and positioning yourself to receive it.

The same applies to healing. By His stripes we are healed, according to Isaiah 53 and 1 Peter 2. Healing is part of the atonement that Jesus purchased on the cross. So when you pray for healing, you're not asking God to do something He's reluctant to do. You're accessing something He's already provided. That changes everything about how you pray. Instead of timid requests that sound more like wishful thinking, you can pray with bold expectation because you're standing on a promise, not just hoping for a possibility.

But here's where many believers struggle. They pray with expectation, but when the answer doesn't show up right away, they start to doubt. They wonder whether they heard God correctly, whether they had enough faith, or whether the promise really applies to them. That doubt weakens the expectation they started with, creating the kind of instability James warned about: a double-minded person who shouldn't expect to receive anything from the Lord.

This is why sustained asking, the consistency we talked about earlier, is so important. When you commit to praying about something daily, you're reinforcing your expectation every single day. You're not letting doubt creep in and take root. You're actively choosing to believe, to expect, to trust that God heard you and is responding even when you don't see evidence yet. That daily choice to re-engage your expectation is what maintains the spiritual posture necessary for breakthrough.

Here's a practical way to build expectation. When you pray for something specific, finish your prayer by thanking God in advance. Thank Him for providing before you see the money. Thank Him for healing before you feel better. Thank Him for breakthroughs before anything changes. This isn't about trying to force God's hand or pretending to have faith you don't feel. It's about aligning your attitude with the truth that God has already heard you and begun the answer. Thanksgiving is the language of expectation. It shows you, and the spiritual world, that you're not just hoping for breakthroughs, you're expecting them.

The fourth part of authentic asking is surrender. This might sound like it goes against expectations and specificity, but it doesn't. They actually work together. You can't truly ask with faith unless you're also willing to trust God with the outcome. There's something special about giving your requests to God, knowing He understands more than we do. This mix of boldness and trust lets God work in ways that surprise us and remind us of His greatness. As you balance surrender and specificity, it might help to ask yourself, 'Is my request anchored in God's larger purpose or just in my preference?' This guiding question invites you to practice discernment, ensuring your surrender doesn't diminish your boldness.

Jesus modeled this perfectly in the Garden of Gethsemane. He prayed with specificity: "Father, if it be possible, let this cup pass from me." That's a clear request. But then He added: "Nevertheless, not my will, but yours, be done." That's surrender. Jesus asked for what He wanted while submitting to what the Father knew was necessary. He demonstrated how to be both specific and surrendered, expectant and yielded.

This is crucial because sometimes what we're asking for isn't actually what we need. Sometimes God's no, not yet, or here's something different is far more loving than giving us exactly what we requested. And if we're so rigid in our asking that we can't recognize God's better answer when it comes, we'll miss the breakthrough He's actually providing while we're still demanding the breakthrough we envisioned.

Surrender doesn't mean praying weak prayers. It doesn't mean adding so many conditions that you never really ask for anything specific. It means praying bold prayers while trusting a God who is even stronger. It means asking with all your heart, while knowing that God's perspective is much bigger than yours. It means being open to being surprised by how God answers, while still expecting Him to respond.

Think of it this way. A small child asks a parent for candy before dinner. The parent says no, not because they don't love the child or because they're being stingy, but because they know candy before dinner will spoil the child's appetite for the nutritious meal they've prepared. The child might be disappointed in the moment, but the parent's no is actually an expression of love and wisdom. Later, when the child enjoys a satisfying dinner and gets dessert afterward, they benefit far more than they would have from the candy they originally wanted.

That's what surrender allows for in our prayers. It creates space for God to respond in ways that serve us better than our original request, even when we can't see that in the moment. And here's the beautiful thing: when you surrender the outcome while maintaining expectation, you actually position yourself to receive more, not less. Because you're not limiting God to your imagination of what breakthroughs should look like. You're opening yourself to however He chooses to provide.

Specificity and surrender aren't opposites: they work together. Being specific focuses your faith. It gives you something real to believe in, something to watch for, and something to measure. Without being specific, prayer gets so vague that you never really know if God answered. You might feel God's presence or provision, but that doesn't build the kind of faith that comes from seeing specific prayers answered in clear ways.

However, specificity must be balanced with surrender. Avoid presumption by trusting in God's wisdom and allowing Him to respond in the best way. Pray specifically to focus your faith and create a tangible measure of God's work, while surrendering to His wisdom to guide the answers. Praying with specificity strengthens your faith, while surrender ensures your prayers align with His will.

Pray specifically, naming your needs and desires, but hold your requests with open hands. Trust that God's answer, even if it's different from what you expect, serves a greater purpose. Balancing specificity and surrender lets you experience breakthroughs beyond what you imagined, as your faith lines up with God's wisdom.

Let's talk now about what asking does beyond just positioning you to receive. The act of asking accomplishes something profound in your relationship with God and in your spiritual formation. It's not just about informing God of your needs, as He already knows them. Asking is truly about transforming who you are. Consider how asking can shape not just your immediate circumstances, but your identity and potential. Who might you become if you embraced the transformative power of asking? This transformation unfolds in several ways.

This is why James writes, "God opposes the proud but gives grace to the humble." Pride creates resistance between you and God's provision. It's not that God is being petty or vindictive. It's that pride that positions you as though you don't need what God is offering. And if you're not postured as a receiver, you can't receive what's being given. Humility, expressed through asking, opens your hands to receive God's grace. It creates the proper posture for breakthrough.

Second, asking builds closeness with God. When you bring your needs to Him regularly and specifically, you're having an ongoing conversation with Him. You're not just coming to God when something big happens; you're inviting Him into the details of your daily life. You're treating Him as a caring Father, not a distant figure you only call on in emergencies.

Think about any close relationship in your life. Intimacy is built through communication, through sharing your life with someone else, through letting them see your needs and vulnerabilities. The same is true with God. When you ask Him for things and bring your worries, concerns, and desires to Him, you're building intimacy. You're letting Him into the deeper places of your life. And that ongoing dialogue strengthens your relationship in ways that casual, generic prayers never will.

Third, asking helps you expect God to move. When you ask for something specific, you begin to look for His response. You notice more of what God is doing in your life. You're alert to opportunities and unexpected help. This expectation changes how you live. Instead of just going through the motions, you're engaged and watching for God's hand in your life. Often, this awareness helps you see breakthroughs you might have missed otherwise.

Fourth, asking generates testimony. When you've prayed specifically for something, and then you see God provide it, you have a story to tell. You have concrete evidence of God's faithfulness that you can share with others who are struggling to believe. Your testimony becomes a tool that builds faith not just in your own life but in the lives of those who hear it. And in the kingdom economy, testimony is incredibly powerful. Revelation 12:11 says that believers overcome by the blood of the Lamb and the word of their testimony. Your story of answered prayer has spiritual force. It defeats lies that say God doesn't answer, doesn't care, doesn't move in people's lives anymore.

This week, consider sharing one specific answered-prayer story with a friend. By turning personal victories into shared narratives, you can amplify hope and faith within your community. Additionally, I invite you to gather with a group this week and exchange these testimonies collectively. Sharing stories in a group not only multiplies faith but also ingrains these breakthroughs into the communal culture, strengthening the collective belief and support within your community.

But you only have a real story to share if you've asked for something specific and then noticed how God answered. Generic prayers lead to vague stories that don't mean much. But if you can say, "I needed exactly twelve hundred dollars by Friday for car repairs, and on Thursday someone I hadn't talked to in years called and said they felt led to bless me with fifteen hundred dollars," that's a powerful testimony. It's specific, measurable, and clear. It encourages others to ask with faith because they see real evidence that God answers specific requests.

Fifth, asking helps you learn to recognize God's voice. When you talk to God regularly and bring your requests to Him, you start to notice how He speaks to you. Maybe it's through Scripture that suddenly stands out, through situations that match your prayers, or through other people who say just what you need to hear. The more you ask and watch for answers, the better you get at hearing God. This skill is important not just for breakthroughs, but for living your whole life with Him.

Now, I want to address something that comes up frequently when I teach on this subject. People ask, "What about praying according to God's will? Doesn't 1 John 5:14 say that if we ask anything according to His will, He hears us? So shouldn't we focus on discerning God's will before we ask for anything?" And that's a valid question that deserves a thoughtful response.

Yes, Scripture does emphasize praying according to God's will. And yes, there's wisdom in seeking to understand what God wants before you make requests. But here's what many believers miss: God's will is often far broader than we think. We tend to assume that God's will is a narrow path in which He cares only about a few specific things and that everything else is outside His concern. But that's not the picture Scripture paints.

God's will includes your provision, your healing, your peace, your joy, your relationships, and your purpose. These aren't peripheral concerns that God tolerates. They're central to His heart for you. So when you pray for provision, you're praying according to His will because He's already promised to supply all your needs. When you pray for healing, you're praying according to His will because healing was part of the atonement. When you pray for wisdom, you're praying according to His will because James says God gives wisdom generously to all who ask without finding fault.

The question isn't whether God's will includes these things. The question is how and when He chooses to provide them. And that's where surrender comes in, which we already discussed. You can ask with confidence for anything that aligns with God's revealed character and promises in Scripture, knowing that you're praying in accordance with His will. Then you trust Him with the specifics of how and when He responds.

But here's what you shouldn't do: use "God's will" as an excuse not to ask. Don't hide behind statements like "If it's God's will" to avoid the vulnerability of specific asking. Don't use surrender as a spiritual bypass that keeps you from actually engaging your faith. God wants you to ask. He wants you to bring your desires to Him. He wants to respond to your requests. And if something you ask for isn't aligned with His will, He's perfectly capable of saying no or redirecting you. Your job isn't to perfectly discern every aspect of God's will before you pray. Your job is to ask and then trust Him to respond in the way that serves you best.

While preaching at a church, I spoke with a man who had been unemployed for 6 months. His prayers were broad, like asking "God, help me find work," but nothing seemed to change. I encouraged him to be specific in his prayers, suggesting he specify the type of job, workplace setting, and salary he sought. Initially hesitant, he decided to write down these specifics, praying with focused intention. A month later, he received a call about a job that perfectly matched his skills and offered a salary beyond his expectations. This demonstrated that specific prayer led to a breakthrough.

Here's another practical tool for this kind of asking: start a prayer journal. It doesn't have to be fancy, just a simple notebook where you write your specific requests, the date you started praying, and notes about how God responds. This helps in a few ways. First, it makes you get specific because you're writing things down. Second, it lets you track your prayers over time so you don't forget what you asked for. Third, it creates a record of God's faithfulness you can look back on when you need encouragement.

Here's how to use it. At the top of a page, write one specific request. Below it, write the date. Then, each time you pray about this request, jot down the date and maybe a brief note about anything significant that happened that day related to the request. When God answers, whether it's in the way you expected or in a different form, write that down with the date. Over time, you'll build a record of God's responses to your prayers that will strengthen your faith and provide powerful testimony material.

Some of your journal requests might get answered quickly. Others could take months or even years. Some might get a different answer than you expected, and you'll note that as you see God provide in other ways. Writing it all down keeps you involved in the process. It helps you remember what you prayed for and stay focused and intentional in your prayer life, something most people never do.

Now, let's address one more critical aspect of asking before we close this chapter. We need to talk about asking in Jesus's name, because this phrase gets thrown around casually but is actually loaded with meaning that most believers don't understand.

When Jesus says in John 14:13, "Whatever you ask in my name, this I will do," He's not teaching us a magic phrase to tack onto the end of prayers. "In Jesus' name" isn't a spiritual password that gives you access to whatever you want. It's much deeper than that. To ask in Jesus's name means to ask according to His character, His authority, and His purposes. It means your request aligns with who Jesus is and what He came to accomplish.

Think about it this way. If someone gave you their credit card and said, "Use this in my name," what would that mean? It would mean you have authority to access their resources, but you're expected to use that authority responsibly, in ways that align with their intentions and values. You wouldn't use their card to buy things they wouldn't approve of. You'd use it in ways that honor the trust they've placed in you.

That's what asking in Jesus's name means. You have access to His authority and His resources. You can bring requests to the Father on the basis of what Jesus accomplished on the cross. But those requests should align with Jesus's character and purposes. You're not trying to manipulate God into giving you things that serve your flesh or your ego. You're accessing the provision that Jesus purchased for you through His death and resurrection.

So when you ask in Jesus' name, you're essentially saying, "Father, based on who Jesus is, based on what He accomplished, based on the relationship He's established between us, I'm bringing this request. I'm asking for this because it aligns with the life Jesus died to give me. I'm trusting that through Jesus, I have access to everything I need for life and godliness."

That's why asking in Jesus's name is so powerful. You're not coming to God based on your own merit or worthiness. You're coming based on Jesus's merit, Jesus's worthiness, Jesus's accomplished work. And that gives you confidence that you could never have if your access depended on your own goodness or spiritual performance. Jesus has already done everything necessary to give you full access to the Father. Your job is to use that access, to ask boldly and confidently, knowing that you're coming through Jesus and that changes everything about how the Father receives you.

This is why Hebrews 4:16 says, "Let us then with confidence draw near to the throne of grace, that we may receive mercy and find grace to help in time of need." Notice the word "confidence." We're not supposed to come to God timidly, apologetically, hoping He might decide to acknowledge us if He's in a good mood. We come with confidence because Jesus has opened the way. We come boldly because our access isn't based on our worthiness but on His.

But that confidence should never become presumption. There's a difference between coming boldly as a beloved child and coming arrogantly as someone who thinks they can demand whatever they want. The balance is this: you have full access because of Jesus, but you use that access wisely, asking for things that align with His character and purposes, surrendering the outcome to the Father's wisdom, trusting that He will respond in the way that serves you best.

When you understand asking in Jesus's name this way, it transforms your prayers. Instead of timid requests that sound like you're not sure God is even listening, you pray with authority. You pray with confidence. You pray knowing that through Jesus, you have every right to bring your needs before the Father and expect Him to respond. Not because you deserve it, but because Jesus made it possible.

Let's finish this chapter with a clear action plan. Information alone doesn't change anything; it's what you do with it that matters. If you want to move forward and see breakthroughs, you need to put what you've learned into practice right away. You can also use this as a 30-day plan to build a habit and break patterns that hold you back.

1. Identify Barriers
First, identify the barriers that have been preventing you from asking well. Is it pride that makes you think you should handle things yourself? Is it unbelief that doubts God will respond? Is it false humility that says your needs are too small to bother Him with? Be honest about which barrier or barriers are operating in your life. Name them. Acknowledge them. Confess them before God and ask Him to help you dismantle them.

2. Write Down Three Specific Requests
Second, write down three specific requests. Make them concrete, measurable, and aligned with what you know about God's character and promises in Scripture. Don't write twenty requests. Start with three. Quality over quantity. These should be things that genuinely matter to you, things you've been carrying anxiety or worry about, things that would make a tangible difference in your life if they were resolved.

3. Commit to Daily Prayer
Third, commit to praying about these three requests daily for the next thirty days. Keep it simple. You don't need long, elaborate prayers. Just bring each request to God with specificity, consistency, expectation, and surrender. Ask as though you're confident He's hearing you and will respond. Thank Him in advance for His provision. And then release the outcome to His wisdom.

4. Start a Prayer Journal
Fourth, start your prayer journal. Get a notebook today, not next week, today, and

write down your three requests with the date. Then every time you pray about them, jot down the date and any notes about what you're observing, sensing, or experiencing related to those requests. Create a record that you can look back on later as testimony to God's faithfulness.

5. Assess and Recalibrate
Fifth, examine your prayers for the past month. How many of them were specific versus vague? How many were consistent versus sporadic? How many carried genuine expectation versus just going through the motions? Use this honest assessment to recalibrate how you approach prayer going forward. Don't beat yourself up about what you've done wrong. Just commit to doing it differently starting now.

And finally, spend some time meditating on what it means to ask in Jesus' name. Read through John 14-16, where Jesus teaches extensively about prayer and about His relationship with the Father. Let the reality of your access through Jesus sink deep into your understanding. Let it build confidence in your prayers. Let it transform how you approach God.

As you finish this chapter, remember: asking isn't just the first step in a process. It's a new way to relate to God and yourself. When you learn to ask well, with honest dependence and expectant faith, everything changes. You stop living as if you're on your own and start living as a child of God with access to all He offers through Jesus. This shift can bring real changes, like unexpected financial help, restored relationships, or better health. These outcomes help you grow and strengthen your faith, showing that breakthroughs are real, not just ideas. Your breakthrough starts the moment you dare to ask.

But asking is only the first dimension. It's essential, but it's not complete. You can ask perfectly, with all the specificity, consistency, expectation, and surrender we've discussed, and still not see a breakthrough if you stop there. Because asking is meant to lead to seeking, and seeking is meant to lead to knocking. It's a progression, a trilogy of escalating intensity and investment. And most believers stop at asking, which is why they're frustrated with their prayer lives.

The good news is that you're not going to stop at asking. You're going to move into the next dimension. You're going to learn what it means to seek, to take the verbal requests you've made and put feet to them, to partner with God in active pursuit of breakthrough. You're going to discover that faith isn't just about what you say in prayer. It's about what you do in response to prayer. And that's where things get really exciting, because that's where you move from spectator to participant, from passive believer to active partner with God.

But before you move into that next chapter, before you learn about seeking, you need to get this first dimension right. You need to learn to ask well. Because if you can't articulate what you need, if you can't sustain consistent prayer, if you can't maintain expectation, if you can't surrender the outcome, then seeking will just become striving. You'll be running around trying to make things happen through your own effort rather than partnering with God in His process.

So take time now to put what you've learned into practice. Follow the action steps. Break down the barriers. Write your requests. Start your journal. Pray daily with specificity, consistency, expectation, and surrender. Give this thirty days of focused effort. Then watch what happens, see your relationship with God grow, notice more of His work in your life, and watch breakthroughs start to appear in ways you didn't expect.

Because here's the truth that I've seen proven over and over in my own life and in the lives of countless others. When you learn to ask well, God responds. Not always in the way you expect. Not always on the timeline you prefer. But always in a way that serves your ultimate good and His ultimate glory. He's a good Father who gives good gifts to His children. And when you position yourself to receive those gifts through authentic, faith-filled asking, you'll discover that the Christian life is far more dynamic and powerful than you ever imagined.

Are you ready? Then close this chapter, grab your journal, write down your three requests, and start asking; today, right now. Don't wait until you feel more spiritual or more confident. Ask from where you are, with what you have. God will meet you there. He's been waiting for you to ask, and the moment you do, everything starts to change.

Your breakthrough is closer than you think. It starts with a prayer. Not just any prayer, but the kind of asking this chapter has equipped you to engage. So ask. Ask boldly. Ask specifically. Ask consistently. Ask expectantly. Ask in Jesus' name. And then get ready for the next dimension, because we're just getting started.

Now let's learn to seek.

CHAPTER THREE

THE SECOND DIMENSION

SEEKING: WHEN FAITH GETS FEET

SHE HAD BEEN BLEEDING for twelve years, caught in a cycle of desperation and hope. Those years wore down her body, drained her finances, and left her isolated. Mark's Gospel says she suffered under many doctors, spent everything she had, and only got worse. She tried every remedy, faced repeated disappointment, and watched her life slip away as those she trusted took her money but gave her nothing in return.

Then she heard about Jesus. People were talking about a Rabbi who healed the sick, cast out demons, and spoke with real authority. Maybe she overheard conversations in the marketplace, even though she wasn't supposed to be there. Maybe she heard about the leper He healed, the paralyzed man who walked, or the man freed from demons. We are not certain how she heard about Him, but we are sure that what she heard sparked a hope she hadn't felt in years. It was the risky hope that maybe Jesus could help when no one else could.

Her story stands out because she didn't just hope or pray for it. She acted. She pushed through a crowd that could have punished her for being there since she was considered unclean. She risked being exposed and humiliated, but still made her way through the crowd to touch the edge of Jesus's robe.

That touch changed everything. Right away, her bleeding stopped, and she knew she was healed. Jesus realized that power had gone out from Him and asked who touched Him. The disciples were confused because the crowd was pressing in, but Jesus knew this touch was different. It wasn't just a random bump. It was the desperate reach of someone desperately seeking something that He alone could give.

When the woman saw she couldn't stay hidden, she came forward, trembling, and told Jesus everything. He said, "Daughter, your faith has made you well. Go in peace, and be healed of your disease." It was her faith, not just hope, that gave her the courage to push through the crowd and reach for healing.

This is what seeking really means. Many believers get stuck because seeking takes more than just asking. Asking uses words and can happen anywhere. But seeking means taking action. It takes movement, risk, effort, and purpose. Seeking is when your prayers become steps, when faith turns practical, and when you start trusting God to meet you as you go.

Let's look at the Greek word Jesus uses for "seek" in Matthew 7:7: *zeteo*. It means to look for, strive for, desire, or search carefully. It's like when you lose your car keys or phone. You don't just hope they show up. You get up, retrace your steps, check everywhere, move things, and even ask others for help. That's zeteo: searching with determination until you find what you need.

Jesus uses the present imperative tense here, just like with "ask." He's telling us to keep seeking. Don't give up after one try or do it halfheartedly. Keep going with steady effort until you find what you're looking for. This is about actively pursuing, not just waiting. It's about working with God for your breakthrough, not expecting Him to do everything while you do nothing.

Let me be clear: we can't earn God's love by working harder, and that's not what I mean by seeking. True seeking is about aligning our actions with God's grace. It's not about earning. You can't earn God's blessing, favor, or provision through your own effort. Salvation comes by grace through faith, not by works. That's non-negotiable. Ephesians 2:8-9 says, "For by grace you have been saved through faith. And this is not your own doing; it is the gift of God, not a result of works, so that no one may boast." If salvation, the greatest blessing, comes by grace through faith, then every other blessing does too.

So what is seeking? It means putting yourself in a place where God's provision can reach you. It's aligning your actions with your prayers and showing your belief by acting on what you ask for. Think of grace like rain. God sends it freely. You can't earn or control it, but you can step into it. Open your hands and receive. Remember, God is already moving toward you, eager to meet you. Seeking doesn't create the blessing; it puts you in a place to receive what God is already providing.

James understood this when he wrote that faith without works is dead. He wasn't disagreeing with Paul about grace, but showing that real faith always leads to action. If you truly believe something, it changes how you live. If your life looks the same as someone without faith, then it's just agreement in your mind, not real faith. Real faith leads to action, and that action is what we call seeking.

The woman with the issue of blood is a perfect example. She believed that touching Jesus's garment would heal her, but her faith didn't stop at belief. It moved her into a crowd she wasn't supposed to be in, pushed her past obstacles and danger, and led her to reach out for what she believed was possible. Her faith and her seeking worked together. Faith led her to seek, and seeking put her in a position to receive what she believed. This is the model Jesus gives us in Matthew 7: ask, seek, knock. These aren't separate activities, but parts of the same journey. Asking states your need. Seeking puts you in a position for the answer. Knocking means you keep going until breakthroughs come. Each step asks more of you than the last. Asking takes humility and faith. Seeking adds action and risk. Knocking needs all that plus persistence and determination. You can't skip steps. Clear asking leads to effective seeking, and diligent seeking leads to persistent knocking.

Let's talk about what seeking looks like in everyday life. This is where faith becomes real, and sometimes uncomfortable. It's also where you find out whether you truly want the blessing or just like the idea of it, because seeking often takes real effort and commitment.

Seeking has three main parts, and you need all of them to put yourself in a position for breakthroughs. These aren't just suggestions; they're necessary steps that work together to move you closer to God's provision. If you skip one, you might end up stuck and wondering why your breakthrough hasn't come.

THE FIRST DIMENSION OF SEEKING: WISDOM

When you start seeking, the first thing you need is wisdom. It's important to know what you're facing, what solutions exist, what challenges might come up, and what resources you have. Think about how much can change when you go beyond just praying for help and begin learning about your goals. Many people ask God for provision but don't look into how it might arrive. They pray for healing but don't learn about their condition. They ask for open doors but don't check which ones are open or how to walk through them.

Seeking wisdom is about learning as much as you can about what you're praying for. If you want a financial breakthrough, learn how to manage money, budget, invest, and find new ways to earn. This might mean reading books, taking classes, or talking to people who are good with money. If you're praying for healing, learn about your diagnosis, treatment options, and how your habits affect your health. If you're praying for a job, update your resume, learn new skills, understand your field, and connect with others in your industry.

Some people worry that seeking wisdom might weaken their faith. They believe that real trust in God should lead to supernatural answers, so learning isn't needed. But learning is actually a way to obey and show trust, not just rely on yourself. While miracles do happen, God often works through what we know and do, multiplying our efforts in ways only He can.

Think about the story of feeding the five thousand. Jesus could have provided food another way, but He asked what was already there. The disciples found a boy with five loaves and two fish. Jesus took what they had, blessed it, and multiplied it. The miracle happened because someone was willing to offer what they had. "God multiplies what you mobilize." God often takes what you bring, blesses your efforts, and uses your wisdom and actions. He blesses the natural and makes it supernatural.

Seeking wisdom doesn't mean you don't have faith. It actually shows your faith in action. It says, "God, I trust You to provide, and I want to be ready to see and receive what You give. I want to understand my situation so I can work with You." This is what active trust looks like. This is what it means to seek.

Here's an example from a pastor friend. A couple came to him feeling overwhelmed by debt. They had prayed for years for a financial breakthrough, asking God to provide or erase their debt, but nothing changed. When my friend asked what they had done besides praying, they admitted they hadn't made a budget, tracked their spending, looked into debt consolidation, talked to a financial counselor, or read any books on managing money. They had asked, but they hadn't truly sought. Like so many others, they never considered seeking.

What about you? Take a moment to think about your financial habits. Are you actively looking for solutions, or just hoping for a miracle? If you're not seeking, I encourage you to please consider some practical steps you can take alongside your prayers for financial help.

He encouraged them to start seeking wisdom. He gave them resources on budgeting and debt management and introduced them to a financial counselor from his church who offered to help. At first, they resisted because it seemed like hard work, but eventually, they decided to give it a try.

In just four months, their priorities changed. By using what they learned, they made real progress. They reduced their debt from $15,000 to just under $9,000, which significantly reduced their stress. As they focused on needs instead of wants, their approach became more practical and less about just hoping for a miracle. God blessed their efforts as they used the wisdom they gained, showing that taking action can really make a difference.

Seeking wisdom means doing your research, getting informed, and learning from people who have faced similar challenges. Gaining knowledge helps you make better choices and find new opportunities. The best part is that God loves to give wisdom. James 1:5 says, "If any of you lacks wisdom, let him ask God, who gives generously to all without reproach, and it will be given him." You don't have to beg or earn wisdom. Just ask for it and be ready to receive it by actively seeking it out.

If you're praying about something right now, ask yourself: What do I need to learn about this situation? What knowledge would help me handle it better? Who has faced this before, and what can I learn from them? What books, courses, or experts could help? To get started, take a small step today. Spend five minutes searching online for articles or videos on your topic. Find one expert to follow for advice. Don't just pray and hope. Pray and learn. That's seeking wisdom, and it's the first key step in effective seeking.

We often struggle because we don't know what we need to know. That's why I wrote *The Unknown: What You Need to Know but Don't Know*. This book equips you with the tools to identify knowledge gaps and effectively bridge them, empowering you to take informed action. If you haven't read it yet, I encourage you to get a copy. I believe it will help you.

THE SECOND DIMENSION OF SEEKING: OPPORTUNITY

After you gain wisdom about your situation, the next step is to look for opportunities. This involves putting yourself in places where breakthroughs can happen. Show up where provision is likely, and be present and ready when God opens doors. Sometimes, this means taking risks, even if it feels uncomfortable. I once hesitated to go to a networking event because I was worried I wouldn't fit in. I missed meeting someone who later helped a friend succeed. No doubt, if I were with my friend, I would have benefited as well. That taught me that taking risks can open doors you didn't expect.

You can pray for a job, but if you don't update your resume, apply, or tell people you're looking, how will you find one? God can do anything, but He often works through everyday situations. He might connect you with someone who knows about a job or bring an opportunity your way. But you need to be ready and in the right place for those connections to happen.

That's what it means to seek opportunity. You pray for what you need, then look for where it could come from. You apply for jobs, reach out to your network, and learn new skills to be more employable. You go to places where the kind of work you want is available. Instead of waiting for God to bring the opportunity to you, you take steps toward it.

Maybe you're seeking breakthroughs in the area of relationships. You might be praying for a spouse, which is a good thing. But if you never leave your house, go to the right places to meet people that you are interested in, or accept invitations, how can God connect you with the right person? God can work anywhere, but most relationships start through shared activities and regular time together. So, seeking opportunity means putting yourself in those situations.

When you begin seeking opportunities, you often face challenges that push you out of your comfort zone. It's about being willing to be seen and trying things that might not work right away. Instead of seeing your comfort zone as safe, think of it as a cage that gets smaller with every missed chance. We all want to avoid rejection or disappointment, but staying in that cage only keeps you stuck. Imagine the joy and fulfillment that come from breaking free, reaching your breakthrough, and stepping into your purpose. Let this hope help you face challenges and move past fear.

I see this a lot in church. members long for opportunities to serve but never volunteer. Someone wants their business to grow, but never markets or promotes it. Someone prays for healing but doesn't change the habits that cause their illness. Someone wants reconciliation but never starts the tough conversations needed for healing. They want a breakthrough, but they're not willing to go where breakthroughs can happen.

There is a difference between seeking and wishing. Wishing is passive; you just hope something good happens. Seeking is active. You move toward what you believe in. You go to the right places, take risks, and make yourself available. You might face rejection or failure, but it's worse to never try and always wonder why nothing changes.

Let me share an experience that taught me more about seeking opportunity than any sermon I've preached. A pastor friend invited me to speak at a week-long conference, and I had been preaching on faith, a theme close to my heart. One night, the service was especially powerful. Lives were touched, hearts were changed, and I left the building still excited about what God had done.

On my way home, I stopped at a gas station to fill up. I was still thinking about the service and amazed at how God had moved. After filling my tank, I went inside to pay. As I walked back out, I saw a man coming toward me. He was smiling, but his eyes showed worry. Even though he tried to look friendly, I could see he was concerned.

He asked if I could help him with five dollars for gas. I checked my pockets for cash, but I remembered I had given everything I had during the service. I had no cash, just my cards, which I had just used to buy gas. Before I could explain, he pointed to his car parked at the front of the station.

"My whole family is with me," he said, and the way he said it made me look closer. There they were: his wife in the passenger seat and two daughters in the back, still in their school uniforms. It was eleven o'clock at night.

My eyes widened. This wasn't just a man asking for gas money. This was a father who had driven his family into the night, with no clear way home. He continued to explain that things had been tough financially. Someone he worked for owed him money and hadn't paid him. So he decided to load his family into their car, even though they didn't have enough gas, and drove to the man's home to collect what he was owed. Unfortunately, the man wasn't there, so the trip was unsuccessful. And he is now, at a gas station after eleven at night, seeking five dollars because he didn't have enough fuel to get home.

I stood there for a moment, speechless; not because of his request, but because of this man's level of faith. This man needed gas, and instead of staying home and praying or waiting for help to miraculously appear, he went to the one place where gas was available. He went to the gas station. He didn't have money, and his situation was desperate, but he knew that if he stayed home, nothing would change. So he went to where the solution was, trusting that somehow, help would meet him there.

The boldness of his faith struck me. It took real courage to load his family into a car with not enough gas and drive to where help might be found. That's what seeking opportunity is at its core: putting yourself in position for breakthroughs even when you don't know exactly how they will come.

"I don't have cash," I told him, "but I have my card. Go pull up to a pump."

I went back inside and paid for forty dollars' worth of gas for him, enough to get his family home and more. When I came back out and told him it was taken care of, the relief on his face was unforgettable. But what stuck with me even more was the lesson he taught me without realizing it.

Many of us pray for help but stay in the wrong places. We ask God for provision while sitting in environments where it can't reach us. We pray for opportunities but remain invisible and unavailable. We ask for breakthroughs but put ourselves in situations where breakthroughs can't happen. This man understood something important: if you need gas, you go to the gas station. You don't wait for it to come to you. You move to where the solution is, trusting that once you're in position, provision will find a way to reach you.

That night still encourages me when I'm tempted to pray passively. It reminds me that seeking isn't just about mental or spiritual effort; it's also about where you are physically. It's about showing up where breakthroughs can happen, even if you don't have everything figured out or if getting there uses up your last resources. When you move toward the answer instead of waiting for it to come to you, something changes. Your faith becomes active in ways that passive prayer never could.

My only regret from that night is that I didn't go to the ATM and get some cash to give him beyond the gas. But that experience taught me something I've never forgotten. God responds to faith that takes action. He responds to people who put themselves in positions for blessing, not just those who wish for it from afar. Sometimes, the breakthrough you're praying for is waiting in the place you're afraid to go or think you can't reach.

That man sought opportunity by going to the gas station with an empty tank and a real need. Because he showed up where the solution was, provision found him; not because he earned it, but because he was in the right place to receive it. That's the power of seeking opportunity. That's what it means to partner with God by putting yourself where His provision can reach you.

Seeking opportunity means showing up and being available. It's about being in places where breakthroughs can happen. It takes faith because you act before you see results. You move before the door opens. You invest your time, energy, and sometimes money, not knowing if it will work out. That can feel risky and uncomfortable, but that's what faith is about.

Hebrews 11:6 says, "Without faith it is impossible to please God, for whoever would draw near to God must believe that he exists and that he rewards those who seek him." Notice that God rewards those who seek Him, not those who just wish, hope, or ask once and then do nothing. He rewards those who actively pursue Him and His provision with effort and faith. This idea appears throughout Scripture. For example, Jeremiah 29:13 says, "You will seek me and find me when you seek me with all your heart." This Old Testament wisdom connects with Jesus's teaching in Matthew 7:7, confirming that when we truly seek, we will find. As you reflect on this, consider who in your circle might join you in this Hebrews 11:6-style pursuit. Imagine the power of a community coming together, each person bringing their unique gifts and perspectives to this shared mission. In what ways could you support and encourage each other as you collectively seek God and His rewards?

Ask yourself right now: Where should I be that I'm not? What opportunities haven't I explored? What environments or communities might be where God's provision is waiting for me? Then ask the harder question: What's stopping me from going there? Is it fear of rejection, comfort with the way things are, laziness disguised as faith, or the belief that if God wanted to bless me, He'd do it without any effort from me?

The truth is, God could do it without your help. He is all-powerful and doesn't need you, but He chooses to work with you because partnership helps you grow in ways that passivity never will. When you seek opportunity, take risks, and make yourself available, you grow in faith, courage, trust in God, and character. Often, who you become through seeking is more valuable than what you receive.

THE THIRD DIMENSION OF SEEKING: ALIGNMENT

The third part of seeking is often the hardest because it means looking within, not just around you. Seeking alignment is about removing anything in your life that could be blocking the blessing you're praying for. It requires being honest about your own patterns, habits, mindsets, or relationships that might be holding you back. It also means working with God as He shapes your character while you wait for your situation to change.

Take a moment to invite God into this time of self-reflection. Pause for two minutes with Psalm 139:23-24: "Search me, O God, and know my heart! Try me and know my thoughts! And see if there be any grievous way in me, and lead me in the way everlasting!" Use this time to think about what might need to change in your life for the breakthrough you want. The Bible teaches that sometimes the obstacle to your breakthrough isn't outside of you; it's within. Until you let God bring your life into alignment with what you're asking for, breakthroughs will be hard to find.

Think about Naaman, the Syrian commander in 2 Kings 5. He was a powerful military leader, yet he suffered from leprosy. When he traveled to Israel seeking healing, the prophet Elisha sent a messenger telling him to wash seven times in the Jordan River. Naaman was furious. He expected something dramatic, not a simple instruction. He wanted healing, but he wasn't ready to follow through on what it would take. Wanting something and being ready to act are not the same.

Naaman's response is telling. Instead of obeying, he complained that the rivers of Damascus were better than the waters of Israel. He focused on what he thought should happen rather than submitting to the path God provided. His servants had to reason with him, asking why he wouldn't do something simple if it meant healing. Finally, Naaman humbled himself, went to the Jordan, and dipped seven times. Only then was his flesh restored. Healing came when he acted, not when he argued.

How often are we like Naaman? We pray for breakthroughs but don't take steps to change or deal with what keeps us stuck. We ask God to heal our relationships but avoid facing our own issues, like unforgiveness or poor communication. We want God to provide for us, but we don't change our spending or learn to manage money. We hope for new opportunities, but don't build the character or skills needed to handle them.

Seeking alignment means asking God to show you what's blocking your breakthroughs and being willing to deal with whatever He points out. Sometimes it's sin that needs to be confessed or unforgiveness that needs to be released. It could be relationships that need healing or ending, or habits and mindsets that need to change. Whatever it is, seeking alignment is about working with God as He changes you while you wait for your situation to shift. Remember, you are already accepted and loved in Christ. Your identity in Him is secure. Aligning with His will is about growing and finding freedom, not about feeling condemned. Looking inward becomes a journey of hope, not judgment.

It also means being open to changing your environment when needed. Sometimes the obstacle to breakthroughs isn't just inside you; it's in your surroundings or the people you're with. Maybe you're praying for spiritual growth, but spend time with people who don't respect your faith. Maybe you want to stay sober but still go to places where temptation is strong. Or maybe you want financial breakthroughs, but work in a toxic place that drains your energy and creativity.

Seeking alignment might require making tough choices about relationships, places, or situations that hold you back. This doesn't mean leaving people who need help or avoiding every challenge. But it does mean being honest about whether your environment supports what you're praying for. If it doesn't, seeking alignment means being willing to make changes, even when it's hard.

Think about Lot in Genesis. He left Abraham and chose to live near Sodom because the land looked rich. It seemed like a smart decision, but the spiritual environment was harmful. The people there were wicked, and over time, that affected Lot and his family. When judgment came, Lot lost almost everything.

His wife looked back and became a pillar of salt, and his daughters made poor choices. The wealth he hoped for by living near Sodom ended up costing him more than he gained.

Sometimes seeking breakthroughs means leaving places that seem successful but are spiritually empty. It's about putting God's purposes first, not the world's values. It takes wisdom to know when to stay and be a positive influence and when to leave to protect yourself. This is a bold prayer because God will answer it and show you things you might not want to see. But it's necessary if you want to move forward.

When God shows you something that needs to change, your response determines whether you'll experience breakthroughs. You can defend yourself, make excuses, blame others, or downplay what God is showing you. Or you can humble yourself, accept the truth, and take action to address it. The first response keeps you stuck. The second response sets you up for breakthroughs.

Here's a practical exercise to help you seek alignment. Take a sheet of paper and draw a line down the middle. On the left side, write what you're asking God for. Be specific. On the right side, write what that blessing would require from you in terms of character, capacity, or skills. Then ask yourself honestly: Do I have what this blessing would require right now?

For example, if you're praying for a leadership position, the right side might include qualities such as integrity, wisdom, good judgment, the ability to handle conflict, and the capacity to manage multiple responsibilities. Now, assess yourself honestly. Do you have those qualities? If not, seeking alignment means working on them instead of just praying for the position. God might be withholding the blessing not to punish you but to protect you, because giving you something you're not ready to handle could harm you rather than help you.

Or maybe you're praying for a restored marriage. The right side might include qualities like good communication, patience, a willingness to forgive, a commitment to change, and emotional maturity. If you're lacking in these areas, seeking alignment means working on them instead of just praying for your spouse to change. Often, the breakthrough in your marriage comes when you focus on becoming the person who can sustain a healthy marriage, not just expecting your spouse to change.

This principle applies to every area where you're seeking breakthroughs. Financial provision requires stewardship. Physical healing often needs lifestyle changes. Ministry opportunities require character growth. Restored relationships need humility and forgiveness. Career advancement requires skill development and professionalism. In every case, there's a character or capacity requirement attached to the blessing. Seeking alignment means honestly checking if you have what the blessing requires and working to develop it if you don't. Before we go on, remember that grace comes before growth. Your identity in Jesus is your foundation, and you are already worthy because of Him. I want to make this clear, because sometimes teaching on seeking can get off track. Seeking alignment isn't about making yourself worthy of God's blessing. You can't do that. You're worthy because of Jesus, not because of anything you do. This isn't about earning favor by improving yourself. It's about putting yourself in a place to receive and care for what God wants to give you. It's about removing obstacles that could cause you to waste the blessing or be hurt by it. It's about working with God as He changes you, so you're ready when breakthroughs come.

It's like preparing for a marathon. If you try to run a marathon without training, you'll probably get hurt because your body isn't ready. But if you train and build up your strength and endurance, you can finish the race. Training doesn't earn you the right to run; the race is open to anyone who signs up. But training prepares you to finish what you started. Seeking alignment prepares you for breakthroughs so you can handle them when they come.

Let me show you what all three steps of seeking look like, working together with a comprehensive example. Imagine you're praying for a job in a field you're passionate about, but you have limited experience in it. Here's what seeking would look like across these steps: Learn, Show, Grow.

Learn (Seek Wisdom): You research the field thoroughly. You find out what skills are required, what credentials are valued, and what the typical career path looks like. You read industry publications and join professional groups. You talk to people in the field and ask how they got started. You take online courses or earn certifications to become more competitive. You're becoming educated about what you're pursuing rather than blindly hoping something works out.

Show (Seeking Opportunity): You start attending industry events and conferences, even if you have to save up to afford them. You reach out to companies you admire and ask for informational interviews, not begging for a job but genuinely seeking to learn from people who are where you want to be. You update your online presence to reflect your interest and growing knowledge in this field. You volunteer for projects or offer to work for organizations that do the kind of work you want to do. You're positioning yourself where connections can happen, where your name becomes familiar to the right people, and where opportunities can find you because you've made yourself visible and available.

Grow (Seeking Alignment): You honestly assess what personal obstacles might be hindering your pursuit. Maybe you need to work on your communication skills or your confidence in professional settings. Maybe you need to address time management issues that would prevent you from performing well, even if you got the opportunity. Maybe you need to deal with the fear of failure that's keeping you from taking the necessary risks. Maybe you need to adjust your current work schedule to free up time to pursue this new direction. You address whatever internal or circumstantial obstacles are blocking your path rather than just hoping they won't matter.

When all three steps work together, when you're learning about the field, showing by positioning yourself strategically, and growing by removing personal obstacles, you create momentum. You're not just praying and waiting. You're praying and moving. You're partnering with God in bringing about the breakthrough you're believing for. More often than not, breakthroughs come through that partnership rather than through passive waiting.

Now, let me address the elephant in the room that some of you have been thinking about since this chapter started. What's the difference between seeking and striving? Because on the surface, they can look very similar. Both involve effort. Both require action. Both demand intentionality and persistence. But there's a crucial difference that determines whether your activity is faith in motion or anxiety in motion.

Striving comes from a place of fear and control. It's frantic activity driven by the belief that if you don't make it happen, it won't happen. Striving doesn't trust God. It tries to force outcomes through sheer willpower and effort. Striving exhausts you because you're carrying weight that was never meant for you to carry. Striving makes you rigid and controlling because you can't tolerate anything that doesn't fit your timeline or your vision. And striving produces burnout because you're operating in your own strength rather than in partnership with God.

Seeking, on the other hand, comes from a place of faith and partnership. It's intentional activity driven by the belief that God is at work and that you're cooperating with His work. Seeking, trusts God while taking responsibility for what's yours to do. Seeking energizes you because you're partnering with divine power rather than operating alone. Seeking makes you flexible because you're watching for how God might answer in unexpected ways. And seeking produces breakthroughs because you're aligning your efforts with God's purposes rather than pursuing your agenda on your own.

Here's a practical way to discern which one you're operating in. Ask yourself: Am I finding rest in this process, or am I constantly anxious? Am I able to sleep at night, or am I tormented by worry about whether things will work out? Do I have peace even when I don't see progress yet, or am I only at peace when circumstances confirm my efforts? Can I hold my plans loosely and adjust when God redirects, or am I so attached to specific outcomes that any deviation feels like failure?

If you're anxious, sleepless, lacking peace, and rigidly attached to specific outcomes, you're probably striving. If you're able to work diligently while maintaining inner peace, if you can adjust course when God redirects, if you trust that God is working even when you don't see evidence yet, you're probably seeking. The difference isn't in the level of effort. It's in the posture of your heart while you're making that effort.

Jesus addresses this distinction in Matthew 11 when He says, "Come to me, all who labor and are heavy laden, and I will give you rest. Take my yoke upon you, and learn from me, for I am gentle and lowly in heart, and you will find rest for your souls. For my yoke is easy, and my burden is light." Notice that Jesus doesn't say His yoke involves no work. A yoke is a tool for work. But His yoke is easy, and His burden is light because you're working in partnership with Him rather than working alone or working against Him.

Seeking is taking up Jesus's yoke. It's working, yes, but working with Him rather than for Him or instead of Him. And there's rest in that partnership even in the midst of effort. Striving is trying to carry burdens Jesus never asked you to carry, trying to accomplish things through your own strength that were only meant to happen through His power working in and through you.

So if you find yourself exhausted, burned out, anxious, and frustrated despite all your efforts, stop and ask God if you've shifted from seeking to striving. Ask Him to show you what you're trying to control that you need to release. Ask Him to reveal where you're working in your own strength rather than in partnership with His power. And then make the necessary adjustments to return to seeking, to faith-filled action that trusts God while taking responsibility for what's yours to do.

Here's another way to look at seeking. It's like a bridge between asking and receiving. Asking is about saying what you need. Receiving is when you get what you asked for. There's usually a gap between these two, and that's where seeking happens. Each step you take on this bridge is a small victory, showing your progress. These moments, like gaining clarity or receiving unexpected blessings, help you stay motivated. Seeking is the journey across the bridge. It's where your faith is tested, your character grows, and you learn to trust God for every step, not just the end result.

Some bridges are short. Some prayers get answered quickly, and the seeking phase is brief. You ask, you take a few steps of obedient action, and breakthroughs manifest almost immediately. But other bridges are long. Other prayers require extended seasons of seeking where you're doing everything right but still not seeing the breakthrough you're believing for. And those long bridges are where most believers give up. They start well. They seek wisdom. They pursue opportunity. They work on alignment. But when breakthroughs don't come as quickly as they hoped, they get discouraged and stop seeking. They abandon the bridge before they've crossed it.

This is why understanding seeking as a dimension between asking and receiving is so important. Because it helps you see that seeking isn't forever. You're not going to be in this phase permanently. You're on a bridge that leads somewhere. Every step of seeking is taking you closer to breakthroughs, even when you can't see how far you've come or how far you have left to go. And if you quit in the middle of the bridge, if you stop seeking before you've completed the crossing, you'll never reach the breakthrough that was waiting on the other side.

So when you're tempted to quit, when you're tired of seeking and want to just give up, remember that you're on a bridge. Remember that every day you seek wisdom, every time you position yourself for opportunity, every step you take toward alignment, you're moving forward. The bridge isn't endless. There's a destination. There are breakthroughs waiting. And everyone who keeps seeking finds. That's Jesus's promise. Not might find. Not hopefully finds. Finds. Present tense. Certain outcome. If you keep seeking, you will find what you're looking for.

But you have to actually keep seeking. You can't take a few steps and then sit down in the middle of the bridge waiting for God to carry you the rest of the way. Seeking requires sustained effort. It requires consistency. It requires getting back up every time you feel like giving up. It means taking one step forward every time you feel like giving up.

Here's your assignment as we close this chapter. I want you to take those three specific requests you wrote down in the last chapter, the ones you committed to praying about daily. Now I want you to add three columns next to each request. Label them: Wisdom, Opportunity, Alignment.

Under Wisdom, write down what you need to learn about this situation. What books should you read? What research should you do? Who should you talk to? What knowledge are you lacking that would help you navigate this more effectively?

Under Opportunity, write down where you need to position yourself. What environments or communities should you be part of? What connections do you need to make? What steps can you take to make yourself available for breakthroughs?

Under Alignment, write down what internal obstacles need to be addressed. What character issues is God highlighting? What habits need to change? What relationships need healing or ending? What mindsets need renewal?

Then commit to taking at least one action in each column every week. Share your weekly progress with a friend or a supportive group. Let others join you on your journey and help keep you accountable. Over time, these small, steady steps will add up. In a month, three months, or six months, you'll be surprised at how far you've come.

But you have to start. You have to move from just asking to actively seeking. You have to put feet to your faith and hands to your prayers. You have to partner with God in the process of breakthrough rather than waiting passively for Him to do everything.

Remember the woman with the issue of blood. She didn't just pray for healing. She pressed through a crowd. She reached out her hand. She sought with everything in her. And when her faith connected with Jesus's power, when her seeking intersected with His provision, breakthroughs happened instantly. Your breakthrough is waiting at that same intersection. The intersection where your faith-filled action meets God's supernatural provision. But you have to move toward that intersection. You have to seek.

So ask God right now to show you what seeking looks like in your specific situation. Ask Him to give you wisdom about what to learn, opportunity about where to position yourself, and alignment about what needs to change in you. Then take the first step. Not tomorrow. Not next week. Today. Right now. Take one action that moves you from asking to seeking, from talking about your need to doing something about it while trusting God to meet you in the action. Reach out to a mentor by text today to set up a conversation that can offer new insights and guidance. Take this bold action within 24 hours to demonstrate your commitment to actively engaging in your journey toward breakthroughs.

Because here's what I've learned over these ten-plus years since God brought me through my wilderness. Breakthroughs don't usually come to those who wait passively. It comes to those who seek actively. It comes to those who partner with God by taking responsibility for what's theirs to do while trusting Him for what only He can do. It comes to those who refuse to let fear, comfort, or passivity keep them from moving toward what they're believing for.

You've learned to ask. Now learn to seek. And in the next chapter, we're going to learn the final dimension, the one that requires more than asking or seeking ever could. We're going to learn to knock. We're going to discover what it means to arrive at the door of your answer and refuse to leave until it opens. We're going to develop the kind of desperate, persistent, shameless audacity that Jesus says is essential for breakthroughs to manifest.

But before we get there, before we learn to knock, you need to get this second dimension right. You need to learn to seek. You need to put your faith into action. You need to move from passive prayer to active pursuit. Because if you can't seek, if you can't take action, if you can't partner with God in the process, then knocking will just be noise. You'll be pounding on doors you never actually positioned yourself to reach.

So seek. Seek wisdom. Seek opportunity. Seek alignment. Remember that everyone who seeks finds. Be confident that your actions are not earning God's favor but putting you in a place to receive what He already wants to give. Trust that God is working even when you can't see it yet, and every step forward brings you closer to breakthroughs, even if the journey feels long.

Let's be people who seek to change our communities and help them change.

When we work together to find wisdom, opportunity, and alignment, we can encourage each other and grow. As we move forward, we can trust that our efforts will help us find what we're looking for and make a real difference.

Your breakthrough is closer than you think. It's waiting on the other side of your obedience and your willingness to seek. So take the next step, and then another, and another. Keep seeking until you find what you're looking for. You will find it. Jesus promised, and His promises never fail.

Now, take action. Your journey isn't over. The best is still ahead. Keep seeking and let faith guide your steps.

Chapter Four

THE GEOGRAPHY OF BREAKTHROUGH

Positioning Yourself Where Miracles Happen

Breakthroughs often come when we're willing to leave our comfort zones and try something new. For thirty-eight years, a paralyzed man waited by the pool of Bethesda, hoping to be healed. He was surrounded by others who were also sick or desperate, all believing that if they could be the first to reach the water when it was stirred, they would be healed. The pool was famous for this: when an angel stirred the water, the first person in would be cured. Many people gathered there, watching and waiting for their chance at a miracle.

When Jesus met the man, He asked, "Do you want to be healed?" At first, this question might seem harsh. After all, why would someone wait by a pool for thirty-eight years if they didn't want to be healed? But Jesus was really asking if the man was ready to try something different and move beyond what he had always done.

"Do you truly want to be healed?"

The man didn't say yes. Instead, he explained, 'Sir, I have no one to put me into the pool when the water is stirred up, and while I am going another steps down before me.' This wasn't just about his situation; it showed how he thought. For thirty-eight years, he relied on a method that needed help he didn't have, waiting in a place where healing was supposed to happen but was never able to reach it. Think about your own life: are you waiting for opportunities that seem out of reach, or stuck in a way of thinking that can't get you what you need? Noticing these barriers is often the first step to finding new ways forward.

Then Jesus did something amazing. He didn't help the man into the pool or wait for the water to move. Instead, He told the man to get up, pick up his mat, and walk. Right away, the man was healed: no pool, no special conditions, just Jesus. When Jesus is present, miracles can happen, no matter where we are or what method we expect.

This story teaches us that breakthroughs often depend on being in the right place, not just the place we know best. Where you are matters. Sometimes, we wait in a spot where we expect miracles and miss what's happening right in front of us. The man at the pool waited for years, focused on one way to be healed, while Jesus, the true source of healing, was right there. Think about your own life: are you waiting by your own 'pool,' hoping for change in a familiar place, when maybe you need to move or try something new? Take a moment to reflect on where you might need to step out in faith and take action.

Maybe you're staying in a job that no longer excites you because it feels safe, or you spend hours on dating apps but never find a real connection. These are examples of how we can stay in our own 'familiar pools' and miss out on new opportunities that could change our lives.

This is the challenge we face when we think about where miracles happen. Location matters, and being in the right place is important. But we also need to notice if we're stuck in the wrong spot, waiting for something that isn't coming, or missing what God is doing right next to us because we're focused on just one way or place. This can happen in many areas of our lives. To put this into practice, take a moment to think about where you are now. Are you in a place that matches your goals, or are you staying somewhere just because it's familiar? Make a list of areas where you feel stuck and choose one small change you can make to move forward.

Let's talk about what it means to position yourself for breakthroughs. We'll discuss how to be strategic while you wait for miracles and how to stay open if God leads you somewhere new or uses an approach you didn't expect.

The first principle is this: proximity creates possibility. Where you are affects what you have access to. For example, in a desert, you won't find ocean fish, and in the Arctic, you'll only find certain fruits like Cloudberries, known as "Arctic Gold". Geography shapes what's available, what opportunities you find, and what resources you can access. This is true both physically and spiritually. The environments you choose determine what you're exposed to, who you meet, and what doors open for you.

Take the example of a software developer named Alex who moved to Silicon Valley, a well-known tech hub. Before moving, Alex struggled to find good networking opportunities and projects that matched his skills. Alex often said, "I feel like my skills are invisible in my current environment." After relocating, Alex found a community of like-minded professionals and innovative companies. This move led to a job at a top tech firm and new opportunities for growth and collaboration. "I finally felt seen and valued for my contributions," Alex said. This story shows how changing your location can open doors that were closed before, proving that proximity really does create possibilities.

Let's look at this in practical terms. If you're praying for a job but live in a rural area with few openings in your field, your location is a challenge. God can still provide, but staying where opportunities are scarce makes it harder for those opportunities to reach you. If you want community but never leave your house, or you want ministry opportunities but aren't involved in a church or group, or you want your business to grow but never network or attend events, you're making it harder for good things to find you by limiting where you put yourself.

I want to be clear: God isn't limited by geography. He can do anything, anywhere. But we are often limited by where we are. God often works through natural means, like connections and opportunities that exist in certain places. When we put ourselves where opportunities are more common, we're working with the way God usually provides, instead of expecting Him to do things differently.

Answer the reflection questions below as a quick self-check. What is one barrier between you and your goals? Write it down. Then, challenge yourself to share one insight with a friend or loved one to boost your accountability.

To help you assess your own geography of opportunity, consider these reflection questions:

1. Are there opportunities within my reach that I have not yet explored due to geographic constraints?

2. What steps can I take to strategically position myself in an environment where the type of breakthrough I seek is more likely?

3. How can I broaden my network and connections to increase my access to opportunities?

4. Am I imposing limitations on myself because of my current physical location, and how can I overcome them?

5. In what ways do I need to stay open to God's provision, even if it leads me to unfamiliar places?

Think about how Jesus lived. He could have stayed in Nazareth and healed people from a distance; He's God, after all. He did heal the centurion's servant from afar, but that was rare. Most of the time, Jesus went to where people needed Him. He traveled from town to town, meeting the sick, the hurting, and the lost where they were. He knew that being present mattered. Even though He had power beyond geography, He still showed that being in the right place opens doors that staying away does not.

This idea applies to us, too. You can pray for breakthroughs anywhere, and God hears you no matter where you are. But putting yourself in the right place makes it more likely you'll notice and receive those breakthroughs. It puts you where the help or resources you need are usually found. It connects you with people who can help, and it opens doors that you couldn't reach otherwise.

Let me show you what this looked like in Scripture through the story of Ruth. After her husband died, Ruth became a childless widow. Her mother-in-law, Naomi, decided to return to Bethlehem, and Ruth chose to go with her despite having no prospects, no security, and no guarantee of provision. When they arrived in Bethlehem, they were destitute. They needed food, and the harvest was just beginning. According to the law, the poor and the foreigner were allowed to glean in the fields behind the reapers, gathering whatever grain was left behind. So Ruth went out to glean.

Here's what's important about Ruth's story. She didn't just pick any field. The Bible says she happened to end up in Boaz's field, who was related to Naomi's late husband. The word "happened" might sound like luck, but with God, nothing is random. Ruth made a wise choice; she went where she could find food during harvest. By putting herself where provision was, she found not only food but also met Boaz, who became her husband and redeemer.

This is strategic positioning at its finest. Ruth didn't sit at home praying for provision to fall from heaven. She didn't wait for Boaz to somehow find her while she stayed in Naomi's house. She positioned herself in the field during harvest season, in the place where provisions were being gathered, in the environment where a man of means like Boaz would be overseeing his workers. And that positioning led to an encounter that changed the entire trajectory of her life.

Notice that Ruth couldn't control whether Boaz would notice her. She couldn't manufacture his favor or force him to redeem her. But she could control whether she was in a position for that encounter to happen at all. She could position herself where possibilities existed. And in doing so, she cooperated with God's providence in a way that passive waiting never would have accomplished.

This is what it means to position yourself wisely. Find out where the kind of breakthrough you want usually happens, and go there. Ask yourself: Where do miracles like the one I need usually take place? Where do the opportunities I'm praying for show up? Where are the connections I need? Then, put yourself in those places with faith, and watch for God to meet you there.

Let me give you some practical examples of what this looks like across different areas of life. If you're praying for employment, strategic positioning means going where employers are. That might mean attending job fairs, networking events, and industry conferences. It might mean relocating to a city where your industry has a strong presence. It might mean joining professional organizations where you can connect with people who have hiring authority or knowledge of opportunities. You're not earning the job through these efforts. You're positioning yourself where job opportunities exist and making yourself available to receive what God provides.

If you're praying for a spouse, strategic positioning means going where potential spouses are. That might mean joining groups or activities where you can meet others who share your values and interests. It might mean saying yes to social invitations even when you'd rather stay home. It might mean serving in church ministries where you can build genuine relationships rather than just showing up for services and leaving. Again, you're not manufacturing a spouse through activity. You're positioning yourself in environments where meaningful connections can form.

If you're praying for healing, strategic positioning might mean seeking out doctors who specialize in your condition, joining support groups where you can learn from others who have experienced similar health challenges, researching treatment options, and being willing to travel to where the best care is available. You're not replacing faith with medicine. You're positioning yourself where healing resources exist while trusting God to supernaturally use them.

If you're praying for ministry opportunities, strategic positioning means serving faithfully where you are, developing your gifts, making yourself available, and building relationships with leaders who might open doors for you. It means saying yes to opportunities, even if they're smaller than you hoped for, because faithfulness in small things leads to being entrusted with larger things. You're not forcing your way into ministry. You're positioning yourself where ministry happens and allowing God to open doors in His timing.

In every situation, wisely positioning yourself means working with how God usually provides, while staying open to His miracles. God can provide anywhere, but He often uses natural channels, connections, and opportunities found in certain places. When you put yourself in those places, you're not limiting God; you're making it easier for His provision to reach you.

But there's an important balance here. Positioning yourself can turn manipulative if you're not careful. There's a difference between putting yourself where opportunities are and trying to force things to happen. It comes down to your attitude. Are you waiting with humble expectation, trusting God's timing? Or are you demanding results, thinking you can make breakthroughs happen just by being in the right place?

Consider this comparison:

Faithful Positioning:

- **Motive:** Humble expectancy.

- **Action:** Trusting God to open doors in His timing.

- **Outcome:** Cooperation with God's sovereignty.

Manipulative Positioning:

- **Motive:** Entitled demanding.

- **Action:** Trying to force outcomes through one's own efforts.

- **Outcome:** Presumption, attempting to control God.

Strategic positioning says, "God, I'm going where provision typically flows, and I'm trusting You to provide according to Your wisdom and timing." Manipulation says, "If I position myself in the right place and connect with the right people, I can force the outcome I want." One is faith. The other is presumption. One honors God's sovereignty. The other tries to usurp it. And the difference shows up in how you respond when you position yourself strategically, and breakthrough doesn't come immediately.

If you're acting in faith, you can put yourself in the right place and wait patiently, trusting that God is working even if you don't see results yet. You can stay calm even when things take longer than you hoped, and you can adjust your approach without losing trust. But if you're trying to force things, you'll get anxious and frustrated when results don't come quickly. You might blame God, yourself, or others for missed opportunities.

So, as we talk about positioning ourselves where miracles happen, we have to constantly check our hearts. Are we cooperating with God or trying to control God? Are we partnering with His providence or trying to manufacture our own? The line can be thin, but the difference is everything.

Now let's talk about recognizing when you're in the wrong place. Because it's possible to be positioned somewhere with good intentions, but wrong timing or wrong fit. Remember the man at the pool of Bethesda who spent thirty-eight years in one location waiting for healing that never came through that method. Sometimes God calls us to leave places we've invested in, to abandon methods we've committed to, to try a completely different location or approach than what we've been doing.

This can be one of the hardest things to figure out because it means admitting that what you've been doing isn't working. It takes humility to see you might be in the wrong place or using the wrong approach, and courage to leave what's familiar for something unknown that could bring the breakthrough you need. I remember a time when I kept working hard in the wrong place, hoping for results that never came. Realizing I needed to change was difficult, but I learned that adjusting your course is a key part of the journey.

How do you know when it's time to change locations or strategies? Here are some indicators to watch for. First, if you've been in the same place using the same approach for an extended period with no fruit, that might be a sign it's time to try something different. I'm not talking about a few weeks or even a few months. I'm talking about years of positioning yourself in a place or pursuing a strategy that consistently produces no results. It's like watering concrete, hoping for flowers to bloom. At some point, faithfulness becomes stubbornness, and persistence becomes an excuse not to change what clearly isn't working.

Before we dive into these indicators, take a moment to reflect: What is your "watering concrete" scenario? Identify where in your life you are exerting effort but seeing no growth. This pause can help you align personally with the path we're about to explore.

Think about planting a seed in poor soil. No matter how much you water it, nothing grows. The problem isn't your effort, it's the soil. You need better ground. In the same way, if you've been serving faithfully in a ministry for years but see no growth or open doors, the issue might not be your actions. You could be in a place that can't support what God wants to grow in you. Staying there out of habit or fear isn't faith; it's just staying stuck.

Second indicator that it might be time to change location or strategy: if you consistently feel like you're forcing doors that won't open, if you're exhausted from pushing against resistance that never yields, that might be God's way of telling you this isn't the path He has for you. Now, I'm not saying every closed door means you're in the wrong place. Sometimes, closed doors are temporary. Sometimes resistance is part of the process. But if every single door is closed, if every effort meets with insurmountable obstacles, if you never sense any forward momentum despite consistent effort, wisdom says it might be time to ask God if He's trying to redirect you.

Jesus talked about this when He sent out His disciples. He told them that when they entered a town and weren't welcomed, they should shake the dust off their feet and move on to the next town. Don't camp out where you're not welcome. Don't waste years trying to force open doors that God isn't opening. Shake the dust off and move to where receptivity exists. That's wisdom. That's strategic positioning. That's recognizing that your time and energy are limited, and they're better invested in places where there's evidence of God's blessing and favor than in places where everything is an uphill struggle.

The third indicator: if you sense in your spirit that God is calling you somewhere different, even if it doesn't make logical sense, even if it feels risky or uncomfortable, that's worth paying attention to. Sometimes God calls us to leave places of comfort or familiarity to position us for breakthroughs that can only happen in new territory. Abraham had to leave Ur. Moses had to leave Egypt, then later leave Midian. David had to leave his father's house. Jesus left the carpentry shop in Nazareth to begin His public ministry. In every case, staying where they were would have meant missing what God wanted to do through them. Breakthrough required a change in geography.

I experienced this firsthand when God called us to launch Faith & Works Ministries. We were comfortable where we served. We had relationships, stability, and familiarity. But I kept sensing that God was calling us to something different, to position ourselves in a place where what He wanted to do through us could actually manifest. It didn't make complete sense logically. This was smack in the middle of the COVID-19 pandemic. Many churches were shutting down, and here we were planting a new ministry. It was extremely risky. It meant leaving behind what was known for what was unknown. But looking back now, I can see that the breakthrough God had for us could only happen through that repositioning. What He wanted to birth through us required us to be in different soil, in a different environment, in a place that was conducive to what He wanted to grow.

So if you're sensing that call, if you feel God tugging at you to leave where you are and position yourself somewhere different, don't dismiss it because it's inconvenient or scary. Don't let comfort or fear keep you in a place God is trying to move you from. Because sometimes the miracle you're praying for is waiting in a location you haven't been willing to go to yet. Sometimes breakthroughs require you to leave the familiar pool where you've been lying for years and go where Jesus is actually working, even if it's not where you expected Him to be.

Now let's flip this and talk about when you should stay where you are. Because repositioning isn't always the answer. Sometimes the breakthrough you need will come right where you're planted if you'll just remain faithful and keep watching for God's movement. How do you know the difference between staying faithfully and staying stubbornly? Here are some markers. A simple checklist can serve as a quick reference tool to guide your decision:

1. Are you seeing any fruit, even if it's small? If yes, consider staying.

2. Do you have peace about your current situation despite challenges? If

yes, it might be wise to remain.

3. Are you experiencing personal growth or learning important lessons? If yes, staying could be beneficial.

If you see some progress, even if it's less than you hoped, that's often a sign to stay. If doors are opening slowly, or you notice small signs of growth, don't give up just because you're impatient. Being faithful during slow seasons can lead to breakthroughs that wouldn't happen if you kept moving around. Some plants take years to bear fruit, and moving them too often keeps them from growing. Sometimes you need to stay put long enough to see what will develop.

If you feel peace about where you are, even when things are hard, that's usually a reason to stay. Peace isn't the same as comfort. You can go through tough times and still know you're where God wants you. But if you're always anxious and can't find rest, it's worth looking at your situation. Peace is a good sign you're in the right place, while constant restlessness can mean it's time for a change.

If you're learning and growing where you are, even without big results yet, that's often a reason to stay. Sometimes God keeps us in a place not for the breakthrough itself, but to prepare us for what's coming. Joseph spent years in slavery and prison, but those years prepared him for leadership. If you're building character and learning important lessons, don't rush to leave. The place of preparation matters.

And if God has specifically told you to be where you are, if you have clear direction that this is where He wants you, even though it's difficult, then stay. Even when it looks like nothing is happening. Even when others are experiencing breakthroughs elsewhere. Even when every logical indicator says you should leave. Obedience to clear direction trumps all other considerations. If God said stay, stay. The breakthrough will come in His timing, and it will be worth the wait.

A local pastor, a dear friend of mine, referred a couple from his congregation to meet with me. He was convinced that my approach could offer the guidance they sought. They had been praying fervently for years to buy a home, but were increasingly frustrated with the financial drain of renting. This common struggle was one I deeply empathized with, having experienced it myself. During our conversation, they mentioned a bold plan: possibly relocating from Sint Maarten to somewhere with a lower cost of living, hoping this drastic move might finally allow them to own a home. That idea struck me as life-altering.

After hearing their story, I asked them three pivotal questions: Do you feel God is calling you to leave, or is it frustration with your current situation driving this decision? They admitted it was more frustration than divine calling. Second, does leaving bring peace, or does it feel like an escape? Here, they recognized it felt like running away from the difficulty. Finally, are there signs of growth and life where you are, or is everything stagnant? They reflected and acknowledged that despite financial strains, their spiritual journey was thriving, their service meaningful, and they felt truly part of their community.

Based on their reflections, I suggested they stay put. It wasn't about knowing when or how their breakthrough would happen, but about recognizing that, spiritually, they were planted where they needed to be. Leaving prematurely could mean sacrificing the very growth and connections that were, in essence, positioning them for a breakthrough they couldn't yet see.

They committed to staying and to shifting their strategy while remaining in the same location. Instead of just praying for a house to somehow materialize, they started seeking wisdom about finances. They took a financial planning course. They met with a mortgage advisor to understand exactly what they needed to qualify for a loan. They identified areas where they could cut spending and increase savings. They looked for additional income opportunities. They remained in the same geographic location but strategically repositioned themselves by gaining knowledge and adjusting their approach.

Within two years, they had saved enough for a down payment and qualified for a mortgage. They bought their first home right here in Sint Maarten, the place they had almost left in frustration. When they shared their testimony, they said that the key wasn't changing their location. The key was changing their strategy while staying in the place God had them. They needed to reposition themselves financially and educationally, not geographically.

That's the wisdom we need when discerning whether to stay or go. Sometimes you need to change locations. Sometimes you need to change strategies in your current location. And sometimes you need to stay exactly where you are and just keep faithfully doing what you're doing while trusting God's timing. The key is learning to discern which one applies to your situation, and that discernment comes through prayer, through counsel from mature believers who know you well, and through paying attention to the indicators we've discussed.

Now let's talk about another dimension of positioning that often gets overlooked. Let's discuss relational geography. Who you surround yourself with matters as much as where you position yourself physically. Your circle sets your ceiling. The people around you shape your environment and can either help or hinder what you're believing God for. Being wise about your relationships is just as important as choosing the right place. By taking these specific relational actions, you begin to align your environment with your goals and set the stage for meaningful progress.

Proverbs 13:20 says it plainly: "Whoever walks with the wise becomes wise, but the companion of fools will suffer harm." Your associations shape your trajectory. The people you spend the most time with influence your thinking, your decisions, your beliefs about what's possible, and your standards for what's acceptable. If you're surrounded by people who don't believe God answers prayer, who mock faith, who settle for mediocrity, who make excuses instead of taking action, that environment will affect you whether you realize it or not. You might pray for breakthroughs while your relationships are programming you for stagnation.

This doesn't mean you abandon everyone who isn't where you want to be. Jesus spent time with sinners, with the broken, with those who needed what He had to offer. But notice that Jesus's closest relationships, His inner circle of disciples, were people He was intentionally pouring into, people who were hungry for what He was teaching, people who were willing to change and grow. He had concentric circles of relationship. The crowds on the outer edge came and went. The disciples in the middle who committed to following Him but still struggled to understand. And the inner three, Peter, James, and John, who were with Him in the most intimate moments of His ministry.

You need the same kind of wisdom about relational positioning. You need to be strategic about who you allow into your inner circle, who has access to your thoughts and dreams, and who has access to your vulnerable moments. Those closest relationships should be with people who strengthen your faith, who sharpen you, who call you higher, who believe with you for breakthroughs rather than talking you out of it. And you need to be equally strategic about limiting access for people who consistently drain you, discourage you, mock your faith, or pull you toward compromise.

This is hard for many believers because we've been taught that loving people means giving everyone equal access to our lives. But that's not biblical. Even Jesus, who loved everyone perfectly, didn't give everyone the same level of access. He taught the crowds. He discipled the twelve. He shared His deepest moments with three. And there was one, John, who reclined on His chest at the Last Supper, who had a level of intimacy that even the other disciples didn't share.

Jesus modeled relational wisdom by being strategic about who He allowed into different levels of proximity.

You should do the same. Love everyone. Serve everyone who's in your path. But be strategic about your inner circle. Be intentional about who influences you most. Because if you're praying for breakthroughs while your closest relationships are pulling you toward mediocrity, your positioning is working against your prayers. You're trying to move forward while your environment is programming you to stay stuck.

Let me ask you some diagnostic questions about your relational geography. This quick quiz will help you reflect more interactively. To increase engagement, I challenge you to tally your scores and share the results with an accountability partner. This can help turn your reflection into communal momentum, enabling you to initiate changes with the support of those who care about your journey.

1. Who are the five people you spend the most time with? Score each relationship (1-5) on how much they encourage you.

2. Do these relationships produce energy or depletion in you? Rate each on a scale of 1 (depleted) to 5 (energized).

3. How much faith do they instill in you? Use a scale from 1 (more doubtful) to 5 (more faith-filled).

4. Do these relationships inspire you to take action or tempt you to give up? Score each from 1 (tempted to give up) to 5 (inspired to action).

The scores will tell you whether your relational positioning is supporting or sabotaging what you're believing God for. By sharing results with your accountability partner, you add an extra layer of commitment and create shared momentum towards strategic improvements.

And if you realize that your closest relationships are toxic or draining, if the people you spend the most time with are pulling you down rather than building you up, you need to make some hard decisions. You might need to create distance from certain relationships. You might need to invest more time and energy in life-giving relationships and less in life-draining ones. You might need to actively seek out new relationships with people who are where you want to be, who model what you're trying to become, who have the kind of faith and breakthrough you're pursuing.

This isn't about judging others or thinking you're better than them. It's about being wise. You become like the people you spend time with, so if you want breakthroughs, you need to be around people who expect them, who have strong faith, and who are actively seeking God, not just talking about Him.

I once had the opportunity to preach at a ministry that created intentional environments where breakthrough-oriented believers could connect with one another. I was so intrigued by this initiative. Small groups where people aren't just studying Scripture but actually applying it and holding each other accountable. Prayer gatherings where they weren't just praying generic prayers but getting specific about what they're believing God for, and then tracking testimonies of answered prayer. Service teams where they're not just volunteering out of obligation but actively using their gifts and watching God multiply their efforts. These environments create relational geography that supports spiritual growth and breakthrough.

If you don't have access to those kinds of environments where you are, you might need to create them. Start a small group in your home. Invite a few people who are hungry for more than surface-level Christianity to meet regularly, pray specifically, and pursue God together. Find a church or ministry that operates at the level of faith you're trying to grow into, rather than staying in a place that accommodates spiritual complacency. Make strategic decisions about your relational positioning, just as you do about your physical positioning.

Here's the truth: you can be in the best place for breakthroughs, but if you're surrounded by people who don't believe it's possible, their doubt will affect your faith. Being in the right place physically but the wrong environment relationally usually doesn't work. Relationships are powerful; they shape your thinking, beliefs, and actions.

So positioning yourself where miracles happen isn't just about physical geography. It's about relational geography. It's about surrounding yourself with people who strengthen your faith rather than weaken it, who speak life rather than death, who believe with you rather than doubt with you. And sometimes that requires painful decisions to create distance from relationships that were significant but no longer serve your spiritual growth. That's hard. But it's necessary if you're serious about breakthroughs.

Let me shift gears now and talk about one more crucial aspect of positioning yourself where miracles happen. It's what I call spiritual geography, and it's perhaps the most important dimension of all. Physical geography matters. Relational geography matters. But spiritual geography, the environments and atmospheres you create and participate in through worship, prayer, and faith, might matter most of all.

Imagine what happens the moment someone decides to turn off the blaring news updates, filled with chaos and worry, and instead puts on calming worship music. Instantly, the room transforms into a haven of peace, anxiety giving way to a profound sense of God's presence. This small shift beautifully illustrates how spiritual geography can alter our internal and external environments, preparing us for the breakthroughs we seek.

But here's what's different in the New Covenant. We don't have to travel to a specific building or location to access God's presence. Jesus told the woman at the well that a time was coming when true worshipers wouldn't worship in Jerusalem or on a mountain, but in spirit and in truth. The temple is now your body if you're a believer. The Holy Spirit lives in you. Which means you can create spiritual geography and cultivate a spiritual atmosphere wherever you are.

So what does it mean to position yourself in spiritual geography that supports breakthrough? It means creating and participating in environments where faith is high, where expectation is normal, where God's presence is welcomed and honored, where miracles are believed for and celebrated when they happen. It means surrounding yourself not just with people who believe in breakthrough, but with atmospheres where breakthrough is actively pursued.

This is why gathering with other believers matters so much. Yes, you can worship God alone. Yes, you can pray effectively on your own. Yes, you have direct access to God through Christ without needing anyone else. But there's something that happens in corporate worship, in united prayer, in gathered community that doesn't happen the same way in isolation. Jesus said that where two or three are gathered in His name, He's there in the midst of them. There's a manifestation of His presence in corporate gatherings that amplifies faith and creates a spiritual atmosphere conducive to breakthroughs.

I've seen this repeatedly throughout my Christian journey. I've had nights of worship and prayer where the atmosphere became so charged with faith and expectation that miracles happened spontaneously. People got healed who we weren't even specifically praying for in that moment. Financial provision was made for families who had been struggling. Relationships were restored. Addictions were broken. Not because we worked up some emotional frenzy or manipulated God through our worship, but because when believers gather in unity with expectant faith, when we create a spiritual atmosphere that honors God's presence and believe for His power, breakthrough happens more readily.

This is what it means to position yourself spiritually. It's more than just being at church; it's about engaging with expectation, joining in worship, and adding your faith to the group. When you show up this way, you're not just attending; you're helping create an atmosphere where God can move. But spiritual geography isn't limited to church services. You can create it in your home through consistent worship and prayer. You can create it in your workplace by maintaining a posture of faith and speaking life rather than participating in negativity and complaints. You can create it in your thought life by choosing to meditate on Scripture and God's promises rather than dwelling on problems and impossibilities. Spiritual geography is about the atmosphere you cultivate wherever you are, and that atmosphere either attracts or repels breakthrough.

Certain physical environments are conducive to certain activities. You wouldn't try to have a serious conversation in a nightclub where the music is deafening. You wouldn't attempt to rest in a construction zone where jackhammers are running. The environment shapes what's possible in that space. The same is true spiritually. If you're constantly immersed in environments characterized by doubt, fear, negativity, and unbelief, those atmospheres will make it harder to maintain your faith and receive breakthroughs. But if you're intentional about creating and participating in environments characterized by worship, faith, expectation, and life-giving truth, those atmospheres will support your pursuit of breakthrough.

So ask yourself right now: what kind of spiritual geography am I consistently positioning myself in? Am I surrounding myself with worship music or with content that feeds anxiety and fear? Am I meditating on Scripture or scrolling endlessly through social media that leaves me feeling inadequate and discouraged? Am I participating in prayer gatherings where faith is high, or am I isolating myself spiritually? Am I speaking life and possibility or rehearsing problems and complaints? The answers to these questions reveal whether your spiritual positioning is working for you or against you.

If you see that your spiritual environment needs a change, you can start right now. Turn off the news and play worship music. Put down social media and read your Bible. Call a friend who builds your faith, not someone who just agrees with your complaints. Find a church or group where faith is strong. These choices can shift the spiritual atmosphere around you.

Let me bring all of this together with a comprehensive framework for strategic positioning. If you're praying for breakthroughs in any area of your life, ask yourself these three questions, and remember the mantra: Place, People, Presence. This will help you recall the importance of physical, relational, and spiritual positioning.

Physical geography: Where should I be physically that I'm not? What locations, environments, or contexts would increase my access to the kind of opportunity I'm believing for? Am I in the right place geographically, or is God calling me to reposition? If I'm in the right place but not seeing fruit, do I need to adjust my strategy while staying put, or is it time to move?

Relational geography: Who should I be surrounding myself with? Are my closest relationships supporting or sabotaging my faith? Do the people I spend the most time with strengthen my belief in what's possible or reinforce limitations and doubt? Do I need to create distance from certain relationships and invest more deeply in others? Do I need to actively seek out new relationships with people who model the breakthrough I'm pursuing?

Spiritual geography: What atmosphere am I creating and participating in? Am I cultivating environments characterized by worship, faith, and expectation, or am I allowing environments of doubt, fear, and negativity to dominate? Am I engaged in corporate worship and prayer where breakthrough is the norm, or am I spiritually isolated? Am I filling my mind with truth that builds faith or with content that breeds anxiety?

When your physical location, relationships, and spiritual atmosphere all line up with what you're believing God for, you're in a strong position for breakthroughs. You're not earning it or trying to control God; you're just working with the way He usually provides. Be where provision flows, surround yourself with people of faith, and create an atmosphere that welcomes God's presence. Breakthrough comes to those who are ready.

Here's your assignment as we finish this chapter: This week, honestly assess where you are physically, relationally, and spiritually. Write down your current position in each area, then write where you should be based on your prayers. Find the gaps. Make one change in each area: one physical move, one relationship adjustment, and one spiritual shift. Don't try to do it all at once. Take one step in each area and see what God does.

Because here's the promise that undergirds everything we've talked about in this chapter. When you position yourself where miracles happen, when you align your geography with God's activity, breakthrough becomes not just possible but probable. Not because you earned it through your positioning, but because positioning is cooperation with how God typically works. And God loves to bless obedience. He loves to meet faith with power. He loves to bring breakthroughs to those who position themselves to receive them.

The man at the pool of Bethesda spent thirty-eight years in the wrong place using the wrong method. Don't be like him. Don't waste decades waiting for breakthroughs in locations or through methods that aren't producing fruit. Be willing to leave familiar pools when Jesus is working somewhere else. Be strategic about where you position yourself physically, relationally, and spiritually. And watch as the geography of your life shifts to accommodate the miracles God wants to perform.

Your breakthrough is out there. It might be in a new place, a new relationship, or a new spiritual atmosphere you haven't tried yet. So take action. Change your position, your circle, or your environment as needed. The geography of breakthrough is real, and being willing to move could be what unlocks everything God has for you.

Let's move to the next part of this journey. Positioning yourself is important, but sometimes you still have to wait. There are seasons when you're doing everything right, but the breakthrough hasn't come yet. These waiting times are important; they build your character and faith. So keep going. The journey isn't over.

CHAPTER FIVE

THE WILDERNESS OF SEEKING

WHEN YOU'RE DOING EVERYTHING RIGHT BUT SEEING NO RESULTS

TRANSFORMATION OFTEN BEGINS IN the wilderness. The Israelites, just a year after leaving Egypt, stood at the edge of the Promised Land, ready for something new. They had seen miracles, crossed the Red Sea, and witnessed God's glory. When the spies returned, they described a land so abundant that two men had to carry a single cluster of grapes. It was a place flowing with milk and honey, just as God had promised. Everything they had hoped for was right in front of them.

But they didn't enter. They felt both excitement and fear. The smell of ripe grapes reminded them of the abundance waiting for them, but the dry desert around them made their hesitation stronger. The grapes meant more than just food; they were a sign of God's promise and His assurance. Still, the gap between this promise and the harsh wilderness made it hard for them to fully trust what God had given them.

Ten of the twelve spies saw the giants and the fortified cities and concluded it was impossible. The people believed the bad report over God's promise. They wept all night. They discussed choosing a new leader to lead them back to Egypt. And because of that unbelief, because they couldn't trust God at the threshold of breakthrough, they wandered in the wilderness for forty years. A short journey became a four-decade tragedy. An entire generation died in the desert, never possessing what God had already prepared for them.

They spent forty years in a wilderness that should have taken just over a year to cross.

Take a moment to think about that. It wasn't because God was harsh; it was because they chose fear instead of faith when it mattered most. Delays like this aren't just about lost time; they can stop growth and change. The Israelites stood at the entrance but turned away because it seemed too hard. God answered their prayers and brought them to the Promised Land, but when it was time to go in, they said no. That choice cost them everything. We see this in our own lives when a work project drags on because of indecision or fear of change. The point isn't to compare stories, but to show how easy it is to hesitate at important moments, which can affect our growth and transformation.

I'm starting this chapter with this story because there's something important you need to know before we go on. You can ask the right way, seek with all your heart, and do everything you can. But if you don't understand what happens between getting your answer and actually receiving it, if you see the wilderness as rejection instead of the final test before breakthroughs, you might give up when you're closer than you think.

Think about a time when you almost gave up. What doubts did you have? How close were you to quitting? Keep that memory in mind as we go through this together. I've been there too. I remember when waiting felt too hard and doubts filled my mind. I almost gave up. In that moment, I had to choose faith instead of running from uncertainty. I reminded myself of the promises, even when they felt far away, and trusted that the end was closer than I thought. Remember that we all feel vulnerable sometimes, and it takes courage to keep going when the way forward isn't clear.

The wilderness isn't a sign that you're lost. It doesn't mean you made a mistake or that God has forgotten you. The wilderness is the final test of faith, often the last part of the journey, where God asks you one last question before opening the door: Do you trust Me enough to keep going when trust is all you have left? The main promise of the wilderness is transformation. It's a journey that builds strong faith, resilience, and readiness for what's next. Embrace this change, because it means you'll come out not just with what you asked for, but with the growth needed to keep it.

Most teaching on prayer stops at asking. Some mention seeking. But few talk about what happens in the wilderness between seeking and receiving. This silence leaves people unprepared for the most important part of the journey. Many see the wilderness as failure, when it's actually the beginning of success. They see big challenges and think God's promise was a mistake when those challenges arise. It helps to picture a simple roadmap: Promise, Process, Possession. The promise is the vision or word from God that begins your journey. The process is the journey itself, often full of challenges and growth in the wilderness. Possession is when the promise is fulfilled. Keeping this framework in mind can help you stay hopeful and find your way.

Remember, the wilderness isn't just empty time while God decides what to do. It has a real purpose in getting you ready for breakthroughs. During this season, God is working in you, helping you grow as you wait. This is when faith becomes real in your daily life, not just a thought. It also makes you think about whether you truly want what you've been asking for, or if you just liked the idea of it.

I want to be honest with you, this chapter will be different from the ones before, and here's why. We've talked about the humility in asking and the action in seeking. Now, we move to a phase that needs a new perspective. The wilderness calls for a different kind of wisdom, focused on endurance and understanding. It's about learning to see what God is doing when it looks like nothing is happening. It's about holding on to hope when everything says you should give up. It's about standing at the edge of breakthroughs and choosing to keep waiting, even when the door hasn't opened yet, and you don't know when it will.

This chapter isn't a set of steps to follow. Instead, it's more like a journey into new territory, where old answers might not help. We'll explore how God works in tough seasons, how to keep going when you feel like quitting, and why some people reach God's promises while others don't.

Before we go on, I want to thank my friend Pastor Marcus J. Raymond, whom I met in Bible School. His book, THE WILDERNESS SEASON: God's Hidden Path to Your Greatest Breakthrough, and our many conversations have shaped how I see these seasons. Some of the ideas and stories here come directly from those talks.

If you're in a wilderness season right now, this chapter can help you keep going until your breakthrough comes. If you're not there yet but are pursuing something important, it will help you prepare. The wilderness is part of the journey for anyone who wants more than surface-level blessings, who asks for things that require real character, and who seeks a purpose bigger than comfort. Many people give up during these waiting times; about 25% quit just before a breakthrough. Knowing this can turn a general warning into a real reason to keep going. The stakes are high, and you'll need determination.

The real question isn't whether you'll face a wilderness, but whether you'll recognize it, keep your faith during it, and still be standing when your breakthrough comes.

Let's walk through this together. We'll look at lessons the Israelites missed and see what happens between God's promise and its fulfillment. When your journey feels long, let's make sure you don't wander for years when your breakthrough might be just ahead if you keep believing.

The wilderness may be ahead, but so is everything you've been praying for. How you handle this season will determine if you reach what you're hoping for.

Let's look at one of the most powerful wilderness stories in the Bible, because I believe you'll relate to it. The Israelites were slaves in Egypt for four hundred years, enduring harsh oppression, forced labor, and the heartbreak of losing their children to Pharaoh's orders. Then God sent Moses, performed miracles, brought plagues on Egypt, and finally led them out through the Red Sea. They saw the waters split, walked across on dry land, and watched their enemies swept away. It was an incredible rescue.

But after all that, they ended up in a desert with no food, no water, and no clear direction. God had promised them a land full of good things, the land of Canaan. The promise was clear, and their rescue was miraculous. Yet now they faced only sand, heat, and uncertainty. What should have been a journey of about a year turned into forty years of wandering because they struggled to trust and obey.

There's something important to know about wilderness seasons: the wilderness itself wasn't the real problem. God led them there on purpose, guiding them by day with a cloud and by night with fire. This was the path God chose to take them from Egypt to the Promised Land. The real challenge was how they responded.

They couldn't see what God was doing while they waited, so they thought He wasn't doing anything. We need to learn how to wait well. In my book, The Meaningful Life: Discovering God's Unique Purpose For You, I wrote, "Waiting can be an opportunity for growth and development. By utilizing 'wait times' effectively, we can heal emotional wounds, develop new skills, save resources, gain valuable life experiences, and build spiritual maturity."

That's why wilderness seasons can be so tough. They seem like abandonment, but they're really preparation. They feel like punishment, but they're actually getting you ready. It can look like God has forgotten His promises, but He's actually working to fulfill them. If you only focus on what you see, you might give up just before your breakthrough.

Let's talk about what God is really doing during wilderness seasons. When you understand the purpose, it becomes easier to get through the process. Noticing what's being shaped in you during these quiet times helps you keep your faith, even when nothing seems to change. There are five main reasons for the wilderness journey: exposing what's in your heart, developing dependency, testing your motives, building endurance, and preparing your testimony. To help you remember, use the acronym 'E.D.T.E.P.' (Exposing, Developing, Testing, Enduring, Preparing). We'll look at each one in detail.

The first thing God does in the wilderness is expose what's really in your heart. When the Israelites left Egypt, they were celebrating. They were singing. They had faith. But within a short time in the desert, their true hearts came out. They complained. They accused Moses of bringing them out to die. They romanticized their slavery, claiming Egypt was better than freedom if freedom meant discomfort. The wilderness didn't create these attitudes. It revealed attitudes that had already been there, hidden beneath the excitement of deliverance.

The same thing happens in your wilderness seasons. When you first start believing God for something, when breakthroughs feel close, and excitement is high, it's easy to have faith. It's easy to worship. It's easy to declare God's goodness. But when months turn into years, when you're still in the gap between promise and fulfillment, when nothing visible has changed despite all your effort, what's really in your heart comes out.

Do you trust God's character or just His blessings? Do you worship Him for who He is or only for what He gives? Do you believe His promises because they're true or only because they're convenient?

These questions get answered in the wilderness. And the answers aren't always what you want to see. You might discover that your faith was more shallow than you thought. You might realize that you've been following God for what He can do for you instead of who He is. You might find bitterness, entitlement, or unbelief that you didn't know was there. That discovery is painful. But it's also necessary. Because if those things aren't exposed, they'll sabotage your breakthrough when it finally comes. You'll receive the blessing but lose it quickly because your character wasn't ready to steward it.

So when the wilderness exposes ugly things in your heart, don't run from that revelation. Don't defend yourself or make excuses. Let God do the surgical work of removing what needs to go and healing what needs to be healed. This is part of why He has you in the wilderness. Not to punish you, but to purify you. Not to harm you, but to prepare you for what's coming.

The Israelites who left Egypt weren't ready for the Promised Land. They still had slave mentalities. They still complained instead of worshiping. They still wanted to return to bondage when freedom got uncomfortable. The wilderness was meant to transform them from slaves into a nation that could possess what God promised. But they resisted the process, and that resistance kept them wandering for forty years.

Don't make their mistake. When the wilderness exposes something in you that needs to change, cooperate with God's work instead of fighting it. Let Him form in you what He needs to form so that when breakthrough comes, you're ready for it.

Your wilderness is teaching you the same lesson. No matter what you're trusting God for, money, healing, restored relationships, or a new job, the wilderness shows you that you can't make it happen on your own. You can ask, seek, and do your part, but in the end, the breakthrough comes from God, in His timing and His way. The wilderness is where you learn to trust Him, even when you can't control the outcome. Try starting your day with a simple prayer at breakfast: "God, provide what I need for today." This helps you focus on trusting God for just enough each day, like the manna He gave in the wilderness.

The second thing God does in the wilderness is cause you to develop dependency on Him. This drove the Israelites crazy. They wanted security. They wanted to know that next week's provision was already in hand. They wanted control over their food supply. But God intentionally designed the manna to spoil if they tried to keep it overnight, except on the day before the Sabbath when He provided a double portion. Why? Because He was teaching them something that slave life had never required: moment-by-moment dependence on a Provider they couldn't see or control.

Your wilderness is doing the same thing. Whatever you're believing God for, whether it's financial provision or physical healing or relational restoration or career breakthrough, the wilderness is teaching you that you can't manufacture the answer through your own effort. You can ask. You can seek. You can position yourself. But ultimately, the breakthrough comes from God, in His timing, through His methods. And the wilderness is where you learn to be okay with that. Where you learn to trust a Provider you can't control. Where you develop the kind of dependency that says, "I've done everything I know to do, and now I'm trusting You to do what only You can do." Think about everyday moments, like when you're unsure if your next paycheck will cover your expenses, when you're anxiously waiting on medical test results, or when you face the daily challenges of parenting. These are modern-day equivalents of relying on manna from heaven, fostering a trust that transcends our understanding and requires us to lean wholly on God's provision.

This can be hard for people who are used to being self-sufficient. We like having backup plans and knowing we have options if our first plan doesn't work. But sometimes God removes all the backup plans. He puts you in a place where there's no plan B, no safety net, and no way forward except for His help. Not because He's unkind, but because He wants to end our self-sufficiency so we can experience His sufficiency. That change only happens in the wilderness, when you have no other options.

I experienced this during the eighteen-month wilderness that I mentioned in the introduction. God had given me a promise about ministry, about using me in ways that would impact others. But for a year and a half, nothing happened. Doors stayed closed. Opportunities dried up. I did everything I knew to do. I prayed. I sought God. I positioned myself. I served faithfully wherever I could. But breakthroughs didn't come. And in that season, God systematically removed every backup plan I had. Every strategy I tried hit a wall. Every door I thought would open stayed locked. Until I finally got to a place where I had nothing left except dependence on Him.

And that's when things started to shift. Not because I finally figured out the right formula, but because I finally stopped trying to figure it out. Not because I did something that earned God's favor, but because I surrendered control and learned to trust Him even when I couldn't see what He was doing. The wilderness forced a level of dependency that I never would have developed if breakthroughs had come quickly. And that dependency has been one of the greatest gifts of my life because it transformed how I relate to God in every area, not just in that one situation.

So when your wilderness strips away your sense of control, when it removes your backup plans and leaves you with nothing but dependence on God, don't fight that. Lean into it. Let the wilderness develop in you what slave life in Egypt or comfortable Christianity never could: genuine, moment-by-moment trust in a God who is faithful even when He's invisible.

The third thing God does in the wilderness is test your motives. Why do you want what you're asking for? What's driving your pursuit? Is it God's glory or your comfort? Is it kingdom purposes or personal validation? Is it faith or just a desire for an easier life? These questions matter because what drives your pursuit determines whether you'll steward the breakthrough well when it comes.

Think about what the Israelites wanted in the wilderness. They said they wanted food and water, which were legitimate needs. But listen to how they asked. They accused God of bringing them out to die. They grumbled against Moses. They longed for Egypt, where at least they had garlic and onions and meat, conveniently forgetting the brutal slavery that came with those meals. Their requests were reasonable, but their hearts were wrong. They wanted provision more than they wanted the Provider. They wanted comfort more than they wanted God's purposes. They wanted the blessings of the Promised Land without the transformation required to possess it.

God gave them what they asked for. He provided manna, water, and even quail when they demanded meat. But He also exposed their divided hearts. They wanted deliverance from slavery, but they didn't want the discomfort of the journey. They wanted the destination, but they resented the process. And that divided heart kept them from entering what God had promised until an entire generation died in the desert and a new generation rose up with different hearts.

Your wilderness will do the same kind of testing. You'll discover whether you want breakthroughs for the right reasons or wrong ones. You'll find out whether you're willing to endure the process or just want the easy result. You'll learn whether you're truly surrendered to God's will or if you're just trying to use spiritual language to get what you want. And this testing isn't meant to condemn you. It's meant to purify your motives so that when breakthrough comes, you'll use it for God's glory rather than just your own satisfaction.

Let me give you an example from a testimony that Marcus shared with me. There was a young man who came to him, desperate for prayer. He wanted a job, and he wanted Marcus to agree with him that God would provide one. So they began to pray together. After the prayer, Marcus asked him, 'What steps have you taken beyond praying?' 'I've applied to a few places,' the young man replied, 'but nothing is working out.' Marcus pressed further, 'Are you limiting yourself in what you're applying for?' The young man hesitated, 'Well, I've only applied to jobs that offer high pay and minimal effort, with a convenient location and an impressive title.' Marcus nodded, understanding, 'It seems like you're more interested in the benefits of work rather than the work itself, don't you think?' The young man looked down, contemplating this revelation. He wasn't actually interested in work. He was interested in the advantages that work could offer, without recognizing the sacrifices it often entails.

Marcus challenged him about his motives. Was he asking God for a job so he could be a faithful steward and provide for his needs? Or was he asking God for a job that would make his life easier while requiring minimal effort from him? The question made him angry at first because it exposed something he didn't want to see. But eventually, he admitted that he wanted the blessing without the responsibility. He wanted provision without sacrifice. And the wilderness he was in, the season of unemployment, was actually God's mercy. Because if God had given him the kind of job he was asking for with the heart he had, he would have squandered it within months.

Over time, this young man's heart shifted. The wilderness did its work. He became willing to take jobs that didn't fit his narrow criteria. He became grateful for opportunities rather than entitled about what he deserved. He learned to see work as service rather than just as a means to a paycheck. And once his motives changed, once the wilderness had purified what was driving his pursuit, breakthroughs came. He got a job that actually exceeded what he had originally wanted, but now he had the character to steward it well.

That's what wilderness testing does. It reveals whether you want the blessing for the right reasons. And if the reasons are wrong, it gives you time to adjust before you receive something you're not ready to handle. So when you're in the wilderness, and it feels like God is withholding what you've asked for, consider that He might be protecting you. He might be waiting for your motives to align with His purposes before He releases what He's been preparing for you all along.

The fourth thing God does in the wilderness is build endurance. This may be the most important purpose, because without endurance, you won't reach the next stage. You might ask and seek for a while, but if breakthroughs don't come quickly, you could give up. Think of each prayer as building your spiritual strength, even if you can't see it. Endurance prepares you for the final push, like a hero standing before a door to their dreams. Without this, you risk starting things you never finish and missing out on breakthroughs, which can lead to disappointment and unfulfilled potential.

James writes about this when he says, "Count it all joy, my brothers, when you meet trials of various kinds, for you know that the testing of your faith produces steadfastness. And let steadfastness have its full effect, that you may be perfect and complete, lacking in nothing." Notice the progression there. Trials test faith. Tested faith produces steadfastness. And steadfastness, when it's fully developed, makes you mature and complete, lacking nothing. The wilderness is where steadfastness gets built, and steadfastness is what carries you through to breakthroughs.

Think about endurance in physical terms. If you've never run more than a mile, you can't suddenly decide to run a marathon. Your body isn't ready. You don't have the cardiovascular capacity, the muscular strength, the mental toughness required to sustain effort over twenty-six miles. But if you train consistently, if you gradually increase your distance, if you push through discomfort and fatigue and the voice that tells you to quit, you build endurance. And once you have endurance, you can accomplish things that would have been impossible when you started.

Spiritual endurance works the same way. You can't develop the capacity to persist in faith through years of waiting if you've never had to wait for anything. You can't build the mental and spiritual toughness required to keep knocking at a closed door if you've always gotten what you wanted quickly. The wilderness is God's training ground for endurance. It's where you learn that you can keep going even when you're tired, even when you don't see progress, even when every circumstance suggests you should quit.

And here's why this matters so much. The things worth having, the breakthroughs that will actually transform your life rather than just provide temporary comfort, these almost always require sustained pursuit over time. Quick blessings come and go just as quickly. But breakthroughs that come after years of faithful pursuit, breakthroughs that required you to develop endurance and character and unwavering faith, that kind of breakthrough tends to be permanent. It sticks. It transforms not just your circumstances but your very nature. And you can't access that level of breakthrough without the endurance that only wilderness seasons can build.

I think about David's wilderness between anointing and coronation. Samuel anointed him as king when he was probably a teenager. But David didn't take the throne until he was thirty. That's somewhere between ten and fifteen years of waiting. And they weren't peaceful years. He spent much of that time running for his life from Saul, hiding in caves, living as a fugitive despite having done nothing wrong. He had been anointed. The promise was clear. But the fulfillment was delayed for over a decade.

What was God doing during those years? He was building endurance. He was developing in David the capacity to lead a nation, to make life-or-death decisions, to handle power without abusing it, and to trust God when circumstances were impossible. The boy who killed Goliath wouldn't have been ready to be king. But the man who emerged from years of wilderness, who had learned to wait on God's timing, who had developed unshakeable faith through sustained testing, that man was ready. The wilderness didn't delay David's destiny. It prepared him for it.

Your wilderness is doing the same thing. It's building in you the capacity to handle what God wants to give you. It's developing the endurance to not just receive breakthroughs but sustain them. And if you'll stop fighting the process and start cooperating with it, if you'll let the wilderness do its work rather than constantly trying to escape it, you'll emerge with strength you never knew you could have.

But here's the hard truth about endurance. It only develops through actual endurance. You can't read about it, you can't pray for it, you can't have someone impart it to you. You have to go through the process that builds it. You have to keep going when everything in you wants to quit. You have to maintain faith when circumstances suggest faithlessness would be more reasonable. You have to hold onto God's promises when letting go would be easier. That's how endurance gets built. Not through comfort, but through sustained effort in the face of difficulty.

So when you're in the wilderness, and you want to give up, when you've been asking and seeking for so long that you can barely remember why you started, that's precisely when endurance is being built. That's the moment when you have a choice. You can quit, which is always an option. Or you can take one more step. Pray one more prayer. Believe for one more day. And every time you make that choice, every time you keep going when quitting would be easier, you're building endurance that will serve you for the rest of your life.

The fifth thing God does in the wilderness is prepare your testimony. Hard-earned testimonies not only show personal victory but also give hope and guidance to others, shaping the faith of whole communities. This might seem less important when you're suffering, but it can have the biggest impact. Your wilderness story, when you're doing everything right but seeing no results, is being written right now. How this story ends will decide if it becomes a powerful testimony that builds faith in others or just another story of someone who gave up when things got hard.

Quick answers are nice, but they don't produce compelling testimonies. Easy breakthroughs are pleasant, but they don't inspire others who are in hard places. The testimonies that actually change lives, that give hope to people who are ready to quit, come from sustained pursuit through difficult seasons. They're the stories of ordinary people who refused to give up despite overwhelming odds, who maintained faith when circumstances contradicted everything they believed, who kept knocking even when their knuckles were bloody from pounding on closed doors.

Your wilderness is writing that kind of story. Every day you keep believing is another page. Every prayer you pray when you don't feel like praying is another chapter. Every time you choose faith over doubt is more testimony material. And when breakthroughs finally come, when this season ends, and you step into what God has been preparing, you'll have a story that will strengthen others for generations.

But here's the catch. Testimony only has power if you finish well. If you give up in the wilderness, if you abandon your pursuit before breakthrough comes, you don't have testimony. You just have a sad story about someone who almost made it but quit too soon. The power of wilderness testimony comes from the ending, from the breakthrough that proves God's faithfulness despite the long delay. So every day you stay in the fight, every moment you refuse to quit, you're not just persevering for your own sake. You're creating testimony that will help others who come after you.

I can't tell you how many people have been encouraged by my story of the eighteen-month wilderness. When I share about that season, about the darkness and doubt and feeling abandoned by God, and then about the breakthrough that came when I finally learned what He was teaching me, something shifts in people who are in similar places. They realize they're not alone. They see that wilderness seasons are normal, not evidence of failure. They gain hope that their story might have a similar ending if they keep going.

That's the power of wilderness testimony. But I only have that testimony because I didn't quit. If I had walked away from faith during those eighteen months, if I had concluded that God wasn't real or wasn't good or wasn't faithful, I wouldn't have anything to offer others except bitterness and disillusionment. The testimony exists because I endured. And your testimony will exist for the same reason, but only if you stay in the fight long enough to see how this story ends.

Now, let me shift from what God is doing in the wilderness to how you survive it without losing faith. Understanding the purpose of wilderness seasons is helpful, but it doesn't make them any easier. You still have to wake up every day in circumstances that haven't changed. You still have to fight discouragement when another prayer seems to go unanswered. You still have to maintain hope when every visible indicator suggests you should give up. In this moment, I invite you to pause. Ask yourself, 'What emotion surfaces as you face the silence?' This reflective question is not just a pause; it is a gateway to deeper understanding and readiness. After you've acknowledged this feeling, let's explore strategies to help you carry on. How do you actually do that? How do you survive the wilderness without becoming bitter, without losing faith, without abandoning the breakthrough you've been pursuing? There are five key practices to help you endure: remember God's promises, find community, celebrate provision, refuse comparisons, and maintain spiritual disciplines. Let's explore each one deeply in the following sections.

First, remember what God said before the wilderness began. This is crucial. The Israelites forgot the promises God made before they left Egypt. They forgot that He said He would bring them to a land flowing with milk and honey. They forgot that He promised to drive out their enemies and give them rest. They forgot because the discomfort of the present obscured the promises about the future. And when you forget what God said, when you lose sight of the promise, the wilderness becomes unbearable.

So go back to the beginning of your journey. What did God speak to you about this situation? What promises from Scripture have you been standing on? What vision or direction or confirmation did you receive when you first started pursuing this breakthrough? Write those things down. Put them somewhere you'll see them daily. Because in the wilderness, you'll need constant reminders of what God said when the memory is fresh, and faith is strong. Those reminders will anchor you when circumstances tempt you to believe that God has forgotten His promises.

David did this throughout his wilderness years. He wrote psalms that rehearsed God's faithfulness, that declared His promises, that reminded himself of who God was even when circumstances suggested otherwise. When you read the Psalms, you see this pattern over and over. David would start with an honest lament about his circumstances, but he would always circle back to remembering God's character and promises. That remembering kept him anchored when everything else was shifting.

Do the same thing. Create your own declarations based on what God has said and what Scripture promises. Speak them out loud every day, especially on the days when you don't feel them. Not to manipulate God or to try to make something happen through positive confession, but to remind yourself of the truth when lies are screaming louder. The wilderness is where the enemy's lies are most convincing because circumstances seem to support them. But truth doesn't change based on circumstances. God's promises don't become less true just because they haven't manifested yet. So speak truth over yourself constantly, whether you feel it or not.

Second, you have to find others who have been where you are and made it through. Isolation is deadly in the wilderness. When you're alone with your thoughts, when you have no one who understands what you're going through, the enemy has a field day convincing you that you're the only one struggling, that everyone else has it easier, that God responds to others but not to you. But when you connect with people who have walked through similar wilderness seasons and emerged with breakthroughs, something shifts. Their testimony becomes proof that wilderness seasons do end, that perseverance does pay off, that God is faithful even when He's silent.

This is why community matters so much, especially in difficult seasons. You need people who won't just sympathize with your pain but will speak faith over you when yours is weak. You need voices that remind you of what God said when all you can hear is what circumstances are screaming. You need examples of people who endured and received so that you know endurance is possible.

Pastor Marcus has an amazing department in their ministry, which I am planning to implement in ours as well. They've created what he calls wilderness groups. Small gatherings of people who are all in difficult seasons, all waiting for breakthroughs that haven't come yet, all tempted to give up but choosing to stand together. These groups don't just sympathize with each other. They don't just share their pain, though that's part of it. They actively choose to build each other's faith. They remind each other of God's promises. They celebrate small evidence of God's faithfulness even in the midst of continued waiting. And they hold each other accountable to keep pursuing when everything suggests they should quit.

If you don't have access to that kind of community, create it. Invite a few people who are in challenging seasons to meet regularly. Don't let it become a complaint session. Make it a place where you strengthen each other, where you speak life, truth, and hope over one another. Because the wilderness is hard enough on its own. Don't try to navigate it alone.

Third, you need to notice and appreciate what God is providing in the wilderness rather than just wishing for deliverance. This can be a hard shift, but it's important. The Israelites were so focused on reaching the Promised Land that they missed the daily miracles God gave them: manna, water, clothes that didn't wear out, and His visible presence. They saw these things as barely enough, not as miracles. They were so focused on what they lacked that they forgot to be grateful for what they had. To help you connect with what God is providing now, try writing a short story, about 50 words, about something you're thankful for today. This will help you practice gratitude and notice God's hand in everyday moments.

Looking back on my own difficult season, I remember a time when I felt stuck in my career and unsure about the future. It seemed like every opportunity had dried up. But even then, I received daily blessings; encouragement from a mentor, helpful connections, and friends who believed in me. These small things were my manna, showing me that provision can look different from what we expect, but it's still a gift. Noticing these moments helped me feel grateful and kept me moving forward.

Yes, you're waiting for breakthroughs. Yes, circumstances haven't changed the way you want them to. But look for where God is providing right now, in the middle of your waiting. Is He giving you strength to make it through each day? That's provision. Is He surrounding you with people who support you? That's provision. Are you learning things about yourself and about Him that you wouldn't have learned otherwise? That's provision. Are you developing character, endurance, and faith? That's provision. To help you recognize these provisions, try this exercise: Take a moment to list one present provision you see in your life right now. Write it down and keep it visible. This practice will help shift your mindset to gratitude, reinforcing the idea that God's presence is with you, even in the smallest details.

When you start to celebrate what God is doing in the wilderness instead of just focusing on what you're still waiting for, something changes inside. Gratitude brings a better attitude than complaining. Worshipping while you wait opens your heart to receive breakthroughs in ways that bitterness never can. Often, what you're praying for comes after you've learned to be content in the wilderness, not just desperate to leave it.

This doesn't mean you stop asking for breakthroughs. It doesn't mean you resign yourself to staying in the wilderness forever. It means you trust that God is with you in the wilderness, that He's working in ways you can't see, that He's providing what you need even if it's not what you want. And that trust changes how you experience the waiting.

Fourth, you have to refuse comparison. This is massive. The wilderness is where comparison becomes most toxic because you're looking around at others who seem to be experiencing breakthroughs while you're still stuck. They got the job you've been praying for. They received the healing you've been believing for. They're walking in the breakthrough you've been pursuing for years. And the enemy uses their success to torment you with the suggestion that God loves them more than He loves you, that He responds to their prayers but ignores yours, that something is wrong with you that isn't wrong with them.

All of that is a lie. God's timing for their breakthrough has nothing to do with His plan for yours. Their journey isn't your journey. Their wilderness might have been shorter, but it also might have been preparing them for something different than what God is preparing you for. You don't know what they went through to get to where they are, and even if you did, it wouldn't change what God is doing in your specific situation.

Comparison steals joy, breeds jealousy, and makes you ungrateful for your own journey because you're so focused on someone else's. But more than that, comparison is actually a form of unbelief. When you look at someone else's breakthrough and feel resentment or despair about your own waiting, what you're really saying is that God is unfair, that His timing is wrong, that He should be doing for you what He's doing for them. And that mindset will keep you stuck in the wilderness longer than anything else.

So make a decision right now to refuse comparison. When you see others experiencing breakthroughs, celebrate with them. Let their testimony encourage you that God is still in the miracle-working business. But don't measure your journey against theirs. Don't use their timeline to judge whether God is being faithful to you. Stay in your lane. Trust your process. Believe that God's timing for you is perfect, even when it doesn't match anyone else's.

Fifth, you have to maintain your spiritual disciplines even when they feel empty. This is where many believers fall apart in the wilderness. They start strong. They pray faithfully, read Scripture consistently, and worship regularly. But when months turn into years with no visible change, those disciplines start to feel hollow. Prayer feels like talking to the ceiling. Scripture reading feels mechanical. Worship feels forced. And slowly, imperceptibly, they stop doing the very things that could sustain them through the wilderness.

I understand this temptation because I've felt it. There were days during my wilderness when opening my Bible felt pointless. Days when prayer felt like shouting into a void. Days when worship felt like lying because I didn't feel grateful, joyful, or hopeful. But here's what I learned: spiritual disciplines aren't about feelings. They're about faithfulness. They're about doing what you know is right, even when it doesn't feel meaningful. They're about continuing to position yourself to hear from God even when He seems silent.

And here's what's miraculous about maintaining disciplines when they feel empty. Eventually, something shifts. Not always immediately or dramatically, but over time, the very act of showing up when you don't feel like it creates openness to God's presence that passivity never would. The prayers that feel like they're accomplishing nothing are actually keeping your heart soft toward God. The Scripture you read without feeling anything is actually renewing your mind in ways you can't perceive. The worship you offer without emotion is actually warfare against the discouragement trying to consume you.

Think of it like exercising when you don't feel like it. You don't always feel motivated to work out. Sometimes your body resists. Sometimes it feels pointless because you don't see immediate results. But if you stay consistent, if you keep showing up and doing the work even when it feels empty, over time your body changes. You get stronger. Your endurance improves. The same principle applies spiritually. Keep praying even when it feels empty. Keep reading Scripture even when it feels dry. Keep worshiping even when you don't feel it. Because those disciplines are doing something in you, whether you feel it or not.

So here's what I want you to commit to right now. Don't wait until you feel like praying to pray. Don't wait until Scripture feels alive to read it. Don't wait until worship feels natural to engage in it. Set a schedule and stick to it regardless of how you feel. Not out of legalism, but out of wisdom. Feelings are fickle, but faithfulness produces fruit over time. And the wilderness is where faithfulness gets tested most severely.

Now, let me address something that's probably been in the back of your mind this entire chapter. What if you're in a wilderness that isn't meant to end in breakthroughs? What if God's answer to your prayer is actually no, not just not yet? What if you're supposed to accept your circumstances and not continue fighting for change? These are legitimate questions that deserve honest answers.

To help clarify, let's consider two scenarios of discernment:

Delay: This is when God is saying, "not yet." You might sense a deep peace amidst the waiting, notice small fruits beginning to emerge, receive affirming words from trusted believers, and experience spiritual life growing within you even in hardship.

Redirection: This is when God is providing a new path. In this case, relentless turmoil persists despite all your efforts; repeated failures yield no fruit; respected mentors express genuine concern about your path; and your spiritual perseverance diminishes.

Understanding these scenarios can help you discern whether you are facing a delay that requires perseverance or a redirection that requires a new approach. Being mindful of these signs can help you navigate with wisdom.

So how do you know the difference between a wilderness you should persevere through and a wilderness that's actually God's way of telling you to change direction? Here are some indicators to watch for.

First, peace versus turmoil. If you have deep peace about continuing to pursue what you've been asking for, even though circumstances are difficult, that's usually a sign to keep going. But if you have persistent turmoil, if you can't rest even when you try, if there's a constant sense that you're forcing something that God isn't blessing, that might be a sign to reevaluate. Peace is a reliable indicator of God's will. Not the absence of difficulty, but the presence of peace in the midst of difficulty.

Second, fruit versus repeated failure. If you're seeing some fruit, even if it's small and slow, that's usually a sign you're on the right path. But if you're experiencing repeated failure in the same area despite faithful effort, if every attempt ends in disaster, if nothing ever seems to work no matter what you try, that might be God's way of closing a door you keep trying to force open. This doesn't mean give up at the first sign of difficulty. But after years of sustained effort with absolutely no fruit, wisdom says it might be time to consider whether God is calling you to something different.

Third, confirmation from mature believers versus isolation. If godly people who know you well are affirming the direction you're pursuing, that's encouraging. But if everyone who loves you is gently suggesting that maybe this isn't God's will, if mature believers are expressing concern about your pursuit, you should at least be willing to consider their perspective. Don't blindly follow it, because sometimes God calls you to things that others don't understand. But don't dismiss it either, especially if multiple wise voices are saying similar things.

Fourth, life versus death. Is your pursuit of this breakthrough producing spiritual life in you, or is it producing spiritual death? Are you growing closer to God through the process, or are you becoming bitter and distant? Is your faith increasing or eroding? Is hope alive in you, or has it been replaced by desperation and despair? God's will, even when it's difficult, generally produces life. It might be painful, tested life, refined life, but it's life. If what you're pursuing is producing death in your spirit, that's worth examining.

If you're sensing through these indicators that maybe God is redirecting you, that maybe the wilderness you're in is actually meant to lead you to a different destination than the one you've been pursuing, don't panic. Don't see it as a failure. See it as God's mercy. Sometimes what we think we want isn't actually what we need. Sometimes the dreams we're chasing aren't the ones God has for us. And sometimes the greatest breakthrough comes when we finally let go of what we thought we wanted and open our hands to receive what God actually wants to give.

I'm reminded of a woman I had the privilege of counseling who spent five years praying for her marriage to be restored. Her husband had left, and she believed God was going to bring him back. She stood on Scripture. She prayed faithfully. She refused to move on. But five years later, he was remarried to someone else, and she was still stuck in a wilderness of waiting for something that would never happen. When she finally accepted that God's plan wasn't restoration of that marriage but healing and a new beginning, everything shifted. She started moving forward. She dealt with her pain instead of just praying it away. She opened herself to the future instead of clinging to the past. And today, she's remarried to a godly man who loves her well, with children she never would have had if she'd stayed stuck waiting for the wrong breakthrough.

As we stand together at the threshold of promise, let us declare as one: We will not wander for forty years. We will not allow fear to dictate our journey. Together, we shall press forward, trusting in the preparation of the wilderness and the breakthroughs it paves the path for. Let our collective resolve be the catalyst that propels us into the next chapter, where knocking becomes our shared testimony of faith and persistence.

But here's what I want to be very clear about. Don't use this as an excuse to give up prematurely. Don't read this section and decide that because the wilderness is hard, it must mean God is saying no. Most wildernesses aren't meant to redirect you. Most of them are meant to prepare you for the breakthrough you've been pursuing. So before you conclude that God is closing a door, make sure you've actually been knocking on it persistently. Make sure you've been faithful in asking, seeking, and positioning yourself strategically. Make sure you haven't just been passively waiting and calling it faith.

Because here's the tragedy I've seen play out too many times. Believers give up right before breakthrough because they convince themselves that the difficulty meant God was saying no when He was actually saying not yet. They were in a wilderness that was meant to prepare them, but they misread it as a sign to quit. And they walked away from promises that were about to manifest because they couldn't endure the final stretch of waiting.

Don't be that person. Don't abandon your pursuit because it's taking longer than you wanted. Don't mistake the wilderness for rejection when it's actually preparation. Stay in the fight. Keep asking. Keep seeking. Keep positioning yourself. And trust that if God wants to redirect you, He'll make it clear in ways that align with the indicators we discussed. But until then, assume that the wilderness you're in is the path to breakthrough, not away from it.

So here's your assignment as we close this chapter. I want you to do an honest assessment of where you are. Are you in a wilderness season right now, where you've been asking and seeking faithfully but seeing no results? If so, take some time to journal about what God might be doing in this season. Look back at the five purposes we discussed. Is He exposing what's in your heart? Is He developing dependency? Is He testing your motives? Is He building endurance? Is He preparing testimony? Write down what you're learning, what's being formed in you, what this season is producing that couldn't have come any other way.

Then make some practical commitments about how you're going to survive this wilderness without losing faith. What promises do you need to remember? What community do you need to connect with? What provision in the wilderness can you celebrate? What comparisons do you need to refuse? What spiritual disciplines do you need to maintain? Write these down as concrete commitments, not just good intentions. And then start implementing them today, not tomorrow, today.

Because here's what I know about wilderness seasons. They do end. They're not permanent. The Israelites eventually reached the Promised Land, though it took a generation. David eventually took the throne. Joseph eventually became second in command in Egypt. Job eventually saw restoration. Every biblical wilderness story has an ending, and that ending almost always involves breakthroughs that were worth the wait.

Your wilderness has an ending, too. And when you finally emerge, when breakthroughs finally come, when the door finally opens, you'll look back on this season and see it differently. You'll see that it wasn't wasted time. You'll see that God was working even when He seemed silent. You'll see that what felt like a delay was actually divine timing. You'll see that the wilderness wasn't punishment but preparation for something bigger than you imagined.

But you have to make it through. You have to endure without becoming bitter. You have to maintain faith without seeing evidence. You have to keep pursuing when everything suggests you should quit. Because the breakthrough you're believing for, the door you've been knocking on, it's closer than you think. And quitting now would mean missing everything God has been preparing through this painful process.

So stay in the wilderness. Not because you want to, but because you know what's on the other side. Not because it's comfortable, but because it's purposeful. Not because you enjoy waiting, but because you trust the One who's making you wait. The wilderness is temporary. Breakthrough is coming. And everything you're going through right now is preparing you for what's ahead.

Now let's move to the next step. We've learned to ask, to seek, to position ourselves, and to endure the wilderness when breakthroughs are slow. But there's one more step that takes even more courage and boldness than anything we've talked about so far. It's time to learn to knock. When you understand what knocking really means, and what it takes and produces, everything changes. Turn the page. The door is waiting.

CHAPTER SIX

THE THIRD DIMENSION

KNOCKING AND THE CRISIS OF PROXIMITY

THE AFTERNOON SUN CAST long shadows on the dusty road as a woman hurried by, desperate to help her suffering daughter. Matthew doesn't share her name, background, or past. He only tells us what she needed and how far she was willing to go. Her daughter was in deep pain, tormented by a demon. But this story is bigger than just one woman; it shows how persistent faith can overcome any obstacle. When she heard Jesus was close, she cried out, "Have mercy on me, O Lord, Son of David; my daughter is severely oppressed by a demon."

This is what it means to ask: be clear, specific, and honest about your need. She knew what she needed and went straight to the only one who could help. But what happened next is where many people might have given up, thinking they misunderstood, that God wasn't interested, or that it just wasn't meant to be.

Jesus didn't answer her. There was only silence. She kept asking for mercy while her daughter suffered, but the one who could help said nothing. The disciples, annoyed by her persistence, asked Jesus to send her away. Then Jesus spoke, not to her but to His disciples, saying, "I was sent only to the lost sheep of the house of Israel."

She wasn't part of Israel. She was a Canaanite, a Gentile, not included in the covenant community. According to Jesus's words, she didn't qualify for what she was asking. If there was ever a time to walk away, this was it. Jesus had basically said the blessing wasn't for her. Most people would have left then, feeling hurt and confused, and wondering why God would let them ask for something He didn't plan to give.

But she didn't leave. She moved closer, knelt down, and said, "Lord, help me." Just three words: no debate, no defense, just persistence. Jesus replied even more directly: "It is not right to take the children's bread and throw it to the dogs." Think about times in your life when you've felt rejected or insulted and wanted to give up. Let this be a moment to reflect on your own challenges to faith and persistence.

He called her a dog. Imagine that for a moment. This woman was desperate for her daughter's healing, crying out to the only one who could help, and Jesus compared her to a dog. Most people would have walked away, feeling offended and rejected. She had asked, been ignored, come closer, and then been insulted. By any measure, she had done enough and had every reason to think the door was closed, and it was time to move on.

But she saw what most people miss. She was at the door, and the resistance wasn't a barrier; it was a test. The harsh words and obstacles weren't signs that the door was closed for good, but challenges to see if she would keep going. Instead of leaving or getting offended, she pressed in even more. Remember, obstacles can be opportunities. They're meant to strengthen your resolve and determination, not stop you.

"Yes, Lord," she said, "yet even the dogs eat the crumbs that fall from their masters' table."

Her answer is one of the most remarkable moments in Scripture. She took Jesus's tough words and used them as her reason to receive. She didn't argue about being called a dog. She simply pointed out that even dogs get crumbs, and even those outside the main group can receive the overflow. She was saying, "I'm not asking for everything, just for what falls to the floor. Surely there's enough from Your abundance to heal my daughter."

Then Jesus, who had been silent, dismissive, and even seemed insulting, suddenly praised her: "O woman, great is your faith! Let it be done for you as you desire." Her daughter was healed immediately. The door that seemed closed opened right away. The breakthrough happened, not because she had perfect beliefs or credentials, but because she refused to give up.

This is what it means to knock. Many people miss their breakthrough here, not because God says no, but because they misunderstand the resistance. We see closed doors and think it's rejection, but these moments test how much we really want the breakthrough. Delays aren't detours; they often mean you're close. Hard times aren't reasons to quit; they're the last challenge before the door opens. Knocking is persistent faith that refuses to give up.

Knocking happens when you've asked and searched and now stand at the door, but it still hasn't opened. You're right at the threshold, sensing something on the other side. You know you're in the right place, but the door is still closed. The real question is whether you'll keep knocking or give up and walk away.

This is the hardest part: being so close to what you've prayed for that you can almost reach it, but not quite. You've done everything right: asked with faith, searched with effort, and put yourself in the right place. But you're still waiting, and the door isn't opening. This is where faith gets tough, and persistence feels uncomfortable. At this point, you have one choice: keep knocking or walk away.

Most lessons on prayer don't address this stage because most people never reach it. They stop asking or give up searching. But for those who make it to the door and keep standing there, this moment means everything. The difference between those who receive and those who don't is often who is still knocking when the door finally opens.

The Greek word Jesus uses in Matthew 7:7 for knock is krouo. It means to strike, to beat, to pound with urgency. It's not a polite tap or a casual knock you do once and then leave. It's insistent, expectant pounding that says, "I'm not leaving until this door opens." It's the knock of someone with no backup, no other options, and no alternative plan. It's desperation shaped by faith. It's a need that shows through persistence. It's the sound of someone who wants breakthroughs more than they fear looking foolish, more than they value their dignity, or care what anyone else thinks.

And Jesus doesn't just tell us to knock. He tells us to keep knocking. The present tense means it's ongoing, just like asking and seeking. This isn't a one-time thing. It's sustained, repeated, relentless knocking that refuses to accept a closed door as the final answer. It's showing up at the threshold day after day, prayer after prayer, refusing to walk away even when everything suggests you should.

Before we go further, it's important to understand what knocking is not. There's a way to misapply this teaching that turns faith into presumption and persistence into stubbornness. Knocking is not demanding. It's not trying to force God's hand through willpower. It's not treating prayer like a vending machine, where if you just press the button enough times, you'll get what you want. That's not faith. That's just trying to manipulate God.

Real knocking comes from humility and desperation, not entitlement or control. The Canaanite woman wasn't demanding anything. She was begging and pleading, saying, "I have nowhere else to go and nothing else to try, and I'm not leaving until You help me." That's very different from insisting God give you what you want just because you've done all the right things and think He owes you.

Knocking is also not mindless repetition. It's not praying the same words over and over, hoping that enough repetition will unlock breakthroughs. Jesus warned against that kind of praying, saying that pagans think they'll be heard for their many words. God doesn't respond to volume or frequency alone. He responds to faith shown through persistent pursuit.

Knocking is an unwavering commitment to faith when you're waiting for your answer. It's the ongoing expression of faith when you're at the door, but the answer hasn't come yet. It's choosing each day to keep believing, keep pursuing, and keep standing at the threshold, even when walking away would be easier. It's showing up to pray about the same need day after day, not to wear God down, but because the need is still real and you're still trusting Him. It's refusing to see a closed door as permanent when God has promised it will open.

Think about knocking on a real door for a moment. When you knock, you're doing a few things at once. You're announcing your presence and showing your need to enter. You're showing respect by waiting for permission instead of forcing your way in. You're also creating urgency with the sound. A knock asks for a response. It says, "I'm here, and I need you to notice me."

That's what spiritual knocking does. It keeps your need before God with both urgency and humility. It says, "I'm still here, I'm still asking, I'm still believing, I'm not going anywhere." Here's what's powerful about that: when you keep showing up at the same door with the same request and faith, something shifts in the spiritual realm. You're not changing God's mind. You're showing that your request is serious, not just a passing thought. You're proving you want this breakthrough more than comfort or avoiding the risk of asking again and again.

Here's another biblical example of knocking in action. In Luke 11, right after Jesus teaches about asking, seeking, and knocking, He tells a parable. A man receives unexpected guests at midnight but has no food, so he goes to his friend's house and knocks, asking to borrow three loaves of bread.

The friend replies from inside, "Don't bother me. My door is locked, my children are in bed with me, I can't get up and give you anything." That's a clear "no." Most people would apologize and leave, but this man stays. Because of his bold persistence, the friend eventually gets up and gives him what he needs.

Jesus isn't saying God is a reluctant friend who needs to be convinced to bless you. The parable shows a contrast. If a tired friend will eventually respond to persistent knocking, how much more will your Heavenly Father, who loves you and never sleeps, respond to your persistence? The lesson is not about wearing God down, but about the power of bold persistence when you need a door to open.

Shameless audacity. That phrase stands out because it describes something we're usually told to avoid. We're taught to be polite, not to impose, and to accept "no" graciously. We learn to value dignity and composure over showing need. While these are good in daily life, they can actually keep you from getting your breakthrough if you bring them into prayer.

The woman with the issue of blood who reached out to touch Jesus's garment showed shameless audacity. She was considered unclean and wasn't supposed to be in the crowd. She risked being exposed and humiliated, but she was so desperate for healing that she didn't care what others thought. She wanted healing more than she cared about appearances.

Blind Bartimaeus also showed shameless audacity. When he heard Jesus was nearby, he shouted, "Jesus, Son of David, have mercy on me!" The crowd told him to be quiet and not make a scene, but he shouted even louder. He didn't let social pressure stop him from seeking a breakthrough. Jesus stopped, called him over, and healed him.

The persistent widow in Luke 18 also showed shameless audacity. She kept coming to an unjust judge, asking for justice against her enemy. The judge didn't fear God or care about people, but because she kept coming, he finally gave her what she wanted just to make her stop. Jesus uses her as an example of how we should pray: never giving up or accepting a closed door as final.

In each of these stories, shameless audacity means you want a breakthrough more than you fear being embarrassed. You need an answer to prayer more than you care about your reputation. You're willing to look desperate because you truly are. You'll risk people thinking you're too persistent or intense because what you're after matters more than their opinions.

This is tough for many of us because we've learned that needing help is a weakness, that asking repeatedly is pushy, and that being persistent can seem like a bother. In human relationships, these social rules make sense. But God isn't like people. He doesn't get annoyed by your requests. He's a Father who loves giving good gifts to His children. When He sees someone who wants His blessing more than they fear looking foolish, He calls it great faith.

That's what Jesus said about the Canaanite woman: "Great is your faith." He didn't say her theology, worthiness, or spiritual track record was great. It was her faith. What made her faith great wasn't fancy prayers or a perfect life, but her refusal to walk away from the door, even when everything suggested she should.

Here's something important about knocking: you might look foolish or feel like you're overdoing it. Sometimes you'll wonder if you're being persistent or just stubborn, if it's faith or just insistence. The line can seem thin, but here's how you can tell the difference.

Persistence rooted in faith has peace beneath the desperation. Even when you're pounding on the door or crying out with everything in you, there's a deep sense that says, "I'm in the right place doing the right thing, even though it's uncomfortable." Stubbornness rooted in pride has anxiety beneath the determination. You're forcing something because you can't accept not getting your way, not because you truly believe God has promised this breakthrough.

Persistence rooted in faith is flexible in its methods but firm in its promise. You're open to God answering in ways you didn't expect, but you don't give up on what He spoke. Stubbornness rooted in pride is rigid about methods and often more attached to a specific outcome than to God Himself. You want things your way, on your timeline, through your preferred channels.

Persistence rooted in faith draws you closer to God even when the door doesn't open. The knocking itself becomes worship, trust, and intimacy. Stubbornness rooted in pride pushes you away from God when He doesn't act as you want. You become bitter, resentful, and convinced He's being unfair.

As we talk about knocking with shameless audacity, check your heart. Are you pursuing breakthroughs because God promised it and you're trusting Him to fulfill His word? Or are you seeking breakthroughs because you think you deserve it and are trying to force God to meet your demands? The first leads to breakthroughs. The second leads to burnout and disappointment.

Now let's talk about what happens while you're knocking. The time you spend at the door, between arriving and the door opening, isn't wasted. Three things are happening as you knock: God is working in the spiritual realm, He's refining you, and preparing the breakthroughs. Understanding this will help you endure the process.

First, knocking is a form of spiritual warfare. When you keep bringing your request to God and refuse to see a closed door as final, you're doing more than just praying. You're fighting against forces that want to keep that door closed. Picture a parent by a hospital bed, praying through the night for their child's recovery. Each prayer is like a small but powerful blow against the illness. This is spiritual warfare in action, where faith stands strong against unseen forces that try to bring doubt and despair. Think of Daniel 10, where an angel told Daniel his prayer was heard from the start, but a spiritual being called the prince of Persia blocked the answer for 21 days. Daniel's steady prayers during those weeks weren't wasted. They were spiritual warfare that helped bring the breakthrough into reality.

The same thing happens when you keep knocking. Sometimes, spiritual forces push back against your prayers, and your persistence keeps the pressure on. The enemy wants you to stop, give up, and believe the door will never open. If you stop knocking and walk away, the spiritual pressure fades. But if you keep showing up, keep speaking God's promises, and keep standing in faith, you're fighting a battle the enemy can't win.

That's why Jesus tells the story of the persistent widow before talking about finding faith when He returns. He connects persistent prayer with lasting faith. Real faith isn't just believing when things are easy. It's sticking with it when the door stays closed, trusting it will open because God promised. Like a student waiting for scholarship news, the widow's persistence shows that with steady faith, anyone facing tough barriers can turn hope into reality.

Second, knocking reveals what you truly value. It's easy to say you want something when it costs nothing. But when it takes effort every day, your persistence shows whether you really want a breakthrough or just like the idea. To make this practical, try a small daily habit: let your morning alarm remind you to spend five minutes in prayer, then write down something you're grateful for. This routine makes persistence feel manageable and turns your desire into action.

Think about the difference between someone who says they want to get fit and someone who keeps going to the gym for months, even without big results. The first wants the outcome. The second wants it enough to stick with the process. The gym responds to your effort, not your intentions. Breakthroughs work the same way. God responds to what you keep pursuing, not just what you say you want.

This is why knocking separates casual believers from committed ones. Casual believers ask a few times and move on when things don't happen quickly. They try different things but never commit. Committed believers, who want breakthroughs more than comfort, keep knocking. They stay at the door and don't leave until it opens. Their persistence shows God, the spiritual world, and themselves that this is something they truly want.

Are there times in your life when you might confuse tiredness with God's redirection? Let this question help you be honest with yourself and notice the areas that challenge you most. It's okay to feel tired; admitting it can help you find the strength to keep going.

I've seen this many times in my ministry. Two people ask for prayer for the same breakthrough. Both seem sincere and talk about faith and commitment. But six months later, one is still coming for prayer and holding onto God's promises, while the other has moved on to something else. One kept knocking; the other got tired and chose a different path.

From what I've seen, people who keep knocking do see breakthroughs. It might not happen when or how they expect, but the door eventually opens. God responds to steady pursuit in a way He doesn't to casual interest. I remember Sarah, who prayed and waited for years before finally getting the job she hoped for. Her joy and gratitude were clear when her persistence paid off. Those who stop knocking rarely see this kind of breakthrough, because they don't build the spiritual strength needed to keep going until the door opens.

Take a moment to think about what you've been praying for. Do you really want it, or just the idea? Are you willing to keep knocking until it takes, or are you looking for an easier way? Knocking will show what you truly value, and that will decide if you're still there when the door finally opens.

Third, knocking helps you recognize when the door is about to unlock. This might sound unusual, but hear me out. When you keep knocking on a door, you get to know it well. You notice its sound, its weight, and how it feels. You start to notice small changes that others might miss. When the lock finally starts to move, you hear it before you see it. Being close to the door makes you aware of shifts that others overlook. To build this awareness, try sitting quietly after each prayer. Spend a few moments listening for any small signs or feelings of change in your spirit or your situation. This habit can help you notice when the latch is turning, making your persistence feel more real.

Spiritually, persistent knocking helps you notice God's movement even before a breakthrough is obvious. You start to see small changes in your circumstances. You recognize moments that others might call coincidences as divine appointments. You sense changes in the spiritual atmosphere around you. You hear God's voice more clearly because you've been listening for it every day. All of this helps you work with breakthroughs as they begin, rather than miss them because you weren't paying attention.

Elijah understood this idea. After praying for rain following three years of drought, he sent his servant to look toward the sea seven times. Six times, the servant saw nothing. On the seventh try, he saw a small cloud, about the size of a man's hand. Most people would have ignored that tiny cloud, but Elijah, who had been praying persistently, recognized it as a sign. He told Ahab to get ready because heavy rain was coming, and it did. Elijah's persistence helped him notice the breakthrough, even when it started small.

This is one of the hidden benefits of knocking that people rarely mention. While you're seeking breakthroughs, you're also building spiritual sensitivity that will help you throughout your life. You learn to notice God's movement. You train yourself to pick up on things others might miss. You become someone who doesn't just wait for obvious breakthroughs, but who sees them when they're small and helps them grow.

Fourth, knocking puts you in the right place to receive breakthroughs when they come. This may seem simple, but it matters. You need to be at the door when it opens, or you might miss what you've been waiting for. Think about the parable of the ten virgins in Matthew 25. Five were wise and kept oil for their lamps, while five ran out of oil. When the bridegroom came, only those who were ready went in, and the door was shut. The others came back too late and were not let in. To help you be ready for breakthroughs, try setting a daily reminder on your phone for a time you set aside to be spiritually open and prepared. This small habit keeps you ready to receive and makes sure you're present in faith and action when the door opens.

By knocking persistently, you make sure you're in the right place when breakthroughs happen. You're not distracted by other options or chasing something else. You haven't given up or walked away. You're right there, ready to knock again when the door finally opens. Because you're in position, you can step into what God has prepared for you.

This is why endurance matters when you're knocking. It's not just about getting a breakthrough, but about being in the right place at the right time when it happens. Often, the difference between receiving what God has for you and missing it is whether you're still knocking when the door finally opens.

Knocking refines your request. When you first start asking for something, your request is often general. Knocking helps clarify what you're really asking for. At first, your request might be general or based on what you think you need. But as you keep coming to God with the same prayer, your understanding grows. Your request becomes more specific. You start to see the deeper need behind your prayer. Ask yourself, "What fear sits beneath my request?" This question can help you look more deeply into your motives and align your intentions with what God truly wants to give you. What you ultimately need is purpose and fulfillment in your work, which might come through a new job or a shift in how you approach your current position. Maybe you started knocking for financial provision, but sustained prayer reveals that what you actually need is freedom from fear and a deeper trust in God's provision, which money alone wouldn't solve. Maybe you started knocking for a spouse, but the process shows you that what you actually need first is healing from past wounds and wholeness in your identity, which makes you ready for a healthy relationship.

Knocking helps refine your request, so when the door finally opens, you receive what you truly need, not just what you first wanted. Often, God gives you something better than you expected because your persistence allowed Him to shape both your request and your readiness to receive it.

Jacob's wrestling with God in Genesis 32 shows this well. He started the night wanting God's blessing. But through the struggle and his refusal to let go, he received much more than he had asked for. God blessed him, changed his name from Jacob to Israel, transformed his identity, gave him a limp as a reminder, and changed his whole approach to God and life. The blessing was bigger and deeper than he could have imagined at the start, and it came through persistent, desperate pursuit.

Let's talk about one of the toughest questions when it comes to knocking: How long should you keep at it? How do you know when it's time to stop? When does persistence cross over into stubbornness, or faith into denial? These are questions many believers face after months or years of waiting with no change, and they deserve honest answers. To help you decide whether to keep going or change direction, ask yourself two things. First, do you feel peace as you pursue this path? If not, it might be time to reconsider. Second, is this process helping you grow spiritually, or is it making you bitter? Growth is a sign of faith, while bitterness could mean you're just being stubborn. Think about these points as you keep knocking. The answers can help guide your next steps.

The reality is, there's no set formula. I can't say that if you knock a certain number of times, the door will open on the next try. There's no one-size-fits-all timeline. What I can offer are some principles to help you decide whether to keep knocking or whether God is leading you somewhere else.

Here are four principles to help you decide whether to keep knocking:

1. Keep knocking as long as you have peace and a sense of God's promise. If you believe God has spoken clearly about your situation, if you have scriptural promises that fit what you're asking for, and if you feel deep peace even when it's hard, keep going. Don't let a long wait make you doubt what God has confirmed. To help keep your peace during the wait, try setting regular checkpoints, maybe every few months, to look for any progress, no matter how small, and celebrate those steps. This helps you stay grateful and focused. Remember, Abraham waited twenty-five years for his promised son, Joseph waited thirteen years for his dream to come true, and David waited over a decade to become king. Waiting doesn't cancel the promise; it shows whether you'll keep believing until it happens.

2. Keep knocking as long as you're growing through the process. If the sustained pursuit is developing your character, deepening your faith, refining your motives, strengthening your dependence on God, that's evidence that the knocking is accomplishing something even if the door hasn't opened yet. God is doing work in you that's as important as the breakthrough you're pursuing. But if the knocking is producing bitterness, cynicism, resentment toward God, spiritual death rather than

spiritual growth, something is wrong. Either your heart needs adjustment, or you're at the wrong door.

3. Keep knocking if you see any signs of progress. Elijah saw a small cloud before the heavy rain came, and that little sign showed his prayers were working. If you notice even small changes, signs that God is working or things are starting to shift, keep going. Don't overlook small beginnings or minor progress. These small steps often mean the door is starting to open.

4. Keep knocking if wise, godly people in your life support what you're doing. If mature believers who know you well encourage you to keep going and see good things happening in your life, that's a good sign. But if those who care about you are worried, or if several wise people gently suggest you might be forcing something that isn't right, listen to them. Sometimes others can see things you can't because you're too close to the situation.

Here's an example of how these principles work together. A friend of mine felt called to start a business. He prayed, got advice, and moved forward. But after two years, the business was failing. He was losing money every month, and things were getting hard at home. One night, he sat at the kitchen table, staring at bills he couldn't pay, while his spouse sat across from him in tears. He kept saying he was "standing in faith" and wouldn't give up, but the stress was overwhelming. When he reached out, we used these four principles to look at his situation. Before I continue this example, think about your own situation. Take a moment to pause and write down your answers to these four questions: Do you feel peace or anxiety? Are you growing, or is negativity taking over? Is there any sign of progress, or does the door seem closed? What do wise people in your life say? This exercise can help you put these ideas into practice and get more involved in the process. Let's get back to the example of my friend. We went through the four principles test.

Peace: He had no peace. He was constantly anxious, his marriage was strained, and he couldn't sleep. Check.

Growth: The process was producing bitterness and resentment rather than character development. He was angry at God for not blessing his effort. Check.

Signs of movement: There were no signs of improvement. Every metric was going in the wrong direction. Check.

Godly counsel: Every mature believer in his life was encouraging him to close the business before he destroyed his family financially. Check.

All four principles pointed in the same direction. He didn't need to keep knocking; he needed to accept that this door wasn't going to open and that God was leading him somewhere else. When he finally closed the business and trusted God with what came next, things changed. He found a job that fit his skills, gave his family stability, and brought peace back into their lives. The door he was knocking on wasn't God's plan for him, and staying there out of stubbornness kept him from the door God really wanted to open.

That's an example of when it's time to stop knocking. On the other hand, consider a couple who believed God for a child. They tried for five years without success. Every pregnancy test was negative, and each month brought more disappointment. Fertility treatments didn't work, and eventually, they ran out of medical options. People even started to suggest that maybe God's plan didn't include biological children for them.

But when they looked at their situation using the same four principles, they saw a different pattern. They felt deep peace about continuing to believe, even though it was discouraging. The process strengthened their marriage and faith, not weakened them. They noticed small signs that God was confirming His promise, even if nothing had happened yet. And wise believers encouraged them to keep standing in faith.

So they kept knocking. They kept trying medical options and prayed with determination. They also prepared for adoption, but still believed God for a biological child. They didn't let the long wait convince them that God had said no. After years of believing, praying, and staying ready, she became pregnant. The door opened because they were still there, knocking, when it finally did.

These two stories show the difference between persistence and stubbornness. The business owner was trying to force a door that God wasn't opening, while the couple waited at a door God was preparing to open in His timing. The four principles helped both of them see which situation they were really in. You can apply these four principles to whatever you're knocking for. Evaluate honestly. Don't make quick decisions in emotional moments, but don't ignore consistent patterns over time either. And remember, choosing to walk away from one door because God is redirecting you isn't failure. It's wisdom. It's hearing His voice and following His lead, even when it means admitting you were pursuing the wrong thing. That takes more courage than mindlessly continuing to knock at a door God has already told you to leave.

But if these four principles show you're at the right door, here's what you need to know: Don't give up. Don't let a long wait make you lose hope. Don't let other people's doubts weaken your faith. Don't let God's silence make you think He isn't listening. Keep knocking. Jesus promises in Matthew 7:8, "To the one who knocks, it will be opened." That's not a maybe, it's a guarantee. And Jesus's guarantees don't run out, no matter how long you've been waiting.

Let's talk about what knocking looks like in real life, because it's more than just prayer. Knocking means your daily choices, your focus, and your commitment to keep going until the door opens. To make this easier, try linking spiritual actions to routines you already have. For example, pray or speak declarations while you commute, or think about your spiritual goals during your morning coffee. By adding these actions to your regular activities, you make persistent knocking a natural part of your day without overloading your schedule.

1. Show up every day, no matter what. This means you're saying, "I'm here, still asking, still believing." Set aside a specific time each day for prayer. Make it a simple routine: start with a moment of silence to focus, read some scripture, then bring your request to God. Let this daily rhythm turn your set time into a spiritual practice. Being consistent builds momentum and strength.

2. Speak out about what you believe in. Keep God's promises fresh in your mind and heart. Write down specific declarations from Scripture and say them every day, even if you don't feel like it. Remember, your feelings don't change the truth; God's Word does.

3. Act as if the door is about to open. Be prepared. If you're hoping for a job, have your resume ready. If you're believing for breakthroughs in your health, make plans for recovery. Living in readiness shows your faith is real. To put this into practice, challenge yourself to take one action in the next 24 hours, like sending your resume, booking a doctor's appointment, or setting up a meeting. Taking action not only prepares you, but it can also help open doors.

4. Celebrate every small sign of progress. Even a tiny cloud can mean rain is coming. Notice and thank God for each step forward, no matter how small. These small wins are signs that the door is unlocking.

5. Don't keep backup plans. Stay focused on what you're pursuing. Having practical wisdom is good, but being divided in your focus can weaken your faith. Commit to this path and keep knocking until the door opens.

That's the power of persistent knocking. This is available to you right now, no matter what breakthrough you're seeking. But you have to take action. Show up every day. Speak words of faith. Be ready. Celebrate small wins. Don't keep backup plans. Do all of this consistently and persistently until the door opens.

Here's what Jesus promises: Not everyone who tries casually will receive. Not everyone who puts in a halfhearted effort will find. But everyone who knocks with real persistence and boldness, who refuses to give up, will see the door open. That's not just a hope, it's Jesus's guarantee. And His guarantees never fail.

So, where are you right now? Have you asked with faith and clear intention? Have you searched with effort and purpose? Have you put yourself in the right place for a breakthrough? If you've done all this and are still waiting, it's time to knock. Dig deeper than before. Want this breakthrough more than you fear looking desperate. Show up with persistence that won't accept a closed door as the final answer.

The door will open. Jesus promised it. But you need to be there, still knocking, when it does. You have to keep believing. Often, the difference between those who receive breakthroughs and those who don't is simply this: who's still knocking when the door finally opens.

Your breakthrough is waiting on the other side of that door. Everything you've prayed for, worked toward, and believed God promised is right there. But you have to knock, not just gently or casually, but with desperate, persistent, bold knocking that says, "I'm not leaving until this opens."

So start knocking, and don't stop. Not when you're tired, not when others say it's not working, not when the door seems locked. Keep knocking. Jesus's promise is about to come true in your life. The door is about to open. When it does, and you step into your breakthrough, you'll see that every knock was worth it.

Keep knocking until the door opens.

Now let's find out what's on the other side of that door and how to handle your breakthrough when it comes. But before moving on, take a moment to think: What door will you knock on today? Choosing and committing to your next step will help you keep moving forward and get ready for what's ahead.

Chapter Seven

THE SOUND OF FOOTSTEPS

Recognizing When Breakthrough is Imminent

Seven times. Elijah sent his servant to look toward the sea seven times. The drought had lasted three and a half years. Rain hadn't fallen in all that time because Elijah had prophesied it wouldn't, and now he was praying for it to return. He climbed to the top of Mount Carmel, bowed down to the ground, put his face between his knees, and prayed. Then he told his servant, "Go up now, look toward the sea."

The servant went, looked, and came back. "There is nothing," he reported.

"Go again," Elijah said. He sent his servant seven times. Six times, the servant returned with the same report: nothing. No clouds, no sign of rain, just clear skies that seemed to contradict Elijah's prayers. Each time, it looked like the prayer wasn't working and that Elijah should give up.

On the seventh time, something changed. The servant returned with a new report: "There is a cloud as small as a man's hand rising from the sea." It was just a tiny cloud, nothing impressive, and most people would have ignored it. But Elijah heard something others missed. He recognized the promise of abundant rain in what seemed like almost nothing.

Elijah told his servant, "Go up, say to Ahab, 'Prepare your chariot and go down, lest the rain stop you.'" Soon, the sky filled with clouds and wind, and heavy rain fell. The tiny cloud became a downpour. What began as something small turned into undeniable breakthroughs. The key is that Elijah recognized breakthroughs when they were still small. He sensed the rain before it started and knew the door was about to open before anyone else noticed.

This chapter is about learning to recognize when breakthroughs are close, even if they haven't fully appeared yet. It's about understanding what the small signs look like in your life so you don't overlook them. Sometimes, people give up just before their breakthrough because they don't see the signs that it's near.

After knocking for so long, they became exhausted. The door still seemed closed, and everything suggested it would never open. They decided their efforts were pointless and that God wouldn't answer, so they gave up. Later, the breakthrough they wanted finally came, but they weren't there to receive it because they had already walked away.

That won't be your story. By the end of this chapter, you'll know what signs to look for. You'll recognize the small beginnings of breakthroughs and have the wisdom to hold on, even when it hasn't fully arrived yet, so you don't give up too soon.

Before we look at these signs, it's important to remember that recognizing breakthroughs is near doesn't mean you know exactly when it will happen. Elijah saw the small cloud but didn't know if rain would come in an hour or a day. He just knew it was coming, and that gave him the confidence to act. In the same way, knowing breakthroughs are close gives you the confidence to keep going, even if you don't know the exact timing.

Let's talk about what breakthroughs look like as we approach it. What are the signs that show the door is about to open, even if it still looks closed? I'll share several markers to watch for, so you'll know when what you've been seeking is getting closer.

The first sign that breakthroughs are close is often increased resistance. This might seem strange, since we usually expect things to get easier as we near a breakthrough. We picture obstacles fading as the door starts to open. But both the Bible and real life show the opposite. Resistance often gets stronger right before a breakthrough, because the enemy senses his time is running out. He sees what you can't yet; that your persistence is about to be rewarded, and he tries one last time to make you give up before you receive what God has for you.

Remember what happened to the Israelites after God promised to free them from Egypt. The Pharaoh made their work even harder by taking away the straw they needed for bricks while still demanding the same amount. Things got worse after the promise, not better. The people complained to Moses, saying, "We were better off before you showed up claiming God was going to deliver us." They thought the extra resistance meant deliverance wasn't coming, but really, it was a sign that deliverance was so close that Pharaoh was desperate.

Think about what happened just before Jesus was born. Herod ordered all boys under two in Bethlehem to be killed. That terrible act happened because the promised King was about to arrive, and the enemy was trying hard to stop what he couldn't prevent. The resistance showed how close the breakthrough was, not how far away it was.

This same pattern happens when you're seeking a breakthrough. If you've been praying, seeking, and doing your best, and suddenly things get harder, it's usually not a sign to quit. It often means you're getting close. The enemy doesn't waste effort on people who aren't a threat or who have already given up. But when he sees someone about to step into something important, he does everything he can to make them give up right before it happens.

So if you notice more resistance in your life, or if new problems show up out of nowhere, don't assume you're on the wrong path. It could mean you're getting close, and the enemy is making a final effort to stop you. Not every obstacle means breakthroughs are near. Sometimes it means you need to change direction. But if you're sure you're following God's call, you still have peace, and the signs we talked about earlier are there, then increased resistance might be a sign that breakthroughs are just around the corner.

I saw this happen in my own life before God started our ministry. The last few months of that long, difficult season were the hardest; not because I was losing faith, but because everything seemed to fall apart at once. It was especially tough since this was during the height of the COVID-19 pandemic, when the whole world was shutting down.

I had traveled to Trinidad for a conference, and while I was there, everything changed overnight. Countries closed their borders, airports shut down, and the world went into lockdown. I was one of the few who made it back to Sint Maarten after the airport closed, but I had to go into quarantine. Alone and isolated, I watched the news as death tolls and economic troubles grew, and I wondered why God allowed me to be caught in this crisis just as I was about to start ministry.

Churches everywhere were closing. The few preaching opportunities I had, which helped support our family, disappeared overnight. I couldn't travel or minister in person. The financial support we depended on while moving into full-time ministry was suddenly gone. We had to use our savings, watching them shrink each week with no sign that things would get better soon. Every forecast and news report said the pandemic would last a long time, and the ministry would never be the same.

My wife and I would sit together, staring at our shrinking bank account as the pressure built. We had followed what we believed God wanted us to do and taken steps of faith to prepare for ministry. But just as we were about to start, the world stopped. The enemy's doubts were constant: "You heard wrong. There's no calling on your life. This pandemic is God's way of telling you to quit and get a real job. Look around; churches are closing, ministries are failing. And you thought this was the right time to start something new?"

To make things harder, some of the relationships we depended on became strained. We thought certain respected leaders would support us as we started the ministry. We expected guidance, open doors, and help during the tough beginning. But when the pandemic hit, everyone was focused on their own struggles, and the help we hoped for didn't come. It wasn't because people were uncaring; they were just overwhelmed. Still, it felt like we were alone, stepping out on a limb with no one to help.

Looking back, I see that the harder things got, the closer I was to breakthroughs. The enemy saw what I couldn't; that God was about to do something big through us, and tried to make me quit before it happened. The pandemic wasn't God's judgment or a sign to stop. It was the final test, the crisis that would either break me or prepare me for what God had planned. At the time, I couldn't see the breakthrough coming. All I saw was a world falling apart and my dreams with it, and I almost gave up. If I had let the pandemic convince me that God's timing was wrong or His calling was a mistake, I would have missed everything He was preparing. But just months after that darkest season, doors opened in ways I never expected. The ministry started, not just in spite of the pandemic, but partly because of it. The shutdown led to new ideas, the isolation made people hungry for real connection, and the crisis showed who was truly seeking God. We were ready to meet needs that no one saw coming until the world stopped and people had to rethink everything.

The second sign that breakthroughs are near is finding unexpected peace in the middle of chaos. This sign is subtle because your situation might not change at all. Everything may still look impossible, and the door may still seem closed. But inside, you feel different. You find yourself calm when you should be anxious, and you have a peace that doesn't make sense given what you're facing, even when others are worried about your situation.

This kind of peace is often God's way of getting you ready for breakthroughs before you see them. He calms your spirit so that when the breakthrough comes, you can handle it with confidence instead of desperation. Think about Jesus sleeping in the boat during the storm. The disciples were terrified, but Jesus was calm because He knew the storm wasn't the end. He knew breakthroughs were just a word away. His peace showed His confidence in the outcome, not a lack of concern for the danger.

If you've been seeking breakthroughs for a long time, doing everything you can and still waiting, and then you suddenly feel at peace, that's important. It's not the peace of giving up or not caring, but a deep, steady confidence that says, "God has this, and I can rest while I keep going." This kind of peace often comes before you see breakthroughs, indicating that something has changed spiritually, even if nothing has changed on the outside yet.

The third sign that breakthroughs are near is getting prophetic confirmation from unexpected places. When breakthroughs are coming, God often uses people who have no way of knowing your situation to confirm it. Someone might say something that speaks directly to what you've been praying about. A stranger's comment, a sermon, or something you read might feel like it was meant just for you, even though the person had no idea about your circumstances.

These confirmations help in several ways. They boost your faith when you feel like giving up, reassure you that you're on the right path, and show that God is working behind the scenes. When you start hearing the same message from different places, it's often a sign that breakthroughs are close.

Joseph went through this before his breakthrough. He spent years in prison after being wrongly accused, and things looked hopeless. Then Pharaoh had dreams that needed interpreting, and the butler suddenly remembered Joseph. That memory was a sign that Joseph's waiting was almost over. The butler couldn't have known how important that moment was, but God arranged it because Joseph's breakthrough had come.

Look for these kinds of confirmations in your own life. Pay attention when people say things that are too specific to be a coincidence, or when different sources mention the same thing about your situation. Don't brush these off as random. They're often God's way of helping you recognize breakthrough and encouraging you to keep going.

The fourth sign that breakthroughs are near is having divine appointments that seem unimportant at first. Breakthrough often comes through connections that look random but are actually planned by God. You might meet someone who knows someone with the resources you need, or be in the right place at the right time to hear about an opportunity. Even a casual conversation can end up being the key to the door you've been knocking on.

Ruth experienced a divine appointment when she ended up working in Boaz's field. The Bible says she just happened to be there, but with God, nothing is by accident. That meeting led to a conversation, then to favor, protection, redemption, marriage, and eventually to her being part of Jesus's family line. If you had asked Ruth that day, she probably wouldn't have thought anything special was happening. It just seemed like another day of survival, and the importance only became clear later.

Don't ignore connections that seem random. If you've been faithfully seeking breakthroughs and suddenly meet someone who can help, or find yourself in conversations that open new doors, pay attention. These could be divine appointments showing that breakthroughs are coming. God may be connecting you with people and situations that will help provide what you've been seeking.

The fifth sign that breakthroughs are near is that your faith grows stronger even though nothing has changed yet. This might seem odd, since you'd expect faith to get weaker the longer you wait. But when breakthroughs are close, something shifts. Your faith doesn't just last; it actually grows. You become more certain that what you're believing for will happen, and more determined to keep waiting at the door until it opens. This stronger faith is often a sign that God is working behind the scenes.

This is different from the excitement you feel when you first start asking for something. That's faith based on hope and possibility. But this is mature faith, built through long pursuit and deep conviction. You've faced hard times and kept going. Instead of getting tired and giving up, you're even more sure that breakthroughs are coming. That's not just natural; it's supernatural, and it often means your breakthrough is close.

Abraham went through this also. As he got older and the promise of a son seemed less likely, his faith didn't weaken. Romans 4 says he didn't lose faith when he thought about his own body or Sarah's. Instead, he grew stronger, trusting that God could do what He promised. That growing faith, even when things looked impossible, was a sign that breakthroughs were near; even though it took twenty-five years for the promise to be fulfilled.

So if you've been seeking breakthroughs for a long time and notice your faith is stronger now than when you started, that matters. It's a sign that something is changing behind the scenes and that breakthroughs are getting closer.

The sixth sign that breakthroughs are near is seeing small steps in the direction you've been praying for. These aren't the full breakthrough yet, but they show things are starting to change. Maybe a door opens a little, or you get a partial answer to your prayers. Circumstances might improve a bit, even if they're not where you want them yet.

These small changes are like Elijah's cloud; easy to overlook because they don't seem big enough. They might not solve everything, but they show that God is working and that your efforts are making a difference. If you ignore these small signs as "not enough," you might miss the start of the breakthrough you've been praying for.

Think about when Jesus fed the five thousand. The disciples brought Him five loaves and two fish; not nearly enough for the crowd. But it was a step in the right direction. Jesus took that small offering and made it more than enough. If the disciples had ignored the boy's lunch because it seemed too small, they would have missed out on the miracle.

When you notice small steps toward your breakthrough, celebrate them and thank God. Let these moments encourage you to keep going. These small changes are often the start of something much bigger. They show that God is working and that your efforts are making a difference, even if you're only seeing the beginning right now.

The seventh sign that breakthroughs are close is gaining clarity about your next steps. When breakthroughs are near, God often gives you clear, specific instructions; not just general ideas, but real action steps that help you get ready for what's coming. This clarity shows that God is preparing to move and wants you to be ready.

Noah got clear instructions to build the ark before the flood. Abraham was told to leave Ur before God revealed the promised land to him. Moses was given specific directions to confront Pharaoh before the plagues started. In each case, clarity about what to do came before the breakthrough, and following those instructions helped bring it about.

If you've been waiting and feeling unsure about what to do, and then suddenly you get clear direction about your next steps, that's often a sign that breakthroughs are coming. God gives you instructions because He's about to act and wants you ready to receive and handle what He's providing.

I went through this before our ministry began. For a while, all I could do was pray, serve where I could, and work on my gifts. Then, over a few months, God gave me clear instructions: connect with certain people, start new projects, prepare specific content, and move in a new direction. The clarity was almost overwhelming after so much uncertainty, but it was God's way of preparing me. Within two months, doors that had been closed for over a year started to open, and the breakthrough I'd been waiting for finally came because I was ready to receive it.

So if you start getting clear direction after a long wait, don't ignore it or think it's just random. Pay attention, write it down, and start taking the steps God shows you. That clarity is often a sign that God is about to do something important and wants you to be part of it.

It's important to remember that these signs aren't formulas; they're just indicators. You might see all seven, or only a few, and they might not come in the same order. There could also be other signs unique to your situation. The goal isn't to use these as a checklist to predict when breakthroughs will happen, but to help you notice when it's getting close so you don't give up too soon.

I've seen this happen many times: believers work hard for breakthroughs, pray, seek, and keep their faith through tough times. But just when breakthroughs are closest, they misread the signs and give up. They see more resistance and think they're off track, when it actually means they're close. They feel unexpected peace and think it means they're quitting, when it's really God preparing them. They see small changes and dismiss them, not realizing they're seeing the start of answered prayer.

Don't make that mistake. Learn to see these signs for what they are. Breakthrough often looks like nothing just before it becomes everything. Train yourself to notice the signs, even when you can't yet see the full picture. Often, the difference between those who receive breakthroughs and those who miss it is simply recognizing how close they were, even when it didn't look that way.

Here's another biblical example that brings all these points together. In 2 Kings 7, Samaria was under siege and facing a terrible famine. People were paying huge amounts for things that weren't even real food. It was a desperate time with no solution in sight. In the middle of this, the prophet Elisha boldly declared that by the next day, flour and barley would be sold at normal prices at the city gate. Breakthroughs were coming within twenty-four hours.

One of the king's officers doubted Elisha's words, saying that even if God opened the heavens, it couldn't happen. Elisha replied that the officer would see it but not eat any of it. That officer stands for people who walk away from breakthrough just before it happens because they can't imagine how God could make it work.

But here's what really happened. That night, God made the enemy army hear the sound of chariots and horses, like a huge army was coming. They panicked, thought they were under attack, and ran away, leaving all their supplies. Four lepers at the city gate, with nothing to lose, decided to go to the enemy camp. When they arrived, they found it empty. They ate, took supplies, and then realized they needed to tell the city that help had come.

By morning, the people of Samaria rushed to the empty camp to get food and supplies. Prices dropped just as Elisha had said. Breakthroughs came within a day of the worst moment. But the skeptical officer, who didn't believe it was possible, was trampled in the crowd and didn't get to enjoy the breakthrough. He saw it happen, but his unbelief kept him from taking part.

This story sums up everything we've discussed. Breakthroughs came when things seemed hopeless, in a way no one expected, and right after a long period of suffering. It happened just as God promised, but only those who believed they were close were ready to receive it. The skeptical officer missed out because he couldn't recognize the signs, even when he was told breakthroughs were near.

Don't be like that officer. Don't let doubt keep you from breakthroughs when it's closer than you realize. Don't ignore the signs just because they don't seem dramatic. Don't give up right before the door opens because you can't see how God will do it. Instead, learn to notice the signs, listen for the footsteps, watch for the small cloud, and get ready to receive when breakthroughs come.

As we finish this chapter, here's something to do: Take some time this week to see if any of these signs are showing up in your life. Review the seven indicators and honestly ask yourself if you're experiencing any of them. Are you facing more resistance, which could mean you're close? Do you feel unexpected peace? Are you getting confirmation from unexpected places? Have you had divine appointments that seemed random? Is your faith getting stronger, even after a long wait? Are you seeing small steps toward your breakthrough? Have you received clear direction after a time of uncertainty?

Write down what you notice. Keep track of the signs so you can see how God is working, even if it's subtle. Most importantly, let these signs encourage you to keep going. If you see any sign that breakthroughs are coming, that's God's way of telling you to hold on. The door is about to open, and what seems small now is about to become something much bigger.

But here's something important: just because breakthroughs are near doesn't mean you stop trying. It's not the time to relax. When you see these signs, keep pushing, be more intentional, and get ready. Breakthrough usually comes to those who stay active, not those who wait passively. One practical way to stay engaged is to set aside five minutes each day for a 'knock again' prayer. This daily habit can turn your excitement into steady discipline and keep you ready for the breakthrough you're seeking.

Think about the lepers in 2 Kings 7. They could have just sat at the gate talking about what God might do, but instead, they got up and went to where help might be found. Because they took action, they were the first to find the empty camp full of food and supplies. Their willingness to move made them part of the story of deliverance.

Do the same in your own life. When you sense breakthroughs are coming, take more action, not less. Keep knocking, keep seeking, and get ready for what's ahead. Passive waiting doesn't bring breakthroughs as well as active pursuit does, even when you know it's close.

As we wrap up, here's a word of caution: don't make up signs that aren't really there. Don't convince yourself you're seeing breakthroughs just because you want the wait to end. Be honest with yourself. Sometimes you're still in the middle of the struggle with no sign of breakthroughs yet, and that's okay. It doesn't mean breakthroughs won't come; it just means it's not time yet. Pretending otherwise can lead to disappointment.

The signs we've talked about are real and show up when breakthroughs are truly near. But you can't force them; they come in God's timing. Watch for them honestly, but don't feel pressured to see them if they're not there. It's better to be honest about where you are than to be misled by false hope.

But if you really are seeing these signs, if several are showing up in your life and you sense God is moving even though nothing has changed yet, stand firm. Keep knocking and don't give up. What you've been working toward is closer than ever, and quitting now would be the biggest loss after all you've put in.

The door is about to open. The small cloud is on your horizon. The footsteps are getting closer. You've prayed, sought, and prepared yourself. You've made it through hard times without losing faith. You've kept knocking, even when it was tough. Now, breakthroughs are building in ways you might not see yet, but you will soon.

So don't stop. Don't quit. Don't walk away. The officer in 2 Kings 7 saw the breakthrough but missed out because he wasn't ready when it came. You won't make that mistake. You'll notice the signs, hear the footsteps, and be ready to knock again when the door opens. When you step into what you've been working for, you'll see that every effort, every tear, and every moment of waiting was preparing you for this breakthrough.

You can hear the sound of footsteps on the other side of your door right now. They're getting closer. Listen closely, watch carefully, and get ready. Breakthrough isn't just a distant hope; it's near for many of you. The door is about to open. The real question is, will you still be there when it does?

So stand firm. Keep knocking. Watch for the signs and get ready. Everything you've been praying for and working toward is about to happen. The waiting is nearly over, and the door is about to open. As you reach this point, ask yourself, 'What will I do when the door opens?' Think about how you'll sustain this breakthrough and ensure it continues to grow. Be as ready to handle the responsibility as you are to celebrate the answer.

Now let's talk about what comes next. Breakthroughs are coming, and you need to know how to handle them when they arrive. The next chapter will cover how to step through the open door and live in the reality of answered prayer. It's about keeping what you've worked for, growing it, and using it to fulfill everything God planned for you.

Turn the page. The door is opening, and what's waiting for you will change your life forever.

Chapter Eight

WHEN THE DOOR OPENS

Stewarding the Blessing You Fought For

T**HE BREAKTHROUGH FINALLY CAME.** The Israelites stepped onto the banks of the Jordan River, feeling the wind and the hope of something new. After forty years in the wilderness, after a whole generation passed away waiting, and after Moses was buried, they finally reached the Jordan. The Promised Land was right in front of them. Everything they had hoped for, and everything God had promised, was now close. But there was still tension. The land was promised, but taking it would take more effort. They had to enter, fight for it, settle, and protect it. This was not just the end of a long journey, but the beginning of a new responsibility to care for this blessing with dedication and wisdom, knowing their purpose depended on keeping this promise alive.

Many people miss something important about that moment. Getting to the Promised Land was only part of the challenge. Actually taking hold of it was a different test. God told Joshua, "Every place that the sole of your foot will tread upon I have given you." There is a tension in that promise. God had already given them the land, but they still had to enter, fight for it, settle, and protect it. The blessing was promised, but caring for it took effort that wandering in the wilderness never required.

This is where many believers struggle. They put all their energy into seeking breakthroughs and often feel worn out. They keep asking, seeking, and knocking until the door finally opens. It's normal to feel tired after such a journey, and it's easy to think the hard part is over once the blessing comes. Some think they can relax and let things run their own course. But I encourage you to be kind to yourself and keep going. Keeping the breakthrough you worked for takes just as much focus, if not more, than getting it. If you approach this with care and understanding, it can feel supportive instead of heavy.

I've seen this pattern happen many times, and it's always hard to watch. Someone prays for a job for months, finally gets hired, but within a year, they lose it because they didn't keep up the same effort they used to get it. Someone believes God for healing, receives it, but then returns to the habits that caused their sickness. Someone stands in faith for a restored marriage, sees progress, but then stops doing the work that made things better, and the relationship falls apart again. Someone finally starts the business or ministry they dreamed of, sees early success, but then lets go of the habits that made it work.

This chapter is here to help you avoid that trap. When the door opens, and you step into your breakthrough, it's not the end; it's the beginning. The blessing you just received marks the start of a new season that requires wisdom, good management, and sometimes new skills. Ask yourself, 'Where am I tempted to take it easy right now?' Taking a moment to reflect can turn this reading into a personal coaching session and help you approach the new season with purpose.

Think about any big life change. Getting into college is hard. Staying in college and graduating is even harder. Getting married is hard. Building a strong marriage that lasts is harder. Starting a business is hard. Growing and keeping that business going is harder. In every case, getting something and taking care of it are two different challenges that need different skills. If you don't see that difference, you might lose what you worked so hard to get.

Let's look at what happens after the door opens. Celebration matters, and we'll talk about that. It's normal to feel relief after working hard. But what matters most is the responsibility that comes with it. How you handle your breakthrough each day will decide if it becomes the start of all God has planned or just a short-lived answer to prayer that fades away.

The first thing you need to understand about stewarding breakthroughs is that you can't maintain it with less than what it took to obtain it. This seems obvious, but it's violated constantly. People often bring great determination and focus to their pursuit of breakthroughs. They pray with fervor, seek diligently, and make sacrifices. They prioritize the pursuit above other things. Yet when the door opens, and they receive what they asked for, they sometimes fall into the trap of thinking they can maintain it without making the same efforts.

Blessings can slip away. Breakthroughs can fade. If you don't actively take care of what God gave you, you'll slowly lose it. There's no standing still. You're either building on your breakthrough, protecting it, or growing it. How you handle it will decide if it becomes a foundation for more or just a memory of something you once had.

Joseph understood this principle profoundly. God gave him dreams about leadership and authority when he was seventeen. But the fulfillment of those dreams came through thirteen years of slavery, false accusation, and imprisonment. Thirteen years of preparation for a moment when Pharaoh would have dreams that needed interpretation. And when that moment came, when the door finally opened, and Joseph was brought before Pharaoh, he didn't waste it. He interpreted the dreams with wisdom. He proposed a strategic plan for handling the coming famine. He demonstrated that he had used his years of waiting to develop the very skills he would need when opportunity arrived.

And then, when Pharaoh elevated him to second in command over all Egypt, Joseph didn't rest on that accomplishment. He immediately implemented the plan he had proposed. He spent seven years of abundance preparing for seven years of famine. He stewarded the breakthrough with the same diligence that had sustained him through the waiting. And because he did, he didn't just save Egypt. He saved his own family, fulfilled the very dreams God had given him decades earlier, and became part of God's redemptive plan for an entire nation.

Notice something important about Joseph's story. The skills and character he developed during his years in slavery and prison were exactly what he needed for his new role. Waiting wasn't wasted; it was training. God was preparing Joseph for what was coming. As you read, think about your own journey and any tough seasons you've faced. What skills are you building during this time? Comparing your timeline to Joseph's 13-year journey might help you find ways to get ready for your own breakthrough. When Joseph's door opened, he was prepared not just to enter, but to build on what was ahead.

The same principle applies to whatever breakthrough you're receiving or about to receive. The asking, seeking, and knocking haven't just been about getting you to the door. They've been about forming in you what you'll need to steward what's on the other side of the door. The faith you developed through persistent asking, the diligence you built through active seeking, the endurance you forged through relentless knocking, these aren't qualities you can abandon once breakthrough comes. These are the very qualities that will allow you to keep, grow, and multiply what you just received.

So when the door opens, when you step through into answered prayer, don't make the mistake of thinking you can now relax the disciplines that got you here. If prayer brought breakthroughs, keep praying with the same intensity. If strategic action positioned you for opportunity, keep taking strategic action. If faithful stewardship in small things led to being trusted with bigger things, keep being faithful even as the scale changes. The tools that unlocked the door are the same tools that will allow you to flourish on the other side of it.

The second thing you need to understand about stewarding breakthroughs is that increase comes with increased responsibility. This is where many believers get surprised and overwhelmed: they wanted the blessing but didn't consider what it would require of them. They prayed for a better job but didn't consider the longer hours or higher expectations that come with greater responsibility. For example, a promotion increases your work hours from 40 to 55 per week. Maybe you believed God for a spouse but didn't prepare for the daily work of building a healthy marriage. Or maybe someone stood in faith for ministry opportunities but wasn't ready for the spiritual warfare and leadership challenges that come with influence. They all got what they asked for, only to feel crushed by the weight of what it required.

Jesus addressed this directly when He taught about counting the cost. He talked about someone wanting to build a tower, but not sitting down first to calculate whether they have enough to complete it. He talked about a king going to war without first considering whether his army was sufficient to win. The point wasn't to discourage pursuit. The point was to help people understand that obtaining something is only the beginning. Stewarding what you obtain is where the real work begins.

This is why the wilderness seasons we discussed in Chapter Five are so important. They're not just about testing whether you really want what you're asking for. They're about developing the capacity to handle it when you get it. God uses the waiting to prepare you for the weight of the blessing. He uses the process of pursuit to build the strength you'll need to carry what He's about to give you. And if you make it through the wilderness, if you endure the testing and arrive at the opened door, you're not the same person who started asking. You're someone who has been shaped by the journey into someone capable of stewarding the destination.

But even with that preparation, even with character formed through the wilderness, you still need to recognize that breakthrough comes with requirements. The better job requires you to deliver at a higher level. The healed body requires you to maintain healthy habits. The restored relationship requires ongoing investment and communication. The launched ministry requires leadership, administration, and sustained vision. Whatever breakthrough you receive, it will demand something from you. And if you're not willing to meet those demands, you'll lose what you fought to obtain.

Let me share how this played out in my own life when God finally brought our ministry to life. I had prayed for years, gone through an eighteen-month wilderness, and kept knocking during the pandemic when things seemed impossible. Then, the door opened. Opportunities appeared, people responded to our message, and the ministry started to grow. It was everything I had hoped and prayed for, and I was excited. But in those early months, I didn't realize how much time administration would take, which led to some disorganization. This mistake taught me the importance of balancing my excitement with good management. I remember missing an important deadline because I took on too much. It disrupted our project and left my team scrambling, which was embarrassing and eye-opening. It showed me I needed to manage my time better and delegate tasks. Even with these challenges, I learned how to handle growth while staying true to my vision.

What saved me was recognizing early that I couldn't maintain the ministry at a lower intensity than it took to birth it. I had prayed fervently during the wilderness. So I must keep praying fervently after breakthroughs come. I had been diligent in preparing myself during the waiting. So, I need to stay diligent in developing my skills after the door opened. I had knocked persistently for the opportunity and must continue to work persistently once I have it in my hands. The disciplines that brought breakthroughs must be e the disciplines that sustain breakthroughs. And because I didn't abandon them once the door opened, the ministry didn't collapse under the weight of its own early success. Remember this: 'Sustain with the same fire that sparked.'

Gratitude is not optional; it's essential. When you've knocked until your knuckles hurt and finally the door opens, gratitude should be your first response. Not relief, not excitement, but gratitude. Picture open hands ready to receive. Deep, genuine gratitude recognizes what you just received as a gift from God.

This matters more than you might think because gratitude does something spiritually that nothing else does. It positions you as a receiver rather than an achiever. It keeps your heart soft toward God instead of hardening with pride. It reminds you that everything you have is grace, even the breakthrough you pursued with everything in you. And it creates a foundation for continued blessing because God gives grace to the humble but opposes the proud.

I've watched believers lose breakthroughs quickly because they failed to cultivate gratitude. They fought for something, received it, and then acted as though they earned it. They took credit for what God provided. They became entitled, assuming that because God gave them one breakthrough, He owed them continued favor without continued faithfulness. And that pride positioned them to lose what they had just gained because pride creates distance from God, and distance from God means distance from the source of all blessing.

Scripture is full of examples of this pattern. The Israelites experienced miraculous deliverance from Egypt, yet instead of cultivating gratitude, they constantly complained. They forgot what God had done and focused on what they didn't have. And that ingratitude kept an entire generation from entering the Promised Land. They had breakthroughs in their hands and lost them because they failed to recognize and appreciate the gift they'd been given.

Or think about the ten lepers Jesus healed in Luke 17. All ten were cleansed. All ten received the breakthrough they desperately needed. But only one came back to thank Jesus. Only one recognized that what he received was a gift that demanded gratitude. And Jesus noticed. He asked, "Were not ten cleansed? Where are the nine?" That question should haunt us because it suggests that most people who receive breakthroughs from God never cultivate the gratitude that sustains a connection with the source of breakthroughs.

Don't be one of the nine. When the door opens, when breakthrough manifests, when you step through into answered prayer, make gratitude your first and most frequent response. Thank God verbally every single day for what He's given you. Write down what you're grateful for so you don't forget when time passes, and the newness wears off. Tell others what God has done so your testimony reinforces your own memory of His faithfulness. Create rhythms of thanksgiving that keep your heart in a posture of grateful receiving rather than an entitled demander.

Gratitude matters because it opens you up to receive more, while entitlement makes you hold on tightly out of fear. Gratitude keeps you connected to God as your source, but entitlement makes you think you're the source. Gratitude sets you up for more blessings, while entitlement can cause you to lose what you have. Often, the difference between keeping a breakthrough and losing it is whether you choose gratitude or let entitlement grow.

The fourth thing you need to understand about stewarding breakthrough is that celebration matters, but it must be followed by consolidation. When the door finally opens after a long pursuit, you should celebrate. Throw a party. Tell your story. Let joy overflow. Breakthrough deserves to be marked and cherished. God gave you something worth having. That's worth celebrating.

But celebration alone doesn't sustain breakthroughs. After the party, after the testimony, after the initial excitement fades, you need to consolidate what you've gained. You need to take stock of what you now have, understand what it takes to maintain it, identify what needs to be protected, and create systems, habits, or disciplines that will allow you to build on this foundation rather than just enjoy it temporarily.

Think about what Joshua did after the Israelites crossed the Jordan River into the Promised Land. They had a moment of celebration. They set up memorial stones to remember the miracle. But then Joshua immediately moved into consolidation mode. He circumcised all the men who had been born in the wilderness. He celebrated Passover to reconnect them with their covenant identity. And then he began the strategic campaign to actually possess the land God had given them. The celebration was appropriate, but brief, because Joshua understood that possessing the land required more than just entering it.

The same principle applies to whatever breakthrough you receive. Celebrate it genuinely and joyfully, but don't let celebration become your permanent state.

After you mark the moment, thank God and share your testimony, then shift into consolidation mode. Ask yourself practical questions. What systems do I need to put in place to maintain this blessing? What habits do I need to develop? What threats do I need to guard against? What relationships do I need to nurture? What disciplines do I need to establish? What knowledge do I need to acquire? What character do I need to continue developing?

To help you internalize these consolidation steps, consider using a simple checklist as a self-audit:

Keep: Identify the practices, relationships, and disciplines that are critical to your current success.
Begin: Determine new systems or habits that will enhance and sustain your breakthrough.
Eliminate: Recognize any actions or behaviors that could undermine the blessing you have received.

Incorporating these micro-exercises can move you from inspiration to implementation, ensuring your breakthrough becomes a lasting foundation for future growth.

These questions help you shift from the excitement of breakthroughs to the wisdom of caring for them. Celebrating is great, but building a life after the breakthrough takes real effort. Think of a breakthrough like a charged battery; if you don't take care of it, the energy will slowly run out. Taking steps to consolidate your gains turns a single moment into a lasting season of blessing. Without this, you might end up celebrating the same breakthrough over and over because you keep losing it and have to fight for it again.

The fifth thing you need to understand about stewarding breakthroughs is that you'll need to defend what you fought to obtain. The enemy doesn't stop attacking just because you received breakthroughs. In fact, his attacks often intensify after the door opens because now he's not trying to keep you from obtaining something; he's trying to steal what you've already received. Jesus said, "The thief comes to steal, kill, and destroy." Stealing is his primary tactic, and what he wants most is the breakthrough you worked so hard to receive. Picture sudden financial temptation that could derail your new career progress, or unexpected distractions that pull you away from the disciplined habits that secured your breakthrough. Specific threats like these illustrate how vigilant you must be to safeguard your accomplishments.

This is why so many believers experience breakthroughs and then lose them within a short time. They fought to obtain it, but didn't fight to keep it. They were vigilant during the pursuit but became complacent after the door opened. They recognized spiritual warfare when they were knocking, but didn't recognize that warfare continues on the other side of the opened door. And that failure to defend allowed the enemy to take back what God had given.

The Israelites went through this many times after entering the Promised Land. They would take over a city and settle there, but often didn't remove all the people as God told them to. Those who remained became problems, leading the Israelites into trouble and even threatening their hold on the land. What they didn't defend, they eventually lost or suffered for. In our lives today, if we don't address issues like endless scrolling, procrastination, or harmful relationships, they can slowly erode our breakthroughs. Like the Israelites, we need to stay alert and deal with these issues before they undo what we've worked for.

Defending breakthroughs looks different depending on what you received, but some principles apply universally. First, you defend breakthroughs by maintaining the spiritual disciplines that brought them about. Keep praying. Keep seeking God. Keep staying in Scripture. Keep surrounding yourself with a faith-filled community. The moment you abandon these disciplines is the moment you become vulnerable to losing what you gained.

Second, you defend breakthroughs by setting boundaries. Whatever your breakthrough is, there are things that threaten it. Relationships that would pull you back into old patterns. Habits that would undermine the new season. Distractions that would steal your focus. Entertainment or media consumption that would shape your thinking away from the truth. You need to identify these threats and establish clear boundaries that protect what God gave you. Not out of legalism, but out of wisdom that recognizes some things aren't compatible with sustained blessing.

Third, you defend breakthroughs by remaining accountable. Pride makes us think we can handle everything on our own once we have breakthroughs. But isolation is dangerous because it removes the checks and balances that keep us grounded. You need people in your life who have permission to ask hard questions, who will tell you the truth when you're drifting, who will help you recognize threats you might not see on your own. That accountability is part of how you defend what you've received.

When our ministry finally launched, one of the smartest things we did early on was establish accountability structures. We brought people into leadership who had permission to respectfully challenge us, to question decisions, to point out blind spots. It was uncomfortable sometimes because I wanted to just run with breakthroughs without anyone questioning my direction. But that accountability has protected the ministry from mistakes I would have made in the enthusiasm of new success. It's defended what God gave us by providing wisdom and perspective I couldn't maintain on my own.

The sixth thing you need to understand about stewarding breakthroughs is that it is not an endpoint but a launching pad. What you do with it determines what comes next. Breakthrough positions you for greater impact, deeper purpose, and expanded influence. What God gives you isn't just for your benefit but meant to empower you for more. How you steward this breakthrough will determine whether God can trust you with what He wants to give you next.

Jesus taught this through the parable of the talents in Matthew 25. A master gave three servants different amounts of money according to their abilities. Two of them invested what they received and doubled it. One buried his out of fear and returned only what he was given. The master praised the two who multiplied their resources and gave them more. But the one who only preserved what he had without growing it lost even that. The principle is clear: faithful stewardship of what you have positions you to receive more. Unfaithful stewardship leads to losing even what you thought you had secured.

This means you can't just sit on breakthroughs and enjoy them passively. You need to ask yourself constantly: How is God calling me to use this blessing? What is He asking me to build with it? Who is He calling me to serve through it? What next level is He preparing me for? How can I multiply this for His kingdom rather than just consume it for my comfort?

The seventh key to stewarding breakthroughs is to help others receive what you worked for. This may be the most important point, because if your breakthrough doesn't help others, it hasn't reached its full purpose. God didn't give you victory just for yourself, but so you could guide others to their own breakthroughs. Ask yourself, 'Who in my life could benefit from my story?' Think of someone who needs to hear about your journey and faith. Reach out to them and let your breakthrough inspire theirs.

Think about what Jesus did throughout His earthly ministry. He could have kept the power to heal, deliver, and transform for Himself. But instead, He trained disciples. He sent out the twelve, then the seventy-two, giving them authority to do what they had seen Him do. He didn't just demonstrate breakthroughs. He multiplied it by empowering others to experience and facilitate the same things. And before He ascended, He commissioned all believers to continue the work He started. His breakthrough paved the way for everyone else's.

That's your calling, too. Whatever door opened for you, whatever breakthrough you received, whatever freedom you now walk in, there are others behind you still knocking at the same door. They need to hear your story. They need to learn from your journey. They need to see that breakthroughs are possible because you're living proof of it. And when you turn around and help them, when you invest in their pursuit the way God invested in yours, you multiply the impact of your breakthrough far beyond your own life.

This is why testimony is so powerful in the Kingdom. When you share what God did for you, when you walk others through the process you went through, when you give them hope by showing them that doors do open if you keep knocking, you're stewarding your breakthrough by multiplying its impact. You're taking what was personal and making it transferable. You're turning your victory into a pathway others can follow.

In our ministry, this has become one of our primary values. Every breakthrough we experience, we document and share. Every testimony we receive, we celebrate publicly so others can be encouraged. Every principle we learn, we teach so others can apply it. Because we recognize that God didn't give us breakthroughs just to build our ministry. He gave us breakthroughs so we could help others experience their own. And the more we steward our blessings by helping others receive theirs, the more God continues to bless us with new opportunities to expand the impact.

So when your door opens, when you step through into breakthrough, don't keep it to yourself. Share your story. Mentor someone who's still pursuing what you now have. Create resources that help others navigate the same journey you walked. Use your platform, however large or small, to point people toward the same God who brought you through. Before proceeding, take a moment to write down the name of one person you'll help. That's how you steward breakthroughs in a way that honors the One who gave it to you and blesses those who are coming behind you.

Now, let me give you some practical action steps for when your door opens, because everything we've discussed needs to translate into concrete decisions you make in the days and weeks after breakthrough manifests. These aren't theoretical ideas. These are practical disciplines that will determine whether you sustain what you just received or lose it through a lack of intentional stewardship.

First action step: Create a testimony document within twenty-four hours of breakthrough. Write down what you asked for, how long you pursued it, what the journey was like, what you learned, how you felt when the door finally opened, and what you're committing to do now that you have it. Date it. Save it somewhere you can access easily. Because human memory is short, and six months from now, when breakthrough feels normal, and you're tempted to take it for granted, you'll need this reminder of what it took to get here and what you committed to when it was fresh.

Second action step: Identify three specific disciplines you'll maintain daily to sustain this breakthrough. Not vague commitments like "I'll keep praying," but concrete actions like "I'll pray for fifteen minutes every morning specifically about stewarding this blessing," or "I'll read one chapter of Scripture daily focused on wisdom for this new season," or "I'll journal three things I'm grateful for about this breakthrough every night before bed." Write these down. Put them on your calendar. Treat them as non-negotiable appointments with yourself and with God.

Third action step: Set up accountability within the first week. Identify someone mature in faith whom you trust and who has permission to ask you hard questions. Tell them about your breakthrough, and ask them to check in monthly on how you're stewarding it. Give them specific questions to ask you. Make yourself accountable for maintaining the disciplines you committed to and for using the blessing for Kingdom purposes rather than just for personal comfort.

Fourth action step: Within the first month, invest your breakthrough in helping someone else. Find one person who's pursuing something similar to what you just received and come alongside them. Share your testimony with them. Pray with them. Encourage them. Help them practically if you can. This early act of generosity positions your heart correctly and establishes the pattern of using your blessing to bless others.

Fifth action step: Create a growth plan for the next six months. Breakthrough isn't static. It's either growing or shrinking. So, within the first thirty days of receiving breakthroughs, sit down and map out how you're going to grow what God gave you. What do you need to learn? What skills do you need to develop? What relationships do you need to cultivate? What next level do you need to prepare for? Write it down as a concrete plan with specific milestones. This moves you from passive enjoyment of breakthrough to active stewardship that builds on what you received.

To provide a tangible example: let's say your breakthrough is landing a new job. In your six-month growth plan, you might start by identifying key competencies critical to your new role, such as mastering specific software or improving your communication skills. Next, outline specific actions, such as enrolling in an online course or joining a public speaking club, to enhance communication proficiency. Set milestones like 'Complete the software course by the end of month three' or 'Deliver a presentation to my team once a month.' Also, plan to network by setting a goal to connect with at least one new colleague each week and schedule quarterly check-ins with a mentor to evaluate your progress and adjust your goals as needed. This detailed approach turns your breakthrough into a solid foundation for further success.

These five action steps give you a simple plan to help you keep your breakthroughs rather than lose them. They aren't hard, but they do take effort, especially when you feel like relaxing after a big answer to prayer. Decide to follow these steps even when you don't feel like it. Emotions come and go, but steady habits will help you stay on track.

Let me close this chapter with a warning and a promise. The warning first: stewarding breakthroughs is harder than obtaining them. You will be tempted to relax, to coast, to assume that because the door opened, you can now stop doing what got you here. Resist that temptation with everything in you. The disciplines that brought breakthroughs are the disciplines that sustain breakthroughs. The character formed through pursuit is the one required for maintenance. And if you abandon what got you here, you will lose what you're here to enjoy.

Here's the promise: If you take good care of what God has given you, keep up your gratitude, discipline, and focus, and help others with your breakthrough, God will keep opening new doors for you. He'll trust you with more because you've shown you're faithful. Your breakthrough will lead to even greater ones, and your story will inspire others. You'll see that the open door isn't the end, but the start of a new journey God has been preparing for you. So remember: How you handle your breakthrough today shapes what comes next.

The Israelites who finally entered the Promised Land after forty years in the wilderness didn't find rest immediately. They found a new kind of challenge, a new season that required different skills than wilderness survival did. But those who remained faithful, who stewarded well what God gave them, who defended their inheritance and multiplied it for the next generation, they experienced the fulfillment of everything God promised. They saw cities built, vineyards planted, families established, and a nation formed. All because they didn't just obtain the blessing. They stewarded it.

That's your calling now. You've asked, sought, and knocked. The door has opened or is about to open. You're stepping through into breakthroughs. And everything depends on what you do next. Will you treat this blessing as a finish line or a starting line? Will you coast on breakthroughs or build on them? Will you hoard what you received or multiply it by helping others receive theirs? The choice is yours. But know this: God is watching how you steward what He just gave you. And your faithfulness in this season determines what He can trust you with in the next.

So steward well. Celebrate genuinely but consolidate intentionally. Maintain the disciplines. Cultivate gratitude. Defend what you gained. Use it to help others. And watch as one breakthrough becomes the platform for the next one, as one opened door leads to another, as what felt like an arrival becomes a departure into something even greater than you imagined when you first started asking.

The door is open. You're right at the start of everything you've worked for. Step forward with wisdom and take care of what you've received. Watch as God does more than you ever expected. This breakthrough isn't the end of your story; it's the start of a new chapter. What you do now will shape what comes next.

Welcome to the other side of the door. Now let's discover what it means to live as someone who doesn't just receive breakthroughs but sustains them, multiplies them, and becomes a source of breakthrough for others. Turn the page. The journey continues, and the best is still ahead.

CHAPTER NINE

THE EVERYONE PROMISE

WHY THIS WORKS FOR ORDINARY BELIEVERS

THE WORD "EVERYONE" IN Matthew 7:8 is of utmost importance. It shapes the conditions of this promise Jesus gave. The 'everyone' promise, as I call it, isn't just for a few people or those with special faith; it's for everyone, and that means all of us. He said, "For everyone who asks receives, and the one who seeks finds, and to the one who knocks it will be opened." No matter your background or spiritual experience, this promise is for you. Look at how God answered Hannah's prayer for a child in 1 Samuel 1, or how Elijah's prayers brought rain in 1 Kings 18 after a long drought. These stories show that God has always responded to people's requests. In this part of the Sermon on the Mount, where the promise is given, Jesus calls us to trust God completely. He shows that God's generosity and care extend to all believers, making this promise part of a larger message about God's faithfulness.

Many of us have read this verse before, but haven't truly believed it's meant for us. It's normal to have doubts and wonder if these promises apply to us. Sometimes we think, 'That's not for me,' because we assume breakthroughs are only for people who seem to have it all together; the ones who pray well, fast for a long time, or seem especially close to God. But we need to challenge these doubts. We often believe the big promises in Scripture are for spiritual giants, and the rest of us should just be grateful for small blessings.

"Why bother?" an inner voice echoes, "You're just one of the ordinary believers; your faith isn't strong enough to see the impossible happen. Maybe if you were more devoted, more like those people at church who have their lives perfectly aligned, then these promises would be yours, too. But not now, not as you are."

These doubts can make us forget God's promise and feel left out of the blessings meant for everyone.

But Jesus didn't say only certain people receive or only the spiritually mature find. He said everyone. This means breakthroughs are possible for regular believers who are willing to try. Each of us needs to decide if we believe this promise is for us, because Jesus made it clear and simple.

On the first day, I wrote down my biggest request; something that felt almost impossible. Each day, I focused on asking, seeking, and knocking. I noticed small changes and signs that things were starting to move. In time, I saw that both my situation and my faith had changed, proving to me that this promise really is for everyone.

Why not try this promise for yourself? Imagine finding new faith and seeing change in just a month. Challenge yourself to ask, seek, and knock for thirty days. Be clear about what you want, keep searching, and don't give up. Watch for changes and new opportunities. This simple step can turn a big idea into something real in your life.

I start this chapter this way because I've seen many believers give up before they even try. They read about asking, seeking, and knocking, but think it's for others, not for them. Maybe they feel they've failed too often, don't have enough faith, or their lives are too messy. Because of this, they never really try, thinking they aren't included in the "everyone" Jesus talked about. But not trying has a cost: it can lead to loneliness, a sense of being cut off from God's promises, and a loss of hope. Doubt can make us give up on our dreams and become cynical. If you take a step of faith, you might not only get answers to your prayers but also find a deeper connection with God.

I know what that struggle feels like. There was a time when I doubted the 'everyone' promise, too. My past felt heavy, and my faith seemed too small. The promise felt far away, as if it were only for others. But when I faced my doubts honestly, I started to see that this promise really does include everyone. My uncertainty didn't disqualify me; it actually helped me understand this truth better. Seeing doubt as a way to talk with God, instead of something to fight, helped me explore my faith more deeply. Carrying doubt while acting in faith is normal and can help us engage more honestly with God's promises.

But here's what matters: when Jesus said 'everyone,' He meant you. He was talking about people living everyday lives; those who work hard, find comfort in simple things, and pray quietly. These are regular believers with regular faith. The only requirement is to make a specific request, keep searching, and keep knocking. You don't need to be perfect or have a spotless past. You just need to be willing to ask, seek, and knock until the door opens.

Think about who Jesus chose as His disciples. They weren't religious leaders or the elite. They were fishermen, tax collectors, and regular working people. Peter worked hard and was impulsive. Thomas doubted. James and John struggled with anger. Matthew had a bad reputation as a tax collector. Jesus chose ordinary people with flaws because His power is shown best in our weakness, not our strength.

So what did Jesus do with these ordinary people? He gave them special access. He gathered the twelve disciples and told them, 'Go, proclaim the kingdom of heaven has come near. Heal the sick, raise the dead, cleanse those who have leprosy, drive out demons.' He gave them the authority to perform miracles and made it clear that their faith, not their status, qualified them. Breakthroughs weren't just for a select few; they were for anyone willing to follow Him and take part in what He taught. By sending out the twelve, Jesus showed that extraordinary gifts are available to those who step forward in faith.

This same offer is for you today. You don't have to be special to see breakthroughs. You just need to be willing. Be willing to ask even if you feel unworthy. Be willing to seek even when you're unsure. Be willing to knock even when the door seems closed. The promise isn't about your qualifications. It's about God's character. God keeps His promises to everyone, not just those who seem impressive.

Here's something practical you can try: take a 72-hour challenge. Write down one specific thing you need and ask God for it over the next three days. Be clear, pray about it each day, and read Psalm 37 as you pray. After you pray, spend 30 seconds writing down what you feel God is saying to you. This simple practice can help you connect your prayers with Scripture and start experiencing the promise for yourself.

Let me show you how this works in real life. The best way to see that the 'everyone' promise is for all of us is to look at the lives of ordinary people who chose to believe it. These aren't stories about spiritual superstars, but about regular people who trusted what Jesus said.

Sarah: Five-Minute Faith

Sarah was a single mom working two jobs to care for her three kids. Her ex-husband had left and wasn't helping. She felt overwhelmed, exhausted, and guilty for not being home more. Many nights, she prayed for help, often in tears as she looked at bills she couldn't pay. But nothing seemed to change. Sarah started to believe that breakthroughs were for other people, not her, because she didn't have the hours to pray, fast, or do all the things she thought were needed to get God's attention. It was at these low moments that Sarah began to wonder, "What could shift in just five minutes a night?"

Then, during a conversation about asking, seeking, and knocking, one phrase stood out to her: 'Everyone who asks receives.' Not just those with time for long prayers or perfect lives; everyone who asks. Sarah realized she had been asking God in a scattered, desperate way, but not with focus or consistency. So she tried what we talked about in Chapter Two. She wrote down three specific requests and prayed for them each day, even if it was just five minutes before bed. She thanked God in advance, even when she couldn't see a way forward. In the second week, she got an unexpected grocery voucher from a local charity. It was a small but meaningful sign that her focused, persistent prayers were making a difference. Celebrating this small win helped her keep going and strengthened her belief in the power of specific and consistent prayer. Sarah's story shows that being specific and consistent in prayer, even for a few minutes a day, can bring real results.

Within five months, things changed. She found a new job with better pay and hours. Her church helped cover some expenses while she got back on her feet. Her ex-husband's wages were garnished, so she finally received steady child support.

Her income went up by 35 percent, bringing stability to her finances. It wasn't dramatic or like something from a movie. It was simply one door after another opening because she kept asking, seeking, and didn't give up.

When Sarah shared her story with me, she said something that stood out: 'I thought breakthroughs were for people who had time to be spiritual. I thought God only answered prayers from people who could give Him hours of worship and prayer. But He responded to my five-minute prayers, prayed in exhaustion because He cares more about my heart than my circumstances. He responds to everyone who asks, even single moms who are too tired.' Sarah's experience shows that God cares about the sincerity of our hearts and our persistence, not just how long we pray.

This is the 'everyone' promise at work. Sarah wasn't special or different; she was just an ordinary person. But she followed the process, and it worked because Jesus promised it would work for everyone, not just those with perfect lives or strong spiritual backgrounds.

Mr. Conrad: Mid-Career Miracle

When I met Mr. Conrad, he was in his fifties and had been unemployed for over a year. He had worked in a specialized field, but the industry had changed, and his skills were outdated. He sent out hundreds of applications and got nowhere. At his age, with his obsolete skill set, he felt invisible to potential employers. He prayed about it occasionally, but mostly he just felt hopeless, like he was too old and too far behind to ever work again in any meaningful capacity.

Then one of our ministry's followers encouraged him to try the ask, seek, knock approach. Mr. Conrad realized he had been waiting for God to give him a job without doing his part to look for one. Inspired by this, he started taking practical steps and trusted God to guide him. He took online courses to update his skills, choosing those that aligned with the current job market. He went to networking events, even though he was nervous, and with each step, he felt God was helping him. By reaching out to old colleagues and applying for jobs that weren't perfect but could get him started again, Mr. Conrad learned that seeking opportunities is about both effort and trusting God to lead the way. His story shows that improving yourself and reaching out to others are important for finding new opportunities.

It took nine more months, but the door opened. A former colleague remembered him when a position opened up at his company. Mr. Conrad got an interview, demonstrated that he had been updating his skills, and was hired. The job wasn't his dream position, but it got him back to work. And within a year, his faithful performance in that role led to a promotion into something better suited to his abilities. Today, Mr. Conrad is thriving in his career again, making more than he did before he was laid off, and he tells everyone who will listen that breakthroughs came because he finally understood that God responds to everyone who asks, seeks, and knocks, even unemployed fifty-somethings who feel like they've been forgotten.

Jennifer: Healing from Invisible Struggles

Or consider Jennifer, a college student dealing with anxiety and depression. She had taken medication for years, seen several therapists, and tried every coping method people suggested. Still, some days she couldn't get out of bed, panic attacks stopped her, and the darkness felt overwhelming. She prayed for healing all the time, but nothing seemed to change. Jennifer started to think maybe God didn't heal mental health struggles, that breakthroughs were only for physical problems, not the invisible battles she faced. It's important to remember that some people need ongoing treatment, and professional help can be a key part of healing. This shows that a full approach to mental health includes both faith and therapy. But then she started using the ask, seek, knock approach. She prayed specifically for healing, naming her depression and anxiety instead of just asking to feel better. She looked up what the Bible said about renewing the mind, found a Christian counselor who combined faith and therapy, and joined a small group where she could be honest about her struggles. She kept praying, even on days when it felt hopeless. Jennifer's story reveals that combining faith with practical support can help overcome mental health challenges.

Her breakthrough didn't come instantly. It came gradually, incrementally, over months of asking, seeking, and knocking. But it came. The depression lifted. The anxiety decreased. She found tools and truths that actually worked, rather than just temporarily managing symptoms. And today, Jennifer is one of the most effective people in their ministry at helping others who struggle with mental health because she knows firsthand that the 'everyone' promise includes people battling invisible illnesses that others often dismiss or misunderstand.

What do Sarah, Mr. Conrad, and Jennifer have in common? They're ordinary people. They don't have special access to God or impressive spiritual gifts. They faced real problems that seemed impossible to solve. But they followed the process

Jesus described, believing that when He said 'everyone,' He meant them. Their belief, and their willingness to ask, seek, and knock, led to breakthroughs that changed their lives.

Now, I want to talk about something that might be on your mind as you read these stories. Maybe you're thinking, "I've been asking, seeking, and knocking for years, but I still haven't seen a breakthrough. Does the everyone promise not include me? Did I do something wrong? Is there something in my life that makes me an exception to what Jesus promised?" Before we get into these questions, take a moment to invite God into your reflection. You might want to pray Psalm 139:23-24: "Search me, God, and know my heart; test me and know my anxious thoughts. See if there is any offensive way in me, and lead me in the way everlasting." Looking at things this way can turn your analysis into worship and help you think more kindly about yourself. As you consider these questions, ask yourself a deeper question: Which part of asking, seeking, and knocking do you tend to skip, and why? Think about whether you naturally avoid one of these steps, and consider what might be holding you back. Taking this time to reflect can help you apply these lessons in a way that fits your own journey.

Those questions deserve honest answers, so let me address them directly. First, the everyone promise is real, and it includes you. There's no hidden exception clause that disqualifies certain people from receiving what Jesus promised. But there are reasons why breakthrough might be delayed even when you're engaging the process faithfully, and understanding those reasons will help you continue pursuing without getting discouraged or concluding you're somehow exempt from God's promises.

One reason your breakthrough might be delayed is that you're still in a wilderness season, like we talked about in Chapter Five. The wilderness doesn't mean God has forgotten you or that the promise isn't real. Think of it like waiting for a slow webpage to load or sitting through a long airport layover. You know the destination is coming, but the waiting can test your patience. It's a time when God is preparing you for what's ahead, helping you grow so you'll be ready for your breakthrough. The Israelites wandered for forty years, not because the promise was false, but because they weren't ready yet. Deuteronomy 8 shows how God used that time to humble and test His people, to see what was in their hearts, and to teach them to trust Him. If you're in a wilderness season now, it doesn't mean the 'everyone' promise failed. Think of it as training, not punishment. It's a step before the promise is fulfilled, helping you grow instead of showing God's displeasure.

Another reason breakthroughs might be delayed is that you're knocking at the wrong door. We talked about this in Chapter Six when we discussed the four principles for discerning whether to keep knocking or redirect. Sometimes what we think we need isn't actually what God knows we need, and He's withholding one thing to give us something better. That's not the 'everyone' promise failing. That's God being a better Father than we are children, knowing what will actually serve us in the long run versus what we think we want in the moment.

A third reason for delayed breakthroughs is spiritual warfare. In Daniel 10, the answer to prayer was sent immediately, but was delayed for three weeks due to spiritual resistance. Your breakthrough might also be facing unseen obstacles. It's like a package that's been shipped but is stuck in transit, with things happening behind the scenes. Your steady asking, seeking, and knocking can help bring the breakthrough, even when you can't see what's going on. The delay doesn't mean the promise failed. It means your persistence is helping the process work, even through the resistance. To strengthen your resolve, consider this prayer: 'Lord, strengthen me while the answer is in transit and help me stay steadfast in faith. Equip me with patience and clarity to perceive Your will and intercede boldly against any forces that seek to hinder progress.'

Or the delay might be about timing. God's timing is rarely our preferred timing, but it's always perfect timing. Abraham waited twenty-five years for Isaac. Joseph waited thirteen years from dream to fulfillment. David waited over a decade from anointing to coronation. In every case, the delay was purposeful, preparing both the person and the circumstances for breakthrough to manifest in the way that would best serve God's purposes. If you're waiting longer than you wanted, that doesn't mean the promise doesn't apply to you. It means God's timing for your breakthrough is different than your preferred timeline, and His timing is better even when it's longer.

Here's the main idea: the 'everyone' promise is real, and it includes you. As you keep following the process, breakthroughs are coming. They might not happen on your schedule or look the way you expect, but knowing this can help you keep going and not feel left out while you wait.

God's choice to give this promise to everyone, not just spiritual elites, changes how we seek breakthroughs. He doesn't want a Kingdom divided by spiritual rank. He wants to show that His power goes beyond human limits. Breakthroughs depend on God's provision, not our qualifications, and we access them through faith.

This is why Paul writes in 1 Corinthians 1:26-29, "Consider your calling, brothers: not many of you were wise according to worldly standards, not many were powerful, not many were of noble birth. But God chose what is foolish in the world to shame the wise; God chose what is weak in the world to shame the strong; God chose what is low and despised in the world, even things that are not, to bring to nothing things that are, so that no human being might boast in the presence of God."

God chooses to work through ordinary people, those who seem weak or unimportant by the world's standards, to show that breakthroughs are about Him, not us. When someone impressive has a breakthrough, people might think it's because of their talent or resources. But when an ordinary person experiences a breakthrough that can't be explained by their own abilities, it's clear that God is at work. That's why the 'everyone' promise exists. It's not about lowering standards. It's about showing that breakthroughs come from God's help, not our qualifications.

Think about Gideon. When God called him to deliver Israel, Gideon was hiding in a winepress, threshing wheat in fear of the enemy. He came from the weakest clan in Manasseh, and he was the least in his father's house. By every measure, he was the wrong person for leadership. But God chose him specifically because of his weakness, not despite it. And when God gave him victory, He made sure Gideon's army was reduced from thirty-two thousand to just three hundred so that no one could say Israel saved themselves by their own strength. God orchestrated the victory in a way that made it undeniable that He did it, not them.

That's your story as well. Whatever breakthrough you're hoping for, God wants to give it to you in a way that shows it was His doing, not yours. Your ordinariness, your weaknesses, and your lack of impressive credentials aren't obstacles; they actually help, because they make you rely fully on God. When your breakthrough comes, you'll know it was Him, and others will see it too.

This is also why Jesus used the word "everyone" rather than "the righteous," "the mature," or "the worthy." Because breakthroughs aren't a reward for spiritual performance. It's a gift accessed through faith-filled pursuit. Yes, character matters. Yes, obedience matters. Yes, how you live affects your relationship with God and your ability to steward blessings. But breakthroughs don't come because you finally got righteous enough to deserve it. It comes because you engaged the process Jesus outlined, believing that His promise applies to you despite your unworthiness.

Now, let me address one more barrier that keeps ordinary believers from experiencing breakthroughs even though the promise clearly includes them. It's the comparison trap we briefly touched on in Chapter Five, but it deserves more attention here because it's one of the primary ways the enemy convinces us we're not part of the 'everyone' Jesus was talking about.

Think of your life as your own race lane, made just for you. Picture marking your lane clearly to help you stay focused on your own path. This reminds us that everyone's journey is different, and it's important to focus on your own progress instead of comparing yourself to others. Stay in your lane. Stay out of the comparison trap by focusing on your own race and what's meant for you.

Comparison hurts our faith because it makes us judge our journey by someone else's results. When we see others get breakthroughs quickly, we might think God loves them more. We might wonder why God blesses others but not us, or feel like failures if our breakthroughs come slowly or in ordinary ways. This kind of thinking can make us believe the 'everyone promise' is for others, not for us. To fight this, try this exercise: Write down three recent comparisons you've made and put them on a sticky note where you pray. Each time you see it, think about how each comparison could actually encourage your faith instead of making you feel less. Turning these thoughts into positive reminders can help you grow and believe in the promises meant for you.

But here's the truth you need to remember: God's blessing in someone else's life doesn't mean He's holding back from you. Their breakthrough doesn't take away from yours. Their quick answer doesn't mean your longer wait is a sign of God's displeasure. God doesn't have a limited supply. His resources are infinite, and His love is unlimited. His promises apply to everyone, including those who receive quickly and those who wait longer, and to those whose breakthroughs come through miracles and those through ordinary means.

The comparison trap makes you focus on someone else's journey when God is calling you to run your own race. It makes you question whether you're part of the "everyone" when Jesus already declared that you are. It creates doubt about God's faithfulness based on someone else's timeline rather than trusting His timing for your specific situation. And that doubt undermines the very faith that makes asking, seeking, and knocking effective.

So what should you do when comparison makes you think breakthroughs are only for others? First, celebrate with them honestly. When someone else gets a breakthrough, let their story encourage you. Their success shows that God is still working and still answers persistent prayers. Let their victory inspire you to keep going rather than letting envy take root. As a practical step, write a short blessing for the person who received their breakthrough. This simple act turns envy into celebration and helps you focus on gratitude instead of comparison. Additionally, consider praying one specific blessing over them; a prayer that God continues to guide and sustain them in their journey. This act of intercession not only redirects negative energy into positive faith but also strengthens your connection to them as spiritual partners in faith.

Second, remember that their journey isn't yours. You don't know what they went through to get where they are. You're seeing the highlight reel, not the behind-the-scenes struggle. What looks like overnight success to you might have taken years to make. And even if their breakthrough did come quickly, that has nothing to do with God's plan for your breakthrough. His timing for them doesn't determine His timing for you, and comparing the two only creates unnecessary pain.

Third, stay in your lane. Run your race. Pursue your breakthrough. Don't let someone else's results distract you from engaging the process Jesus outlined for you. Keep asking with specificity. Keep seeking with diligence. Keep knocking with persistence. Trust that the same promise that worked for them applies to you, and breakthroughs are coming if you stay faithful to your pursuit, regardless of how long others waited or how quickly they received.

The 'everyone' promise isn't a competition where some win and others lose. It's an invitation extended to all believers to engage the process that accesses what God has already made available. And when you stop comparing your journey to others and start focusing on your own faithful pursuit, you position yourself to receive what Jesus promised to everyone, including you.

Let me end this chapter with one more encouragement. You don't need to be exceptional to see breakthroughs. You don't need perfect faith, a dramatic story, or a life without struggles. You just need to be willing: to ask even when you feel unworthy, to seek even when you're unsure, and to knock even when the door seems closed. Stand up with courage. Move forward with determination. Take the step of faith that turns hope into reality. May your asking be bold, your seeking steady, and your knocking persistent. May you find strength in the promise that breakthroughs are not just possible, but promised to those who keep going.

The 'everyone' promise isn't a reward for exceptional people. It's meant to help ordinary people connect with an extraordinary God and receive what they need. If you feel ordinary, weak, broken, or like you have nothing to offer, you're exactly who Jesus meant when He said "everyone."

Asking, seeking, and knocking aren't complicated. You don't need special training or deep spiritual experience. Anyone can do it. A tired single mother praying for a few minutes, an unemployed man learning new skills and hoping for a job, a college student fighting depression and searching for help, an addict desperate for freedom, or a woman struggling with health but still hoping to be a mother; these are the people the everyone promise is for. Ordinary people with simple faith, doing what they can, trusting that God will answer everyone who asks, seeks, and knocks.

Don't count yourself out. Don't believe that breakthroughs are only for others. Don't compare your journey to someone else's, because you might be looking at their success without knowing their struggles. You might be at the beginning while they're much further along. Don't wait until you feel worthy or ready. Just start. Ask with whatever faith you have, even if it's small. Seek with whatever ability you have, even if it doesn't feel like enough. Knock with whatever strength you have, even if you're tired. The promise isn't about your qualifications. It's about God's character. He keeps His promises to everyone, not just those who think they deserve it.

The door will open for you. Answers will come. Breakthroughs will happen in your life, not because you're special, but because you're willing to trust what Jesus promised works for everyone. When you experience your breakthrough, you'll see it wasn't about your worthiness, but about God's faithfulness. It wasn't about your ability, but about His power in your weakness. It wasn't about being special, but about God keeping His promise to everyone who asks, seeks, and knocks.

I want you to remember this phrase, 'Included, therefore engaged.' Let this remind you each day that you are part of 'everyone,' and your participation is important for experiencing God's promise.

You'll become proof that the 'everyone' promise is real and includes people like you. God responds to ordinary believers who don't count themselves out. Your story will encourage others who feel unqualified, showing them that if it worked for you, it can work for them, too. The 'everyone' promise creates a chain reaction; one person's breakthrough inspires another, and the Kingdom grows through regular believers who trust what Jesus said.

So go ahead; ask, seek, and knock. Do it not because you're special, but because you're included. Not because you deserve it, but because it's promised to you. Not because you have all the answers, but because this process works for everyone, including you.

The 'everyone' promise is yours. Claim it. Live it. Watch as God does for you what He's done for many ordinary believers before; He opens doors that seemed impossible, provides what seemed out of reach, and proves His promises are real for everyone who believes and keeps going until breakthrough comes.

You're part of "everyone." Live like it. The next chapter will show you why God designed breakthrough this way, why He wants ordinary believers to experience extraordinary provision, and how knowing His character changes how you seek His promises. Turn the page and see that God wants to answer even more than you want to ask.

CHAPTER TEN

THE FATHER'S HEART

UNDERSTANDING WHO'S ON THE OTHER SIDE OF THE DOOR

> "Your theology about God determines your tenacity in prayer."
> -*Apostle Dr. Ivon L. Valerie*

JANE WANTED TO FEEL closer to God, but often felt alone when she prayed. She sometimes wondered if anyone was really listening or if God was far away. These thoughts kept her up at night, and she longed for a sign that her prayers mattered. Peter also wanted a deeper relationship with God, but he chose to keep his faith even when answers didn't come right away. He worried about giving up too soon, so he often reminded himself, "I trust in God's perfect timing." This helped him see waiting as a chance to grow, not a reason to doubt. To build his faith, Peter started to see himself as a student of Jesus, learning from His example and trying to follow His way of life. This helped him view persistent prayer as a journey with Jesus, not something he had to do perfectly. Peter began using a simple prayer each day: 'God, grant me patience and trust in Your perfect timing.' Whenever he felt doubt, he repeated this prayer to remind himself to keep trusting. By seeing himself as walking with Jesus, Peter realized that knowing who God is matters most. You can learn all the steps of asking, seeking, and knocking. You can understand tough times, notice signs of breakthrough, and know how to handle blessings. But if you don't really know the character of the God you're seeking, or if your view of Him is off, you won't develop the kind of faith that keeps knocking until the door opens. The question, 'Who is the God we're reaching out to?' isn't just basic; it shapes how deep our prayer life can go. If you think God is reluctant, stingy, unpredictable, or harsh, why would you keep knocking?

Many lessons about prayer miss this key point. We often focus on how to pray, having enough faith, being persistent, and following the right steps. But we rarely ask the most important question: Who is the God we're praying to? Do we see God as someone who wants to bless us, or as someone who just watches from far away? The way you see God shapes how you pray. Remember: "Your perception of God is the compass of your prayer life." Just as a compass always points north, your view of God can guide your prayers with confidence and direction. If your view of Him is off, it's like following a broken compass, which can lead to confusion and uncertainty in your spiritual life. Knowing God's true nature is the foundation for building the confidence you need for persistent faith. Take a moment to write down how you see God right now. How might your view of Him affect the way you approach Him? Thinking about this can help you connect more deeply with what you're learning and open up new insights into your prayer life.

How you answer these questions changes everything. It shapes whether you pray with confidence or fear, with hope or doubt, and whether you keep going or give up. Persistent prayer isn't about trying harder; it's about learning with Jesus and growing in faith. Think about how you usually approach prayer. Do you feel hopeful or hesitant? Let your view of God guide you, since it is the compass of your prayer life. Take a moment to write down your thoughts: How do you see God today? What challenges or doubts are shaping your prayers? When you see prayer this way, it becomes a time to learn and walk with God, who is good and will open the door at the right time. What you believe about God will either help your faith grow or hold you back before you even begin. 'Your perception of God is the compass of your prayer life.' Let this guide your journey and help you build your practice on understanding and trust.

This chapter will take a different approach from the earlier ones. Instead of focusing on what you need to do, we'll focus on who God is. First, let's meet the Father behind the door. Before we talk about the wrong ideas that keep people from praying with confidence, think about this: How do your beliefs about God's character shape the way you pray? Reflecting on this can help you connect personally with what we're about to discuss. As you learn more about God's true character, persistent prayer will feel more natural. By the end of this chapter, you'll be able to build a confident relationship with God, turning prayer from a duty into a partnership with a Father who is eager to give. You'll see how knowing God's character deepens your prayer life and makes it more meaningful. When you really know who is on the other side of the door, prayer becomes about relationship, not just about trying to get God to respond.

Before we talk about specific misunderstandings, I want to point out some common ways people get God's character wrong when they struggle with prayer. Some see God as a reluctant giver, others as a random responder, and others as a strict taskmaster. These ideas can weigh us down emotionally. If you've ever felt like you had to beg God to care, worried your prayers weren't good enough, or thought that praying longer or fasting might finally get His attention, this view is shaping your beliefs, even if you don't notice it. Studies show that many people feel anxious about prayer, thinking they need to bargain with God or be perfect to earn His favor. Knowing this is common can help us feel less alone. When we recognize these patterns, we can start to make changes and approach God with a healthier, more accurate view of who He is.

But let's look at what Jesus said about this. After teaching His disciples to ask, seek, and knock, He talked about who they were asking. He said, "Or which one of you, if his son asks him for bread, will give him a stone? Or if he asks for a fish, will I give him a serpent? If you then, who are evil, know how to give good gifts to your children, how much more will your Father who is in heaven give good things to those who ask him!" In Jesus' time, offering bread or fish was a sign of real generosity and kindness. Imagine a mother at dinner, with her child nervously asking for more bread, afraid she might say no. Instead, she quietly gives him the bread, showing trust and care. In the same way, Jesus' teaching shows that God is eager to give good gifts.

Jesus uses this example to challenge the idea that God is a reluctant giver. He points to human fathers, who have their own flaws and limits, but still know how to give good gifts to their children. They don't give stones when asked for bread or serpents when asked for fish. Even if they sometimes say no for good reasons, their natural response is to be generous, not reluctant. Human fathers, even at their best, are only a small reflection of what God is like all the time. If fathers who are imperfect still want to give good things to their children, then God's generosity is far greater.

This changes everything about prayer. If you see God as a reluctant giver, prayer feels like trying to convince Him to give what He would rather withhold. But if you believe God is eager to give, prayer becomes about getting ready to receive what He already wants to give. This shift is about moving from striving to receiving. If you think God usually says no, you may feel you have to work hard for a yes. But if you believe He usually says yes, then a delay is about timing or preparation, not reluctance. Ask yourself: Do you see God as someone you have to persuade, or as a Father who already wants to bless you? Seeing prayer this way helps you move from cautious requests to a more open and trusting conversation. This makes your prayers stronger, because God, in His great generosity, is ready to bless us and give us good things as we come to Him with faith and perseverance.

Think about your own experience as a parent, or how you were raised. When a child comes to you with a real need, do you hold back or make them prove they deserve help? Most parents want to provide and help. You might not always give exactly what they ask for, because you know what's best or the timing isn't right. But your heart is generous, and you look for ways to give good things. That's how a loving parent feels.

God is that kind of Father. He isn't a reluctant giver who needs convincing. He is eager to respond to requests, delights in giving good gifts, and seeks opportunities to bless rather than reasons to hold back. When you knock on His door, He isn't thinking about making you wait or suffer. He's thinking about the best timing, what preparation is needed, and how to give in a way that truly helps you, not just meets your immediate wants.

These two attitudes make a big difference. One makes you timid in prayer, while the other makes you bold. If you expect God to be reluctant, you might give up quickly. If you trust His generosity, you'll keep going. Seeing delay as God preparing the best for you, not holding back, changes how you pray. What you believe about God shapes whether you keep knocking or walk away. As you think about this, remember there are practical tools to help. In the next sections, we'll look at four practices: memorizing Scripture, keeping a record of God's faithfulness, surrounding yourself with people who speak truth, and practicing daily gratitude. These will help you as you learn more about prayer. For example, memorizing Scripture can help you stay steady during times of doubt. These verses give you clarity and strength when anxiety feels overwhelming.

Let's look at another common misunderstanding about God that can make it hard to keep praying. Some people think God is unpredictable, blessing one person one day and someone else the next, without any clear reason. For instance, David, who is faithful at church, tells his pastor, Charlie, "Pastor, I pray every morning, but it feels like God isn't listening. My neighbor, who doesn't seem as committed, keeps sharing stories of answered prayers. It feels unfair." Pastor Charlie replies, "I know that's tough, David. But remember, we only see part of the picture. Just because you don't see answers yet doesn't mean God isn't listening. Trust that He has a reason for His timing, even if it's hard to understand." For David, prayer starts to feel like a game of chance, and this feeling of randomness makes him question why God answers some prayers but not his. If you've ever felt like God's actions are so mysterious that you stop trying to understand, this belief is shaping how you see God.

The Bible gives us a different picture. God is not random or unpredictable. Even if we don't always understand His ways, His character never changes, and we can trust His promises. God's responses follow patterns we see in Scripture, but they aren't formulas we can use to control Him. His love is bigger than any set of rules, and He is not a God of confusion. He is faithful, keeps His promises, and always follows through on what He says.

When Jesus spoke about asking, seeking, and knocking, He was showing us a pattern, not a formula to control God. Everyone who asks receives, everyone who seeks finds, and everyone who knocks has doors opened. This is not random; it's dependable. God's faithfulness gives us a solid foundation. In the Bible, a covenant is a serious promise between God and people, showing that He keeps His word. This is about a relationship built on trust, not just following steps. Imagine two gardeners: one follows strict instructions and gets upset by any change, while the other adapts to the seasons and succeeds by following steady principles. God is like the second gardener. He is reliable and clear about how things work. If someone you loved acted randomly, sometimes generous and sometimes not, you would feel unsure. In the same way, it's hard to trust someone who acts without reason, but God is not like that.

God is not arbitrary. He is faithful to His promises and responds to faith in a consistent way. He is the same yesterday, today, and forever. When you come to Him, you are not taking a chance on His mood. You are approaching a Father whose character does not change, whose love is steady, and whose promises last. If you experience a delay, it is not random. It is part of His purposeful timing. The different ways He answers prayers are not random, but show His wisdom in knowing what is best for each situation. The more you understand how steady He is, the more confidence you will have to keep praying, even when you have not seen an answer yet.

There is another false idea about God to address before we talk about who He truly is. Some people see God as a strict taskmaster who only blesses those who are perfect. This view makes you feel like God is always disappointed, focusing on your mistakes and holding back blessings because you haven't met impossible standards. If you have ever felt you need to have everything together before God will answer, that your past failures keep you from being blessed, or that one more mistake will make God give up on you, this belief is hurting your confidence in prayer.

Look at how Jesus describes the Father in the parable of the prodigal son in Luke 15. The son takes his inheritance, wastes it on wild living, and ends up feeding pigs and feeling unworthy. Yet the father waits for his child to come home, runs to meet him even when he is still far away, and interrupts his words of unworthiness with love, acceptance, and restoration. God cares about holiness. Sin has consequences. Obedience matters. But God's attitude toward you is not harsh condemnation. He is eager to love, bless, restore, and celebrate your return whenever you turn to Him.

There have been times when I felt like nothing I did was good enough and was weighed down by my own failures. I remember being afraid that I could never meet God's expectations. But then I experienced God's steady love, like the father in the story of the prodigal son, welcoming me with open arms rather than criticism. In my self-doubt, I felt God's embrace, which took away my fear of rejection. This changed how I prayed, helping me approach God with confidence rather than hesitation. Knowing who God really is, I can approach Him as a loved child, not someone trying to earn approval.

This is important for persistent prayer because harsh taskmasters only respond to perfect performance, not to someone knocking. Since none of us can be perfect, believing God is a harsh taskmaster stops us from trying. Why keep knocking if you think the door will only open when you have everything right? Why keep going if you believe every mistake adds another lock to the door? Think about Nathan, a devoted believer who hesitates to pray because he feels he must be perfect. Every time he fails, he imagines another barrier between himself and God's favor. This belief leads him to believe that his prayers are pointless unless he first becomes perfect. This kind of thinking keeps him from coming to God at all, afraid that trying will only reveal his flaws rather than opening the door to God's grace.

A taskmaster demands perfection and scrutinizes every flaw. A father rejoices in his child's presence and celebrates every step toward growth. When you understand that God's heart is like the father in the prodigal son story, when you know He is running toward you even when you are far away, and when you see that He wants to bless you more than you want to receive, then knocking becomes natural. You are not trying to earn something God is reluctant to give. You are getting ready to receive what He is eager to give to anyone who comes to Him, even with imperfect faith.

Let's take some time to get a clear idea of who God really is, since fixing misunderstandings is just one step. God isn't a reluctant giver who holds back blessings. He doesn't answer prayers without reason, and He isn't a strict taskmaster who demands perfection before blessing us. Think about which of these mistaken ideas you might connect with most. This is a good moment to reflect and get ready for change. You need a biblical view of God's character that helps you keep seeking breakthroughs. Scripture shows us three key truths about who God is.

The first truth is that God is good, and His goodness doesn't depend on what's happening in your life. This might sound simple, but it's the foundation for everything else. When Jesus said, "If you then, who are evil, know how to give good gifts to your children, how much more will your Father who is in heaven give good things to those who ask him," He was showing that God's goodness is part of who He is. It's not something that changes with His mood or your situation. God's goodness is steady and unchanging.

Emily was a committed believer who lost her home in a fire. Even while standing in the ruins, she chose to say, "God is still good," as she worked through her grief. Her story encouraged her community and showed that God's goodness doesn't disappear when we suffer. Instead, it can become even clearer. Emily's faith reminds us that God's goodness carries us through our hardest times.

This matters because our situations can mislead us. When you're going through a tough time, waiting for an answer, or praying without seeing results, it might feel like God isn't good or that He's forgotten you. If you let your situation decide what you believe about God, you might give up before things change. But if you trust in God's proven goodness, not just what you see right now, you can hold on to your faith no matter what, because your current situation doesn't change who God is. Remember the psalmist's words, 'Oh, taste and see that the Lord is good!' Like Emily, who lost her home in a fire but still chose to declare God's goodness, we are invited to experience God's goodness for ourselves. Her choice to 'taste and see' shows that God's goodness does not depend on our circumstances but is always present in our lives.

The psalmist got this when he wrote, "Oh, taste and see that the Lord is good! Blessed is the man who takes refuge in him!" This isn't just about watching God's goodness from afar or thinking about it in theory. It's about experiencing it for yourself, so it becomes real to you. The more you see God's goodness in answered prayers, unexpected help, or new opportunities, the more this truth becomes a solid part of your faith.

That's why sharing stories of God's help is so important. Every answered prayer and breakthrough isn't just about that moment; it's about building a history with God that reminds you of His goodness. Think of Rosie, who saw her son recover after prayer, or Ettiene, who received financial help just in time. Stories like these remind us that God is faithful. When you face new challenges, you can look back and remember that the God who helped before will help again, even if your situation hasn't changed yet.

The second truth is that God is incredibly generous, and His generosity comes from having more than enough, not from a limited supply. We often think in terms of limits, like our time, money, and energy running out. Helping one person might mean less for someone else. But God's generosity isn't like that. It's like a never-ending supply, always overflowing. God doesn't just give enough; He gives more than enough, so you can enjoy His love and care without worrying it will run out.

God doesn't work with limits. He has endless abundance. When He gives to you, it doesn't take away from anyone else. If He opens a door for you, it doesn't close one for someone else. God's generosity isn't based on a limited supply. No matter how many people He blesses or how much He gives, there's always more than enough.

Paul explained this in Ephesians 3:20, "Now to him who is able to do far more abundantly than all that we ask or think, according to the power at work within us." God doesn't just meet our needs; He goes beyond them. He gives more than we can imagine, not by rationing, but by overflowing generosity.

Knowing this changes how you pray. Instead of making careful requests, you can pray boldly, trusting that God has unlimited resources. You don't have to worry that your prayers take away from others. You can keep asking without guilt, because God's abundance never runs out, no matter how many people He blesses.

The third truth is that God's timing is always right, even if it's not what you hoped for. Waiting can be a time when God is preparing you for what's next, not just making you wait. A delay doesn't mean God doesn't want to bless you; it means He cares enough to get you ready for the best moment. While you wait, remember you're not alone. Others are on this journey too, and God is with you. Use this time to learn and grow, not just to wait.

Think of it this way: a parent wouldn't give a five-year-old the car keys just because they ask. It's not because the parent is mean, but because the child isn't ready. Saying no or not yet is a sign of love and wisdom. When the child is older and ready, getting the keys means much more than if they'd gotten them too soon.

God uses that same kind of wisdom, but He knows perfectly what you need and when you're ready. He sees things you can't and gives at the right time for your best, not just for your comfort. Romans 8:28 says God works all things together for good for those who love Him and are called according to His purpose. This doesn't mean everything is good, but that God is working things out for your good in ways that quick answers never could.

Waiting is still hard, but knowing there's a purpose makes it easier. When you trust that delay is part of God's perfect timing, not a sign He doesn't care, you can stay strong in your faith. You can keep asking, even if the answer hasn't come yet, trusting that when it does, the timing will be right.

Let me share how these three truths helped me keep praying during a tough season. For eighteen months, the door to ministry stayed closed, and I struggled with questions: If God is good, why wasn't He answering? If He's generous, why was He holding back? If His timing is perfect, why did I feel forgotten? I wasn't alone. My peers and our congregation supported me and walked through it with me. During this time, my wife often reminded me, 'Our faith is strongest when we lean on each other and trust that God's plan is unfolding, even when we can't see it.' This type of encouragement was vital, underscoring the communal nature of persistence. Even though I didn't hear anything, I kept praying and seeking. Over time, I saw that waiting was preparing me for what was ahead. God's goodness wasn't about giving me what I wanted right away, but about using the waiting to grow our gifts and character as a community. His timing was about setting us up for the best results, not just making me comfortable.

When the door finally opened and our ministry began, I could see that every moment had a reason. My questions about God's goodness were answered as His generosity exceeded my expectations, and the timing that once frustrated me turned out to be perfect. This experience helped me understand God better and gave me the confidence to keep moving forward in faith.

That's what knowing God's heart does for you. It gives you a solid foundation to keep going, even when things are tough. It helps you trust in who God is, not just what you see. Prayer becomes less about trying to get God's attention and more about confidently seeking what He's already prepared for you.

Here are some practical ways to build this foundation in your life. Knowing about God's character is important, but letting it shape your prayers is even more powerful. These are not quick fixes, but habits that can change how you see and seek God over time. Try these four practices: memorize Scripture, keep a record of God's faithfulness, spend time with people who speak truth, and practice daily gratitude.

First, memorize Bible verses that show God's character. Don't just read them now and then; learn them by heart so you can remember them when you're struggling. Verses like James 1:17, "Every good gift and every perfect gift is from above, coming down from the Father of lights, with whom there is no variation or shadow due to change." Or Lamentations 3:22-23, "The steadfast love of the Lord never ceases; his mercies never come to an end; they are new every morning; great is your faithfulness." Or Psalm 84:11, "No good thing does he withhold from those who walk uprightly." When you know these by heart, you can remind yourself of God's truth when you start to doubt.

Second, keep a journal of God's faithfulness in your life. Write down every answered prayer, every time God provided, and every door that opened. Include dates and details about what you asked for and how God responded. When you face new challenges, you can look back and remember that God, who was faithful before, will be faithful again, even if things are hard right now.

Third, spend time with people who speak truth about God's character. Look for teachers, authors, and friends who remind you of God's goodness, generosity, and perfect timing. Try to avoid voices that make God seem reluctant or harsh, even if they're from church. The people you listen to shape what you believe about God, and that, in turn, shapes how you pray. Be careful about who you let influence your view of God.

Fourth, make gratitude a daily habit. Thank God for who He is, not just for what He gives you. Thank Him for His goodness, even when life is tough. Thank Him for His generosity, even while you're waiting. Thank Him for His timing, even if it's not what you hoped for. Focusing on gratitude helps you remember God's character, which keeps your faith strong. You can also share what you're thankful for with a friend or loved one. This can encourage both of you.

As we finish this chapter, I want you to try something. Close your eyes and picture a banquet table filled with abundance being prepared for you on the other side of the door. Imagine yourself not as a guest waiting to be let in, but as a beloved child invited to enjoy the feast. Focus on the one who is preparing this feast for you. He's not a reluctant giver, not unpredictable, and not demanding perfection. He's a loving Father who is incredibly good, generous, and always on time, even if it's not your timing.

That Father hears every time you knock. He sees every tear and knows every need. He's not waiting to decide if you're worthy. He's preparing the best way to open the door, so when it opens, what you receive will help you more than if you got it right away. He's working for your good and timing everything perfectly. He's even more committed to your breakthrough than you are, because He sees not just what you want, but who you'll become along the way.

What you believe about God shapes how you pray. If you think He's reluctant, you might give up when things get tough. If you think He's unpredictable, you might lose hope when answers take time to come. If you think He's harsh, you might be afraid you'll never be good enough. But if you believe He's good, generous, and always on time, you'll keep praying with confidence, knowing that delay isn't denial, silence isn't indifference, and a closed door isn't forever.

God's heart is for you; not just in theory, but in real, personal ways that matter to you right now. He wants to open the door for you even more than you want to walk through it. He cares about your breakthrough more than you do. He's ready to respond to everyone who asks, seeks, and knocks, not out of duty, but because He loves giving good gifts to His children.

So keep praying and asking, not to convince a reluctant giver, but because you have a loving Father who is waiting for the best moment to open the door. What you believe about Him makes this kind of faith possible. When the door finally opens, you'll see that every moment of waiting was preparing you, that God's goodness was always there, His generosity was greater than you thought, and His timing was perfect, even if it wasn't what you expected.

God's heart is for you. So pray with confidence, knowing who is on the other side of the door and what He wants for you. In the next chapter, you'll see how to live with this kind of persistent faith. Turn the page and know that your journey from passive believer to persistent knocker is almost complete.

Chapter Eleven

THE LIFE OF THE KNOCKER

Becoming A Person of Relentless Faith

THE MOMENT YOU REALIZE you are not the same person you were when you first started your journey is profound. That realization crystallizes the fact that your old thoughts and beliefs no longer define you. This transformation is so meaningful, going back isn't an option. You've arrived at a new place, and there is genuinely no turning back now.

If you've come this far and started asking, seeking, and knocking, you're nearing a turning point. You're not the same person who started this book. You're becoming a knocker, and this new way of living changes your prayers and your whole life.

This last chapter isn't about another technique. It's about bringing everything together and letting it shape your whole life, not just your prayers. Asking, seeking, and knocking aren't just for hard times; they're meant to be a way of living, a mindset for any situation.

To become a knocker, it's important to see why breakthrough living is so powerful. Living this way helps you face challenges with purpose and turn them into chances to grow. Let me show you what it looks like to be a knocker. It's not just a good idea that's hard to follow; it's a practical way of life anyone can choose. The real difference between people who see breakthroughs and those who stay frustrated isn't talent or luck. It's that some choose to live as knockers, while others only ask now and then.

Being a knocker means learning from Jesus and making asking, seeking, and knocking a regular part of your life. It's not about doing rituals only when things are hard. It's about building a steady connection with God and letting Him guide you. As you follow Jesus, you're not just looking for quick answers. You pay attention to where God leads and stay open to new opportunities. Even when doors seem closed, your faith helps you keep going, trusting that every challenge brings a lesson and a chance to grow.

Living this way takes time. You won't develop relentless faith just by reading a book. But you can start making choices today that move you forward. Over time, these choices and habits will shape you. Years from now, you'll see that you live with breakthrough faith every day, not just sometimes.

Here's what a typical day looks like for a knocker. They wake up knowing each day is a gift and that what they do matters. Before getting out of bed, they talk with God; not to seem extra spiritual, but because it feels natural. As they sit up and feel the cool floor beneath them, they whisper a simple prayer of thanks for the new day. They pause to breathe deeply, asking for wisdom and seeking God's presence for whatever comes next.

Their morning prayer is simple, not long or complicated. Sometimes it's just a few minutes connecting with God, admitting they need Him, and preparing to notice Him during the day. They ask before knowing what they'll need, seek before knowing what to look for, and keep a spirit of faith in all they do.

During the day, a knocker sees challenges as hidden opportunities rather than setbacks. When problems come up, they look for how God might use them for something greater. Instead of panicking, they see needs as chances to grow, ask God for guidance, and look for ways to move forward. If a door seems closed, they see it as a chance to build resilience. They keep knocking with calm confidence, knowing each obstacle brings them closer to an opening.

Knockers still feel discouraged or overwhelmed at times; they're human. But these feelings don't stop them, because they know feelings pass, but God's faithfulness remains. They've seen enough answers and breakthroughs to know that if they keep knocking, doors will open, and if they keep asking and seeking, God will respond.

A knocker sees relationships in a unique way. Instead of just hoping for reconciliation when things go wrong, they take action. They look for ways to heal, ask God for help in restoring what's broken, and seek wisdom to bridge gaps. They don't wait for someone else to start the process; they step up first. Even when conversations are tough or the process is hard, they keep going. Knockers don't believe relationships have to end, especially when God is able to bring new life.

At work, knockers stand out for their energy and initiative. They don't just wait for things to happen; they look for opportunities, ask for guidance, and pursue advancement while doing their current job well. Their job isn't just about earning money. It's a place where God can show His faithfulness, and success in one area can lead to more breakthroughs. They do their work well, not to earn God's approval, but because they want to reflect God's excellence.

When it comes to money, knockers take a different approach. They don't just hope their needs will be met; they look for wisdom in managing what they have, ask God for guidance, and look for new opportunities. They give generously out of faith, believing God will provide. They don't hold back out of fear or spend carelessly. Instead, they work with God to manage their resources well, aiming to honor Him and help His kingdom grow. Simply put, knockers are sowers; they sow.

Knockers are intentional about growing spiritually. They don't wait until they feel like praying, reading Scripture, or worshiping. They stick to these habits because they know steady effort brings real results. They ask God to show Himself more, look for truth that changes them, and seek a deeper relationship with God, even when it means being open and honest. They aren't content with just the basics; they want all that God offers and are willing to go after it with determination.

You might be thinking this all sounds tiring. With so much focus and effort, isn't it easy to burn out? Isn't rest important too? These are good questions, and I want to answer them honestly. I don't want you to feel weighed down by new expectations or think this way of living is out of reach.

But it's important to see what you lose by staying passive. If you just coast and avoid putting in the effort, you might miss out on breakthroughs, growth, and a closer relationship with God. When you settle for passivity, you miss the changes that only come from real effort. The biggest risk is missing out on growth and blessings that could have been yours if you had acted. Realizing what you could lose can motivate you to live with more purpose and commitment.

Living as a knocker is different because it comes from a real relationship with God, not just a sense of duty. It's fueled by hope, not fear, and it's supported by God's presence, not just your own effort. When this identity is genuine, you find rest, peace, and joy that lasts for years, not just for a short time.

Think of it like this: when you're close to someone you love, being with them gives you energy instead of draining you. Talking with them is enjoyable, not a chore. Wanting a deeper connection doesn't feel like work; it feels natural. That's what living as a knocker is like when it's based on a real relationship with God. Asking, seeking, and knocking become ways to show how much you value that relationship.

That's why it's so important to understand God's heart, as we talked about before. If you think God is reluctant to help, then being persistent will feel tiring and like hard work. But if you see God as a loving Father who wants to give good things, then persistence feels like working together with someone who wants your success even more than you do. The real difference is in how you see God, not just in what you do.

How do you build a life of relentless faith without burning out? How do you keep going as a knocker for years, not just a few intense months? I want to share some principles that have helped me and many others. My aim isn't just to inspire you, but to give you practical wisdom you can use for the long haul.

The first principle is to build rhythms, not strict routines. Routines can be rigid, tiring, and hard to keep up. They demand perfection and make you feel guilty if you slip. Rhythms, on the other hand, are flexible and life-giving. They become natural habits over time, rather than forced tasks that require constant effort. A knocker doesn't force themselves through a strict prayer schedule out of guilt. Instead, they have a morning rhythm with God that feels as natural as brushing their teeth. Once these rhythms are set, they keep going on their own.

So what does this look like in real life? Start small and build up slowly. If you only pray for two minutes a week now, don't try to jump to two hours a day. That's a recipe for frustration. Instead, try five minutes of focused prayer each morning for thirty days. Just five minutes. Let that become your new habit. After a month, if it feels natural, add another five minutes. Build in a way that fits into your life, not one that turns everything upside down. Over time, these small habits add up to a lifestyle of prayer that feels natural, not forced.

The second principle is to celebrate progress, not perfection. Knockers aren't perfect. There are days when they don't pray, feel discouraged, or want to give up. But they don't let those days stop them. Instead of beating themselves up for not being perfect, they focus on how far they've come. They get back up after setbacks and keep knocking, knowing that being consistent over time is more important than being perfect right now.

This is important because all-or-nothing thinking can hold you back. You might hear thoughts like, 'If you can't do it perfectly, don't bother,' or 'If you failed yesterday, why try today?' Knockers don't listen to those lies. They know that trying, even imperfectly, is better than doing nothing. They celebrate showing up, even on hard days, and keep going even when their faith feels weak.

The third principle is to remember your reason. When things get hard, and you want to quit, think about why you started. What are you hoping for? Why does it matter? What could happen if you keep going? Who are you becoming as you stick with it? Try writing one clear sentence that sums up your purpose, like 'I persist because…'. This simple statement can help you refocus when you feel unmotivated. Your reason is what keeps you moving forward when willpower fades.

That's why sharing your story matters. Every time you experience a breakthrough, write it down. Note what you asked for, how long you waited, what you learned, and how it felt when things finally changed. These stories remind you why you keep going, especially when the next breakthrough takes longer than you hoped. Looking back helps you remember that God is faithful and that persistence works. Your past experiences with God give you strength when things get tough.

The fourth principle is to find others who live as knockers. It's hard to keep this up alone. You need a community of people who understand the journey, who can encourage you when you want to quit, and who will celebrate with you when things finally happen. The people around you shape your ability to keep going. Faith is contagious, but so is giving up. If you spend time with people who have stopped trying, their attitude can rub off on you. But if you're with people who keep asking, seeking, and knocking, their faith will help strengthen yours.

That's why our ministry is focused on building community for knockers. We bring together people who are seeking breakthroughs, who won't settle, and who keep asking, seeking, and knocking no matter what. In this kind of group, faith stays strong, hope stays bright, and persistence is possible. You're not alone. You have others who understand, who can encourage you when your faith is low, and who remind you that the door will open even when you feel like giving up.

Look for this kind of community, or start one if you can't find it. Invite a few people who want more than passive faith to meet regularly. Share what you're praying for, what you're seeking, and what you're knocking on. Pray together, celebrate wins, and encourage each other when things are tough. Help each other keep going, even when quitting seems easier. This kind of group will help you stay a knocker, even when it feels impossible to do it alone. To take a small step toward building this community, text one friend today who might be interested in joining you on this journey. A simple message can be the start of something meaningful.

The fifth principle is to pass it on. One of the best ways to keep living as a knocker is to help others do the same. When you teach someone else how to ask, seek, and knock, you strengthen those habits in yourself. Sharing your story with someone who's still waiting reminds you of God's faithfulness. Encouraging others to keep going also helps you stay committed. Passing it on multiplies your impact and deepens your own commitment. A simple way to do this is to give someone a copy of this book.

That's why I wrote this book. It's not just about my own breakthrough, though that's important. I want to help raise up a generation of believers who don't accept closed doors as the end, who make asking, seeking, and knocking a way of life, and who show that God still answers persistent faith. Every person who becomes a knocker multiplies what God has taught me. And when knockers help others become knockers, whole communities can be changed by people who refuse to live passively.

As you start living as a knocker, look for chances to help others do the same. If you see someone stuck, teach them to ask clearly. If you meet someone who prays without much hope, show them how to seek. If you find someone ready to give up, encourage them to keep knocking. Your breakthrough is not just for you; it should help others. Sharing this with others strengthens your own identity as a knocker and helps grow God's kingdom through changed lives.

Now let me address something that's probably been on your mind during this chapter. What about seasons when you're not actively pursuing a specific breakthrough? What about times when life feels relatively stable, when there aren't any urgent needs or closed doors demanding attention? Does the life of a knocker apply then, or is this identity only relevant when you're in crisis mode?

This is a key question. If you only ask, seek, and knock when you're desperate, you won't build the lasting lifestyle I'm talking about. You'll swing between chasing after God when problems come up and coasting when life is easy. That pattern doesn't build the spiritual strength of a true knocker. Let me show you how this identity grows strongest during stable times.

When you're not chasing a big breakthrough, you're actually getting ready for the next time you'll need one. You're building habits of prayer, reading Scripture, worship, and faith that will help you in tough times. You're growing closer to God, so that asking, seeking, and knocking become natural when needs arise. You're collecting stories of God's faithfulness that will encourage you later. You're learning to walk with God every day, not just in emergencies.

Think of it like physical training. Athletes don't wait until game day to start working out. They train consistently when there's no game scheduled so that when game day comes, their bodies are prepared for the demands. The same principle applies spiritually. Knockers maintain their identity even in stable seasons so that when storms come, when doors close, when needs arise, they're already positioned to engage with faith rather than having to scramble to find faith in the middle of a crisis.

In stable times, you ask God for wisdom to manage what you already have, not just for things you lack. You seek to grow in character and get closer to God, not just to solve problems. You knock on doors for deeper spiritual growth and greater impact, not just for quick fixes. Your approach stays the same, but your focus shifts from urgent needs to long-term growth.

Here's the great part: when you keep living as a knocker during calm times, you often avoid problems that would come from living passively. You ask for wisdom that helps you make good choices. You seek knowledge that opens doors others miss. You keep habits that protect your health, relationships, finances, and spiritual life. By living this way, you prevent doors from closing in the first place.

This is the compound effect of living as a knocker over years and decades. Early on, you're mostly responding to problems, knocking on doors that circumstances forced you to approach. But over time, as the lifestyle becomes embedded, you're increasingly preventing problems before they arise and creating opportunities before you need them. You're living from a place of faithful proactivity rather than desperate reactivity. And that shift transforms everything about your life experience and your testimony.

Let me show you what this has looked like in my own journey. When our ministry first launched, I was constantly in reactive mode. Problems arose, and I was knocking on doors for solutions. Needs surfaced, and I was seeking provision. Challenges emerged, and I was asking for wisdom. I was living as a knocker, but mostly in response to circumstances that demanded it. And that's fine. That's where everyone starts. Crisis creates the urgency that teaches you to engage the trilogy.

Now, after years on this journey, I'm more proactive. I ask for wisdom before problems show up. I look for opportunities before I need them. I knock on doors for greater impact because I want to grow, not just survive. Being a knocker is now part of who I am, whether life is hard or easy. This change has transformed not just my prayers, but how I live, lead, and handle everything God has given me.

That's what I want for you; not just one breakthrough, but a life full of them because you refuse to see closed doors as the end. Not just a win in your current struggle, but a lifestyle of faith that helps you through every season and challenge. Not just one answered prayer, but a close relationship with God where answered prayers come naturally.

That's the life of a knocker. And it's available to you right now if you decide to embrace this identity. Not perfectly. Not instantly. But progressively, consistently, over time, through rhythms that become natural and a community that sustains you and grace that empowers what willpower alone could never accomplish.

As we finish this chapter and book, it's time to set your life on a new path with a declaration. Choose to be a knocker starting today. This identity isn't something you become eventually; it's who you decide to be now. Who you believe you are shapes what you do. Let your belief as a knocker drive your actions, defining you over time.

Stand up wherever you are right now. I mean it. Actually, stand up. Let this be a physical act that marks a spiritual decision. And speak these words out loud, not just in your head, because there's power in spoken declaration that silent agreement doesn't carry:

> *"I am a knocker. I refuse to accept closed doors as permanent. I will ask God with specificity and faith for everything I need. I will diligently seek and, with wisdom, position myself where breakthroughs can reach me. I will knock with persistent faith, refusing to walk away until the door opens. I will not be discouraged by delay. I will not be defeated by difficulty. I will not give up when others quit. Because I know who's on the other side of the door I'm knocking on, and I trust His heart toward me. I will live this way, not just until I get breakthroughs, but for the rest of my life. I am a knocker. This is my identity. This is who I am."*

Now sit back down. Take a breath. And let the weight of what you just declared settle into your spirit. You didn't just make a wish or express a hope. You established an identity. You drew a line in your spiritual development and said, "This is who I'm becoming." And that declaration, reinforced by daily choices and sustained by God's grace, will transform you over the coming months and years into someone who lives with relentless faith.

But just saying it isn't enough. You need to act on it. Here are your final steps: practical things you can do right now to start living as a knocker.

First, return to the door you left behind. You know the one; the prayer you stopped praying, the dream you let go, or the breakthrough you thought would never happen. Start knocking again, not because your situation is different, but because you are. You're a knocker now, and knockers don't quit just because the door hasn't opened yet. As you go back to this door, let yourself feel new hope and face the challenge with fresh determination.

Second, write down your vision for the next three years as a knocker. Where will you be if you keep living this way? What doors will open? What breakthroughs will you see? What will your story and your relationship with God look like? Write it in the present tense, as if it's already happening. This vision will help you stay focused, even when things get tough. Knowing where you're headed brings peace and clarity.

Third, find your core knocking community. Who are the two or three people you'll walk this journey with? Choose people who will pray with you, celebrate your wins, and encourage you when you feel like quitting. Invite them to join you in this commitment. Meet regularly, share your goals, and help each other keep knocking. This community will help you stick with this lifestyle for the long run. Enjoy the support and friendship that come from sharing dreams and encouraging each other.

Fourth, set up your daily rhythms starting tomorrow. Don't make them complicated or overwhelming. Choose simple, steady habits that help you ask, seek, and knock each day. Spend five minutes in morning prayer, asking for what you need and thanking God. Read Scripture for ten minutes to find wisdom and truth. In the evening, reflect on your progress and renew your commitment to faith. These small habits will become the foundation of your life as a knocker. Let these rhythms help you feel steady and strong in your faith.

Finally, decide to share this message with someone in the next ninety days. Find one person who needs to hear it and tell them your story. Give them this book or buy them a copy. Show them how to ask, seek, and knock. Share your experience on social media. Helping someone else become a knocker will grow God's kingdom and strengthen your own faith. You'll feel fulfilled knowing you're making a real difference and helping others on their journey.

As we close, I want you to know something. The journey you're beginning right now, the decision to live as a knocker, is going to cost you. It will require more faith than you currently have, which is why you'll have to trust God to provide the faith you need as you transform. It will demand more persistence than feels comfortable, which is why you'll need community to sustain you when your own resolve weakens. It will stretch you in ways that ordinary Christianity never would, which is exactly why it produces breakthroughs that ordinary Christianity never sees.

But it's worth it; truly worth it. Living a life where prayers are answered, doors open, and you see God's faithfulness again and again is better than just surviving.

When you learn to ask, seek, and knock, you get to experience all that God has for you. Every hard moment, every wait, and every door you knocked on is worth it. You're not going to accept closed doors as permanent. You're not going to settle for the spiritual mediocrity that characterizes so much of modern Christianity. Because you're a knocker now. And knockers refuse to quit. Knockers keep asking until they receive. Knockers keep seeking until they find. Knockers keep knocking until the door opens.

The door you've been approaching throughout this entire book, the one you could hear movement behind but couldn't get to open, is about to swing wide. Not because you finally figured out the secret formula, but because you've become someone who refuses to walk away. Not because God suddenly decided to bless you, but because you've positioned yourself through persistent pursuit to receive what He's been wanting to give all along. Not because you earned it through your effort, but because grace responds to faith that refuses to quit.

So keep knocking. Your persistence is making a difference, even now. God is pleased to see you trust Him enough to keep going, and the angels are cheering you on because they know what's coming when the door finally opens.

And the door will open. Jesus promised: everyone who asks receives, everyone who seeks finds, and everyone who knocks has the doors opened to them. You've asked, sought, and knocked. Now you're living as someone who will keep doing all three until the promise comes true in your life.

The door is opening. Can you sense it? The lock is turning, the hinges are moving. Everything you've been hoping for is about to become real; not far off, but soon, closer than you think. You're still here because you're a knocker, and knockers are there when the door finally opens.

Welcome to a life of relentless faith. Welcome to breakthrough as your new way of living. Welcome to walking with a God who loves to give good gifts to His children who keep asking, seeking, and knocking.

The door is opening. Step through it. Everything is about to change.

Remember, once you know how to knock, you never have to stay stuck again. There will be more doors, more seasons, and more breakthroughs ahead. But you'll face each one as a knocker; someone who doesn't see closed doors as the end, who knows that persistent faith brings breakthrough, and who has learned to access all God has for you by asking, seeking, and knocking.

This is your life now. Live it with confidence and joy. Live it with relentless faith that never gives up. The best isn't behind you; it's ahead, and you're about to step into it.

Now, go knock.

APPENDIX A

Thirty-One Days of Knocking

This 31-day devotional is designed to be used after you complete reading the book, though you can also use it as a standalone daily guide for developing the lifestyle of a knocker. Each day includes Scripture, a reflection that builds on the book's content, and a prayer that models how to talk to God about that day's theme.

Use the Notes section at the back of this book to journal your thoughts, document answers to prayer, and track breakthrough as you work through these 31 days. Many readers cycle through this devotional multiple times, each time focusing on different breakthroughs they're pursuing.

Days 1-7: Foundation and Asking

Day 1: The Trilogy Begins

Scripture: Matthew 7:7-8
Ask, and it will be given to you; seek, and you will find; knock, and it will be opened to you. For everyone who asks receives, and the one who seeks finds, and to the one who knocks it will be opened.

Reflection:
This isn't just a verse about prayer. It's a roadmap for breakthrough. Notice the progression: ask, seek, knock. Three distinct actions, each building on the previous. Most of us stop at asking and wonder why the door never opens. We pray once, maybe twice, then settle into resignation when nothing changes. But Jesus gave us three dimensions for a reason. Asking is where faith begins, but it's not where faith stops. Today, as you start this devotional journey, recognize that breakthrough requires all three levels. You can't skip from asking to open doors. There's work in between. There's seeking that puts feet on your faith. There's knocking that refuses to quit until you see results. The promise is absolute: everyone who goes through the full progression sees the door open. Not some. Not the spiritually elite. Everyone. That includes you.

Prayer:
Father, teach me to pray with the tenacity You intended. Show me how to move beyond words into action, beyond asking into seeking and knocking. I don't want to quit one level before my breakthrough. Give me faith to believe that Your promise applies to me, that I really am part of "everyone" who receives, finds, and sees doors open. Today I choose to start the journey. In Jesus's name, amen.

Day 2: The Death of Self-Sufficiency

Scripture: James 4:2
You do not have, because you do not ask.

Reflection:
The first barrier to breakthrough is pride disguised as self-sufficiency. We don't ask because we believe we should be able to handle it ourselves. We don't want to admit need, don't want to look weak, don't want to burden God with problems

we think we should solve alone. But here's the truth: God gave you needs you can't meet on your own specifically so you'd learn to ask. Your insufficiency isn't failure. It's the design. Every closed door, every unmet need, every impossible situation is an invitation to acknowledge that you need Him. Until you can say "I can't do this without You," you'll never experience breakthrough. Asking isn't just about getting what you need. It's about killing the lie that you don't need God in the first place. What do you need that you've been too proud to ask for? Ask for it today.

Prayer:
God, I confess my pride. I've tried to handle things on my own that were always meant to drive me to You. Forgive me for treating prayer as a last resort instead of a first response. I need You. Not just for this specific breakthrough, but for everything. Teach me to ask without shame and bring my needs to You without apology. I choose dependence over self-sufficiency. Amen.

Day 3: Asking in Jesus's Name

Scripture: John 14:13-14
Whatever you ask in my name, this I will do, that the Father may be glorified in the Son. If you ask me anything in my name, I will do it.

Reflection:
Asking in Jesus's name isn't a magic formula you tack onto the end of a prayer. It means asking according to His character, His will, His authority. When you pray in Jesus's name, you're saying, "I'm asking for this because Jesus would ask for it. I'm pursuing this because it aligns with who He is and what He wants." That changes everything about how you pray. You can't ask for things that contradict His nature and expect Him to answer. But when your request aligns with His heart, when you're asking for breakthrough He wants you to have, you pray with absolute confidence that the answer is coming. Today, examine what you're asking for. Is it something Jesus would pursue? Does it align with His character? If yes, then ask boldly. The authority of His name backs your prayer.

Prayer:
Jesus, I come in Your name, not my own. I'm asking for breakthrough because I believe it aligns with who You are and what You want for my life. Search my heart. If what I'm pursuing contradicts Your character, redirect me. But if this request honors You, if it's something You would pray for me, then I'm asking

with confidence that You hear me and will answer. Let Your name carry weight in my prayer. Amen.

Day 4: Specificity in Asking

Scripture: Mark 10:51
And Jesus said to him, "What do you want me to do for you?" And the blind man said to him, "Rabbi, let me recover my sight."

Reflection:
Jesus knew Bartimaeus was blind. Everyone knew. But He still asked, "What do you want Me to do for you?" Because God wants you to articulate your need. Vague prayers get vague results. "Bless me" doesn't carry the same weight as "open this specific door." "Help my finances" doesn't move heaven the way "provide the $3,000 I need by Friday" does. Specificity forces you to identify exactly what breakthrough looks like. It makes the answer undeniable when it comes. Today, write down three specific requests. Not general blessings, but concrete breakthroughs you need God to provide. Name them. Date them. These become the doors you'll learn to knock on as you move through this devotional.

Prayer:
God, I'm done praying vague prayers and wondering why nothing changes. Today I'm getting specific. Here are three breakthroughs I'm asking You for: [name them]. I'm writing them down. I'm dating this prayer. And I'm believing that when these doors open, I'll know it was You. Make my faith specific so my testimony can be specific. In Jesus's name, amen.

Day 5: Asking with Expectation

Scripture: Mark 11:24
Therefore I tell you, whatever you ask in prayer, believe that you have received it, and it will be yours.

Reflection:
There's a difference between hoping God will answer and expecting Him to. Hope is passive. Expectation is active. When you ask with expectation, you pray like someone who believes the door will open, not someone who's bracing for

disappointment. You make room for the answer. You prepare for breakthrough. You live like it's already on its way even though you can't see it yet. This isn't presumption. It's faith. And without faith, it's impossible to please God. Today, examine how you've been praying. Are you asking with expectation or just going through the motions? Do you really believe God will answer, or are you hedging your bets in case He doesn't? Breakthrough requires you to believe that you have received it before you see it. That's not easy, but it's essential.

Prayer:
Father, I confess that I've asked without really expecting You to answer. I've prayed like someone hoping for a miracle instead of someone confident in Your promises. Forgive my unbelief. Today I choose to ask with expectation. I believe the breakthrough I'm pursuing is already on its way. I'm preparing for it. I'm making room for it. I trust that what I've asked for in faith, You will provide. Increase my expectation. Amen.

Day 6: Consistency in Asking

Scripture: Luke 18:1
And he told them a parable to the effect that they ought always to pray and not lose heart.

Reflection:
Jesus told the parable of the persistent widow specifically to teach us that we ought always to pray and not give up. Always. Not once, not occasionally, not when we feel like it. Always. Because consistency in prayer isn't about wearing God down until He finally relents. It's about aligning your heart with His promises until faith becomes stronger than circumstances. Every time you pray the same request, you're choosing to believe God's Word over what you see. You're building spiritual muscle that will carry you through the wilderness between prayer and breakthrough. Today, commit to consistent prayer for the three specific breakthroughs you identified two days ago. Not just today, but every day until the door opens. Consistency is what separates those who receive from those who quit one prayer away from their miracle.

Prayer:
God, I commit to consistent prayer. I won't pray once and walk away. I won't give up when the answer doesn't come immediately. Every day, I'm bringing these three requests to You. Every day, I'm choosing to believe Your promises over my

circumstances. Give me the discipline to keep asking when I don't feel like it, when nothing seems to be moving, when I'm tempted to quit. I will not lose heart. In Jesus's name, amen.

Day 7: Surrender in Asking

Scripture: Luke 22:42
Father, if you are willing, remove this cup from me. Nevertheless, not my will, but yours, be done.

Reflection:
There's a tension in asking that most believers never navigate well. You have to ask specifically, with expectation, with consistency, but also with surrender. You pursue breakthrough with everything in you, but you hold it loosely enough that if God has something better, you won't miss it by clinging to what you thought you needed. Jesus modeled this in Gethsemane. He asked for the cup to be removed. Specific request. Honest desire. But He ended with surrender: not my will, but Yours. That's the balance. You don't pray with passive resignation, accepting whatever happens as God's will without fighting for breakthrough. But you also don't pray with such rigid demands that you can't receive what God wants to give instead. Today, examine whether you're truly surrendered. Are you asking for breakthrough or demanding it? There's a difference, and it matters.

Prayer:
Father, I bring You my specific requests with expectation and consistency. I'm asking for breakthrough, and I believe You hear me. But I also surrender the outcome to You. If You have something better than what I'm asking for, I don't want to miss it by clinging to my own plan. Not my will, but Yours. I trust that what You give will always be better than what I demanded. Teach me to hold my requests with open hands. In Jesus's name, amen.

Days 8-14: Seeking and Positioning

Day 8: Faith Gets Feet

Scripture: James 2:17
So also faith by itself, if it does not have works, is dead.

Reflection:
You've been asking for seven days. Now it's time to seek. Asking is about what you say to God. Seeking is about what you do in response to what you've asked for. Faith without works is dead, not because works save you but because real faith always produces action. If you're asking God to open a door but doing nothing to position yourself for that opportunity, your faith might be dead. Seeking means you press toward the breakthrough while you pray for it. You pursue wisdom about how to move forward. You look for opportunities that align with what you've asked for. You reposition yourself physically, relationally, and spiritually to be ready when the door opens. The woman with the issue of blood didn't just pray for healing. She pressed through the crowd to touch Jesus's garment. Today, what action does your faith require? What do you need to do while you wait for God to move?

Prayer:
God, I don't want dead faith. I want faith that moves, that acts, that presses toward breakthrough while I pray for it. Show me what actions You're requiring. What do I need to do while I wait for You to answer? Where do I need to reposition myself? Give me wisdom to seek while I ask, to move while I believe. Make my faith active. In Jesus's name, amen.

Day 9: Seeking Wisdom

Scripture: James 1:5
If any of you lacks wisdom, let him ask God, who gives generously to all without reproach, and it will be given him.

Reflection:
The first dimension of seeking is wisdom. You need divine insight about how to navigate toward breakthrough. What's the next step? Which door should you approach? Who do you need to talk to? What needs to change? These aren't questions you can answer through human reasoning alone. You need God's perspective. The good news is that God gives wisdom generously to all who ask. He doesn't withhold it. He doesn't make you beg. He doesn't shame you for needing it. You lack wisdom. Ask for it. Expect Him to provide it. And when it comes, often through Scripture, through counsel, through sudden clarity about

your next move, act on it immediately. Today, specifically ask God for wisdom about the breakthrough you're pursuing. Then pay attention to how He answers.

Prayer:
Father, I need wisdom I don't have. I don't know how to navigate toward this breakthrough. I don't know what my next step should be. But You do, and You've promised to give wisdom generously to all who ask. So I'm asking. Show me what I can't see. Give me insight I couldn't access on my own. Make the path clear. And when You speak, give me courage to act on what You reveal. In Jesus's name, amen.

Day 10: Seeking Opportunity

Scripture: Colossians 4:3
Pray also for us, that God may open to us a door for the word.

Reflection:
Seeking wisdom tells you how to move. Seeking opportunity tells you where to move. Opportunities are the doors God opens in response to your asking. But you have to look for them. You have to recognize them when they appear. And you have to walk through them even when they don't look like what you expected. The woman with the issue of blood sought opportunity. She heard Jesus was passing through, and she pressed through the crowd to reach Him. That was her moment. She didn't wait for a more convenient time or a more comfortable setting. She seized the opportunity when it appeared. Today, ask God to open doors for the breakthrough you're pursuing. Then pay attention. Watch for unexpected invitations, sudden connections, circumstances that align in ways they shouldn't. When opportunity appears, move quickly.

Prayer:
God, open doors for me. Create opportunities I couldn't create on my own. Bring the right people across my path. Align circumstances in my favor. And when opportunities appear, help me recognize them quickly and move through them boldly. I don't want to miss my moment because I was looking for something different. Make me alert to what You're doing. In Jesus's name, amen.

Day 11: Seeking Alignment

Scripture: Psalm 37:4
Delight yourself in the Lord, and he will give you the desires of your heart.

Reflection:
The third dimension of seeking is alignment. Your heart has to match God's heart. Your desires have to sync with His desires. When they do, breakthrough comes naturally because you're pursuing what He already wants to give. But when they don't, when you're chasing something that contradicts His will or His timing, you'll exhaust yourself seeking doors that were never meant to open. This is why the Psalmist says to delight yourself in the Lord first. When your greatest pleasure is knowing Him, when you're more concerned with His glory than your comfort, the desires of your heart start to shift. They align with His. And suddenly what you're asking for and what He wants to give are the same thing. Today, examine whether your pursuit is aligned with God's heart. Are you seeking breakthrough He wants you to have, or are you demanding something that serves your agenda?

Prayer:
Father, I want my heart to match Yours. I don't want to waste energy pursuing breakthrough You never intended for me. Search my desires. Align them with Yours. If what I'm seeking doesn't serve Your purposes, redirect me. But if this breakthrough honors You, if it's something You want me to have, then confirm it. Let my delight in You shape what I desire. In Jesus's name, amen.

Day 12: Physical Geography

Scripture: Ruth 2:3
So she set out and went and gleaned in the field after the reapers, and she happened to come to the part of the field belonging to Boaz.

Reflection:
Sometimes breakthrough requires you to physically move to a different location. Ruth didn't sit in Moab praying for provision. She moved to Bethlehem and positioned herself in Boaz's field. That physical repositioning put her in the path of breakthrough. Your closed door might open somewhere else. Maybe you need to move to a different city, join a different church, work in a different field. Maybe the breakthrough you're praying for is waiting in a location you haven't considered yet. Today, ask God if physical geography is part of your seeking. Do

you need to go somewhere? Is there a place you're avoiding that He's calling you toward? Don't assume your breakthrough has to happen where you are. Sometimes the door opens when you move.

Prayer:
God, show me if I need to move. Is there a physical location where my breakthrough is waiting? Am I staying somewhere out of comfort when You're calling me elsewhere? Give me courage to go where You send me, even if it's unfamiliar, even if it's uncomfortable. I don't want to miss breakthrough because I refused to reposition myself. In Jesus's name, amen.

Day 13: Relational Geography

Scripture: Proverbs 13:20
Whoever walks with the wise becomes wise, but the companion of fools will suffer harm.

Reflection:
Breakthrough often comes through relationships. Who you're connected to determines which doors you can access. Ruth's breakthrough came because she was in Boaz's field, yes, but also because she built relationship with him. The man at Bethesda was healed when Jesus entered his relational space. Some doors will only open through people God places in your path. Others stay closed because you're surrounded by people who don't believe breakthrough is possible. Today, examine your relational geography. Who are you walking with? Are they knockers or quitters? Do they strengthen your faith or drain it? Are there relationships you need to pursue? Connections you need to make? Toxic relationships you need to leave? God may be repositioning you relationally to get you where breakthrough is waiting.

Prayer:
Father, show me if my relationships are helping or hindering my breakthrough. Are there people You want me connected to that I've been avoiding? Are there relationships draining my faith that I need to release? Give me wisdom to know the difference. Surround me with knockers who will strengthen my faith and refuse to let me quit. Position me relationally for breakthrough. In Jesus's name, amen.

Day 14: Spiritual Geography

Scripture: Hebrews 4:16
Let us then with confidence draw near to the throne of grace, that we may receive mercy and find grace to help in time of need.

Reflection:
Physical and relational geography matter, but spiritual geography matters most. Where are you positioning yourself spiritually? Are you drawing near to God or drifting away? Are you in His Word daily or only when crisis hits? Are you worshiping in the middle of the wait or complaining? Your spiritual posture determines what you can access. The throne of grace is available, but you have to approach it with confidence. You have to position yourself there consistently. The woman with the issue of blood repositioned herself physically to get to Jesus, but her spiritual posture, her faith that if she just touched His garment she'd be healed, that's what released breakthrough. Today, examine your spiritual geography. Are you positioned where breakthrough can reach you? Or have you drifted from the throne of grace while you waited for answers?

Prayer:
God, I come boldly to Your throne of grace. I'm positioning myself spiritually in Your presence. I refuse to drift from You while I wait for breakthrough. Keep me close. Keep me in Your Word. Keep me worshiping even when the door stays closed. My spiritual posture matters, and I choose to stay near You. In Jesus's name, amen.

Days 15-21: Knocking and Persistence

Day 15: The Crisis of Proximity

Scripture: Matthew 15:23
But he did not answer her a word.

Reflection:
The Canaanite woman was close enough to speak to Jesus, but He didn't answer. That's the crisis of proximity. You're at the door. You've asked. You've sought. You've repositioned yourself for breakthrough. But the door is still closed. This is where most believers quit. They assume silence means no. They interpret the

closed door as rejection. But Jesus wasn't rejecting the Canaanite woman. He was testing her tenacity. And when she kept knocking, when she refused to let silence stop her pursuit, the door opened. You're closer than you think. The fact that you're at the door means asking worked. Seeking positioned you. Now you have to knock until it opens. Today, if you're in the crisis of proximity, if you're at the door but it's still closed, don't walk away. This is where breakthrough happens. This is where knockers are made.

Prayer:
Father, I'm at the door. I've asked. I've sought. I've positioned myself for breakthrough. But the door is still closed, and the silence is deafening. Help me understand that closed doesn't mean rejected. It means not yet. Give me strength to keep knocking when everything in me wants to quit. I'm closer than I think. I won't walk away now. In Jesus's name, amen.

Day 16: Krouo – The Pounding

Scripture: Luke 11:8
I tell you, though he will not get up and give him anything because he is his friend, yet because of his impudence he will rise and give him whatever he needs.

Reflection:
The Greek word for knock is krouo. It doesn't mean a polite tap. It means to pound, to strike with force, to demand entrance. When Jesus tells the story of the friend at midnight, the man doesn't knock gently and walk away. He pounds on the door until his friend gets up and gives him what he needs. That's shameless audacity. That's the kind of knocking that refuses to be ignored. You've been too polite in your pursuit of breakthrough. You've knocked once or twice and then apologized for bothering God. But He's not bothered by your persistence. He's moved by it. Today, stop knocking politely. Pound. Show God that you're serious about this breakthrough, that you won't walk away until the door opens.

Prayer:
God, I've been too polite. I've knocked gently and walked away when You didn't answer immediately. But You're not looking for polite knockers. You're looking for persistent ones. Today I'm pounding on this door. I'm refusing to be ignored. This isn't disrespect. It's faith that believes You hear me and will answer. Give me shameless audacity to keep knocking until breakthrough comes. In Jesus's name, amen.

Day 17: Knocking as Warfare

Scripture: Daniel 10:12-13
Fear not, Daniel, for from the first day that you set your heart to understand and humbled yourself before your God, your words have been heard, and I have come because of your words. The prince of the kingdom of Persia withstood me twenty-one days.

Reflection:
Daniel prayed, and heaven heard immediately. But the answer was delayed for twenty-one days because of spiritual warfare. Your knocking isn't just about asking God to move. It's about breaking through spiritual resistance that's holding your breakthrough hostage. Every time you knock, you're engaging in warfare. You're declaring that the enemy doesn't get to keep this door closed. You're contending for what belongs to you. The resistance you're feeling, the obstacles that keep appearing, the delay that makes no sense, that's not God withholding. That's the enemy fighting to keep you from breakthrough. Today, recognize that knocking is warfare. And warriors don't quit because the battle is hard. They press through until victory comes.

Prayer:
Father, I recognize that this delay isn't just about Your timing. There's spiritual warfare happening that I can't see. But I'm not backing down. Every time I knock, I'm declaring that the enemy doesn't get to keep this door closed. I'm contending for breakthrough in Jesus's name. Give me strength to fight. Give me tenacity to keep knocking until every spiritual obstacle is removed and the door opens. I refuse to surrender what belongs to me. Amen.

Day 18: Don't Stop at Two

Scripture: 1 Kings 18:43
Go up now, look toward the sea." And he went up and looked and said, "There is nothing." And he said, "Go again," seven times.

Reflection:
Elijah sent his servant to look for the cloud seven times. Not once. Not twice. Seven times. Imagine if the servant had given up after the sixth time and reported

back, "There's nothing coming." He would have quit one look before breakthrough arrived. That's what happens when you stop knocking too soon. You ask once, seek a little, knock twice, then walk away convinced God isn't going to answer. But the breakthrough was coming. You just quit before it arrived. Today, commit to not stopping at two. If you've knocked twice and nothing happened, knock a third time. A fourth. A seventh. However many times it takes. The door will open, but only if you're still knocking when it does.

Prayer:
God, I confess I've given up too soon. I've knocked a few times and walked away when I didn't see immediate results. But breakthrough was coming. I just didn't stay long enough to see it. Today I commit to persistent knocking. I won't stop at two. I won't quit after a few attempts. I'll keep knocking until the door opens, no matter how long it takes. Give me endurance to stay at this door. In Jesus's name, amen.

Day 19: Shameless Audacity

Scripture: Luke 11:8
I tell you, though he will not get up and give him anything because he is his friend, yet because of his impudence he will rise and give him whatever he needs.

Reflection:
The word translated "impudence" literally means shameless audacity. The friend at midnight wasn't embarrassed to wake his neighbor at an inconvenient hour. He wasn't apologetic about his need. He knocked boldly, persistently, shamelessly, until his friend gave him what he needed. That's how you're supposed to approach God with your breakthrough. Not timid, not apologetic, not afraid you're bothering Him. Bold. Persistent. Shameless. You have every right to knock because Jesus gave you permission. You have every reason to expect an answer because He promised everyone who knocks will see the door open. Today, approach God with shameless audacity. Stop apologizing for your need. Stop feeling guilty for asking again. Knock boldly. The door will open.

Prayer:
Father, forgive me for approaching You timidly, like I'm bothering You with my needs. You told me to knock, and I have every right to do so boldly. Today I come with shameless audacity. I'm not apologizing for asking again. I'm not embarrassed about my need. I'm knocking persistently, confidently, expecting

You to answer because You promised You would. Give me holy boldness to pursue this breakthrough. In Jesus's name, amen.

Day 20: When the Door Stays Closed Longer

Scripture: Hebrews 10:35-36
Therefore do not throw away your confidence, which has a great reward. For you have need of endurance, so that when you have done the will of God you may receive what is promised.

Reflection:
Some doors open quickly. Others require sustained knocking over months or years. When the door stays closed longer than you expected, your confidence starts to waver. You begin to question whether God heard you, whether breakthrough is really coming, whether you should just walk away and accept that this door isn't meant to open. Don't throw away your confidence. You need endurance now. The long wait doesn't mean God forgot you. It means He's developing something in you that can only be built through sustained pursuit. Your faith is being refined. Your character is being shaped. Your testimony is being written. The door will open, but first you need endurance to outlast the wait. Today, choose to maintain confidence even though the door is still closed.

Prayer:
God, the door has been closed longer than I expected, and my confidence is wavering. But I refuse to throw it away. I know You heard me. I know breakthrough is coming. Give me endurance to outlast this wait. Strengthen my faith. Build my character. And when the door finally opens, let my testimony be proof that persistent knocking always produces breakthrough. I'm not quitting. In Jesus's name, amen.

Day 21: The Promise for Knockers

Scripture: Matthew 7:8
For everyone who asks receives, and the one who seeks finds, and to the one who knocks it will be opened.

Reflection:
Everyone. Not some. Not the spiritually elite. Not people with perfect faith or spotless records. Everyone who knocks will see the door open. This is the promise you're standing on. This is why you don't quit when the wait gets long or the resistance gets strong. Because God doesn't lie, and His Word doesn't fail. If you're knocking, the door will open. It's not a question of if but when. Your job isn't to figure out the timing or force the door open through your own strength. Your job is to keep knocking until God opens it. Today, anchor yourself in this promise. Everyone who knocks will see the door open. That includes you. The breakthrough you're pursuing is already decided. Now you just have to outlast the wait.

Prayer:
Father, I'm standing on Your promise. You said everyone who knocks will see the door open. I'm knocking, and I believe You. I don't know when the door will open, but I know it will. I don't know how You'll provide breakthrough, but I know You will. Your Word doesn't fail. I'm anchoring my faith in this promise, and I refuse to let go. The door will open because You said it would. In Jesus's name, amen.

Days 22-28: Wilderness and Waiting

Day 22: Wilderness Isn't Where You Got Lost

Scripture: Deuteronomy 8:2
And you shall remember the whole way that the Lord your God has led you these forty years in the wilderness, that he might humble you, testing you to know what was in your heart.

Reflection:
The Israelites thought the wilderness was punishment. They believed they'd somehow gotten off course, that if they'd done things right they'd already be in the Promised Land. But God led them into the wilderness. It wasn't where they got lost. It was where He was doing something they couldn't see. The same is true for you. The delay you're experiencing, the closed door that won't open, the silence that feels like abandonment, that's not punishment. It's purpose. God is exposing what's in your heart, developing dependency, testing your motives, building endurance, and preparing a testimony you can't have without the wait.

Today, reframe how you see this season. You're not lost. You're exactly where God wants you to be, and He's doing something in the wilderness that couldn't happen anywhere else.

Prayer:
God, I thought this delay meant I did something wrong. I thought the wilderness was punishment. But You led me here. You have purpose in this wait I can't see yet. Show me what You're doing. Expose my heart. Develop my dependency on You. Test my motives. Build endurance I'll need for what's coming. I'm not lost. I'm exactly where You have me. In Jesus's name, amen.

Day 23: Wilderness Exposes the Heart

Scripture: Deuteronomy 8:2
...that he might humble you, testing you to know what was in your heart, whether you would keep his commandments or not.

Reflection:
The wilderness shows you what's really in your heart. When breakthrough delays, when the door stays closed, when God doesn't answer on your timeline, what comes out? Bitterness or worship? Complaint or gratitude? Doubt or faith? The wilderness doesn't create these things. It just exposes what was already there, buried under comfort and convenience. God isn't surprised by what He sees. Today, let the wilderness do its work. When frustration rises, acknowledge it. When doubt surfaces, confess it. When worship feels impossible, do it anyway. What's being exposed isn't meant to condemn you. It's meant to refine you. Let God address what the wilderness reveals so you're ready when the door opens.

Prayer:
Father, the wilderness is showing me things about my heart I didn't want to see. Impatience. Unbelief. Bitterness. Complaint. Forgive me. Refine me. Use this season to address what wouldn't surface any other way. I don't want to enter breakthrough with a heart that isn't ready. Do the deep work now so I'm prepared for what's coming. In Jesus's name, amen.

Day 24: Wilderness Develops Dependency

Scripture: Deuteronomy 8:3
And he humbled you and let you hunger and fed you with manna, which you did not know, nor did your fathers know, that he might make you know that man does not live by bread alone, but man lives by every word that comes from the mouth of the Lord.

Reflection:
God let the Israelites hunger so they'd learn to depend on Him for daily provision. Your closed door serves the same purpose. When you can't make breakthrough happen through your own effort, when every door you try to open yourself stays closed, when you're forced to wait on God's timing instead of forcing your own, you're learning dependency. This is uncomfortable. You want to be self-sufficient, to figure it out, to make it happen. But God is killing that instinct because breakthrough requires you to know that you can't live on your own strength alone. You need Him. Daily. Desperately. Completely. Today, embrace the dependency this wilderness is teaching you. It's not weakness. It's the foundation for everything that comes after.

Prayer:
God, sometimes, I dislike depending on You for things I think I should be able to handle myself. But this wilderness is teaching me that I can't live on my own strength. I need You. Daily. For provision, for wisdom, for breakthrough I can't create. Kill my self-sufficiency. Build dependency that will sustain me long after this door opens. I'm learning to need You, and I'm grateful even though it's hard. In Jesus's name, amen.

Day 25: Wilderness Tests Motives

Scripture: Deuteronomy 8:2
...testing you to know what was in your heart...

Reflection:
Why do you want this breakthrough? The wilderness tests your motives. Are you pursuing this door because it serves God's purposes or your comfort? Because it advances His kingdom or your reputation? Because it's what He wants for you or what you decided you deserve? These questions only get answered in the wait. When breakthrough delays, when pursuit requires more than you expected, your

real motives surface. If you're chasing this for the wrong reasons, the wilderness will expose that. And God, in His mercy, might redirect you to something better. Today, let Him test your motives. If what you're pursuing honors Him, He'll confirm it. If it doesn't, He'll redirect you. Trust that either outcome is better than getting breakthrough for the wrong reasons.

Prayer:
Father, test my motives. Why am I really pursuing this breakthrough? Is it for Your glory or my comfort? Your purposes or my agenda? If I'm chasing this for the wrong reasons, redirect me. I'd rather wait longer and get what You want for me than force open a door I was never meant to walk through. Purify my motives in this wilderness. In Jesus's name, amen.

Day 26: Wilderness Builds Endurance

Scripture: James 1:3-4
For you know that the testing of your faith produces steadfastness. And let steadfastness have its full effect, that you may be perfect and complete, lacking in nothing.

Reflection:
The wilderness builds endurance you can't develop any other way. Quick breakthroughs produce shallow faith. But sustained pursuit through long delay, that produces steadfastness. The kind of faith that doesn't quit when circumstances don't change. The kind of tenacity that keeps knocking when the door stays closed for months. The kind of endurance that will carry you through every future wilderness you'll face. You're not just getting breakthrough. You're becoming someone who can sustain breakthrough. Today, recognize that the wait is building something in you that's worth more than the breakthrough itself. Let endurance have its full effect.

Prayer:
God, I want breakthrough now. But You're building endurance that will serve me for the rest of my life. I see it. The wait is producing steadfastness I didn't have before. Faith that doesn't quit when circumstances don't change. Tenacity that outlasts delay. Let this endurance have its full effect. Make me perfect and complete, lacking in nothing. The breakthrough is coming, but first make me someone who can sustain it. In Jesus's name, amen.

Day 27: Wilderness Prepares Your Testimony

Scripture: 2 Corinthians 1:4
...who comforts us in all our affliction, so that we may be able to comfort those who are in any affliction, with the comfort with which we ourselves are comforted by God.

Reflection:
The wilderness you're walking through right now is writing your future testimony. Someone will stand where you're standing, at a closed door, wondering if they should quit. And your story of sustained pursuit through long delay, of doors that finally opened after months or years of knocking, will give them courage to keep going. Your breakthrough isn't just for you. It's for everyone who will need proof that persistent knocking really works. Today, let that shift how you see this wait. You're not just enduring delay. You're collecting a testimony that will strengthen someone else's faith when they want to quit. The longer the wilderness, the more powerful the testimony.

Prayer:
Father, I see it now. This wilderness is writing a testimony I can't have without the wait. Someone needs to hear that I kept knocking when the door stayed closed for this long, that breakthrough came even when delay felt endless. I'm not just enduring this for me. You're writing a story that will strengthen someone else's faith. Let that give me courage to keep going. In Jesus's name, amen.

Day 28: Survival Strategies for the Wait

Scripture: Lamentations 3:22-23
The steadfast love of the Lord never ceases; his mercies are new every morning; great is your faithfulness.

Reflection:
You need practical strategies to survive the wilderness while you wait for breakthrough. First, celebrate what God is doing even when He hasn't done what you asked yet. His mercies are new every morning, and gratitude keeps your heart soft. Second, maintain spiritual rhythms even when you don't feel like it. Read your Bible. Pray. Worship. These aren't optional when the door stays closed. Third, surround yourself with people who refuse to let you quit. Isolation will destroy your faith. Fourth, document small movements. Write down when resistance increases, when peace comes, when unexpected provision appears. These are signs

the door is about to open. Fifth, remember your why. Why did you start knocking in the first place? That's what will keep you going when everything in you wants to quit.

Prayer:
God, give me wisdom to survive this wilderness well. Help me celebrate what You're doing even though You haven't done what I asked yet. Keep me in Your Word, in prayer, in worship even when I don't feel like it. Surround me with people who won't let me quit. Show me small movements that prove the door is about to open. And when I want to walk away, remind me why I started knocking in the first place. In Jesus's name, amen.

Days 29-31: Breakthrough and Identity

Day 29: Steward Breakthrough Well

Scripture: Luke 16:10
One who is faithful in a very little is also faithful in much, and one who is dishonest in a very little is also dishonest in much.

Reflection:
The door is about to open. Maybe it already has. Now comes the most critical part: stewarding breakthrough well. You can't maintain what you obtained with less than what it took to get it. If persistence opened the door, persistence keeps it open. If prayer brought breakthrough, continued prayer sustains it. If repositioning created opportunity, staying positioned protects it. Many believers fight for breakthrough and then immediately relax, assuming the hard part is over. But sustaining breakthrough requires the same faith that accessed it. Today, commit to stewarding well whatever God gives you. Be faithful in little so He can trust you with much.

Prayer:
Father, I've knocked with persistence for this breakthrough. Now teach me to steward it well. I won't take it for granted. I won't relax the disciplines that brought me here. What You've given me, I'll protect with the same tenacity I used to pursue it. Make me faithful in little so You can trust me with much. In Jesus's name, amen.

Day 30: I Am a Knocker

Scripture: Hebrews 11:6
And without faith it is impossible to please him, for whoever would draw near to God must believe that he exists and that he rewards those who seek him.

Reflection:
You're not someone who tried knocking once. You're a knocker. It's your identity now. Knockers don't quit when doors stay closed. They don't walk away when breakthrough delays. They don't give up one prayer before their miracle. They ask, seek, knock, and keep knocking until the door opens. This isn't just about one breakthrough. It's about a lifestyle of tenacious pursuit. There will always be another door, another promise to contend for, another breakthrough to pursue. Today, embrace this identity. Say it out loud: I am a knocker. Let that shape how you approach every closed door for the rest of your life.

Prayer:
God, I am a knocker. This is who I am now. I don't quit when doors stay closed. I don't walk away when breakthrough delays. I ask, I seek, I knock, and I keep knocking until the door opens. This is my identity. This is my lifestyle. Every closed door I face from now on, I'll approach it the same way. Persistent. Tenacious. Refusing to quit. I am a knocker. In Jesus's name, amen.

Day 31: The Door Will Open

Scripture: Matthew 7:8
For everyone who asks receives, and the one who seeks finds, and to the one who knocks it will be opened.

Reflection:
This is the promise you've been standing on for thirty-one days. Everyone who knocks will see the door open. You've asked. You've sought. You've knocked. You've navigated wilderness, weathered delay, maintained faith when circumstances didn't change. You've built endurance, embraced shameless audacity, engaged in warfare, and refused to quit. Now the promise stands: the door will open. Maybe it already has. Maybe you're seeing breakthrough right now. Or maybe you're still knocking, still waiting, still believing. Either way, the promise doesn't change. The door will open. Keep knocking until it does. And when it finally swings wide, walk through with gratitude, steward what God gives you

well, and remember: there's always another door ahead. This devotional ends, but the lifestyle of a knocker never does.

Prayer:
Father, thank You for these thirty-one days. Thank You for teaching me to ask, seek, and knock with tenacity I didn't have before. The door will open. I believe that with everything in me. If it already has, I'm grateful. If I'm still waiting, I'm not quitting. I'm a knocker now, and knockers don't walk away from closed doors. They pound until breakthrough comes. This journey doesn't end here. There will always be another door, another promise, another breakthrough to pursue. And I'll approach every single one the same way: persistent, tenacious, refusing to quit. My door will open. In Jesus's name, amen.

APPENDIX B

THE KNOCKER'S CREED

I am a knocker. This is my declaration over my life:

I believe that God is good, generous, and perfect in His timing. His character doesn't change based on my circumstances. His promises don't expire based on how long I wait. His heart toward me is always for my ultimate good, even when His methods don't match my preferences.

I refuse to accept closed doors as permanent. I will ask with specificity and faith. I will seek with diligence and wisdom. I will knock with persistence and expectation. I will not quit when breakthrough delays. I will not give up when others abandon their pursuit. I will stand knocking at the door until it opens because Jesus promised that everyone who knocks will see breakthrough.

I acknowledge that I am dependent on God for everything. My asking doesn't inform Him of needs He doesn't know. It positions me to receive what He's already prepared to give. My seeking doesn't earn His favor. It demonstrates my willingness to partner with Him in the process. My knocking doesn't manipulate Him into responding. It proves that I trust His heart enough to persist through the waiting.

I commit to living this way not just until I get one breakthrough, but for the rest of my life. I will help others become knockers by sharing my testimony, teaching these principles, and refusing to let closed doors in my life discourage others from pursuing their own breakthrough.

I am a knocker. This is who I am. And I will live with relentless faith until the day I see Jesus face to face.

APPENDIX C

Testimony Collection Template

Use this template to document your breakthroughs. Date each entry and be specific about what you asked for and how God provided. This becomes your personal record of God's faithfulness that you can reference when new doors need knocking.

Date I Started Asking: _____

What I Asked For (Be Specific):

Why This Matters to Me:

How I'm Seeking (Actions I'm Taking):

Where I'm Knocking (Doors I'm Pursuing):

Obstacles I'm Facing:

Date of Breakthrough: _____

How God Answered:

What I Learned Through the Process:

Who I Can Share This Testimony With:

STUDY GUIDE

How to Use This Study Guide

This guide is designed for individual reflection or small group discussion. Each chapter includes 3-5 questions that move from observation *(what does the chapter say?)* to interpretation *(what does it mean?)* to application *(what will I do about it?)*.
For small groups: Don't rush through these questions. Pick 2-3 that resonate most with your group and go deep rather than skimming through all of them. Create space for honest vulnerability, and hold each other accountable to keep knocking.
For individual study: Write out your answers in the Notes section at the back of this book. Be specific. Date your responses so you can track how your understanding and faith develop as you work through the book.

For Group Leaders:

Don't rush. One chapter per week allows time for reading, reflection, and implementation before discussion.

Create safety. Some questions require vulnerable honesty about doubt, unbelief, and wanting to quit. Your group needs to know it's safe to admit struggle.

Focus on transformation, not information. The goal isn't to finish the study. It's to develop knockers who refuse to walk away from closed doors.

Celebrate breakthrough. When someone in your group experiences a door opening, stop everything and celebrate. Let their testimony fuel faith for those still waiting.

Hold people accountable. If someone shares they're about to quit knocking, the group's job is to remind them why they started and refuse to let them walk away.

End each session with prayer. Pray specifically for the breakthroughs people shared. Pray for endurance. Pray for increased faith. Pray that everyone in your group becomes a knocker who outlasts delay.

Stay connected between meetings. Text check-ins, accountability partnerships, and sharing small wins throughout the week keep momentum going.

Remember: This study guide is a tool, not a script. Let the Holy Spirit lead your discussions. Skip questions that don't resonate. Add questions that your group needs. The goal is simple: develop a community of knockers who refuse to quit until the door opens.

Chapter 1:
The Anatomy of Unanswered Prayer

Question 1: Observation

The chapter identifies four main reasons prayers seem unanswered: wrong motives, divine delay, spiritual warfare, and God's better answer. Which of these four categories best describes your current experience with unanswered prayer? What specific examples from the chapter helped you identify where you are?

Question 2: Interpretation

Why do you think God allows prayers to go "unanswered" rather than immediately correcting our wrong motives or explaining His delays? What purpose might the waiting serve in developing your relationship with Him?

Question 3: Personal Application

The chapter validates the pain of unanswered prayer while providing a diagnostic framework. How does understanding the "why" behind delay change your emotional response to closed doors? Does it make you more or less likely to keep praying?

Question 4: Group Discussion

Have you ever experienced a time when God's "no" or His silence turned out to be His better answer? Share that story with your group. How did you recognize later that delay or denial was actually protection or redirection?

Question 5: Action Step

Choose one unanswered prayer you've been carrying. Using the four categories from this chapter, diagnose which reason might explain the delay. Write down what action this diagnosis requires from you. If it's wrong motives, confess and realign. If it's divine delay, commit to sustained pursuit. If it's spiritual warfare, engage. If you sense God has something better, ask Him to reveal it.

Chapter 2:
Asking and Self-Sufficiency

Question 1: Observation

The chapter identifies three barriers to asking: pride, unbelief, and false humility. Which of these three resonates most with your experience? Can you identify a specific instance where one of these barriers kept you from asking God for something you needed?

Question 2: Interpretation

James 4:2 says "You have not because you ask not." Why do you think asking is the first step in the trilogy rather than seeking or knocking? What does God accomplish in us through the act of asking that couldn't happen any other way?

Question 3: Personal Application

The chapter teaches four elements of authentic asking: specificity, consistency, expectation, and surrender. Rate yourself honestly on each of these four (1-10 scale). Which one is your weakest area? What practical step will you take this week to strengthen it?

Question 4: Theological Reflection

What does it mean to ask "in Jesus's name"? How is this different from just adding that phrase to the end of a prayer? Give an example of a request that would align with Jesus's character and one that wouldn't.

Question 5: Action Step

Write down three specific requests you're bringing to God in the Notes section at the back of this book. Make them concrete enough that you'll know when they're answered. Date this list. Commit to praying for these three things daily with expectation and surrender. Share these requests with your group or an accountability partner who will check in with you regularly.

Chapter 3:
Seeking/Faith Gets Feet

Question 1: Observation

The woman with the issue of blood is the primary example in this chapter. What specific actions did she take that moved beyond asking? How did her seeking demonstrate faith that mere words couldn't?

Question 2: Interpretation

The chapter teaches three dimensions of seeking: wisdom, opportunity, and alignment. Why do all three matter? What happens if you seek opportunity without wisdom, or pursue alignment without looking for opportunity?

Question 3: Personal Application

Think about the three specific requests you wrote down in Chapter 2. For each one, what does seeking look like? What action does your faith require? What wisdom do you need? What opportunities should you be watching for? What alignment needs to happen?

Question 4: Challenge Question

The chapter distinguishes between seeking and striving. Seeking is faith in action; striving is self-sufficiency in overdrive. How can you tell the difference in your own life? Are you seeking the breakthrough or striving to make it happen through your own strength?

Question 5: Action Step

Choose one of your three requests from Chapter 2. This week, take three concrete actions that demonstrate seeking. Ask God for wisdom about next steps. Look for one opportunity that aligns with your request. Make one move to position yourself physically, relationally, or spiritually. Report back to your group what happened when you put feet on your faith.

Chapter 4: Geography of Breakthrough

Question 1: Observation

The man at Bethesda pool waited 38 years in the same location and never experienced breakthrough until Jesus showed up. What kept him stuck? What changed when Jesus asked, "Do you want to be healed?"

Question 2: Interpretation

The chapter identifies three types of geography: physical, relational, and spiritual. Why might God require us to move to a different location (physically, relationally, or spiritually) rather than bringing breakthrough to where we already are? What does repositioning accomplish that staying put cannot?

Question 3: Personal Application

Examine your current geography in all three dimensions. Physically: Are you in the right location for breakthrough, or has God been nudging you to move? Relationally: Who are you walking with? Are they knockers or quitters? Spiritually: How close or distant are you from God's presence right now? Which geography needs the most attention?

Question 4: Group Discussion

Ruth's story demonstrates strategic repositioning. She moved to Bethlehem (physical), positioned herself in Boaz's field (relational), and maintained faithfulness to God throughout (spiritual). Share a time when repositioning opened a door that had been closed. What did that move require from you? What did it produce?

Question 5: Action Step

Based on this chapter, identify one specific way you need to reposition yourself for breakthrough. Maybe it's a physical move, a new connection you need to pursue, a toxic relationship you need to release, or a spiritual discipline you need to reestablish. Write down the repositioning God is requiring and one step you'll take this week to begin that move. Don't wait for the breakthrough to happen where you are if God is calling you somewhere else.

Chapter 5:
The Wilderness

Question 1: Observation

The Israelites turned an 11-day journey into a 40-year wilderness. What specific behaviors or attitudes prolonged their wilderness? How did their complaining, unbelief, and backward focus keep them from breakthrough?

Question 2: Interpretation

The chapter reframes wilderness as purposeful rather than punitive: "Wilderness isn't where you got lost." How does this shift in perspective change how you navigate delay? If God led you into the wilderness, what does that mean about what He's doing there?

Question 3: Personal Application

The chapter identifies five purposes God has for wilderness seasons: expose your heart, develop dependency, test motives, build endurance, and prepare your testimony. Which of these five purposes do you recognize in your current season? What is God exposing, developing, testing, or building in you right now?

Question 4: Survival Strategies

The chapter offers five survival strategies for wilderness seasons. Which one do you need most right now: celebrating what God is doing, maintaining spiritual rhythms, surrounding yourself with the right people, documenting small movements, or remembering your why? Be specific about how you'll implement this strategy this week.

Question 5: Action Step

Wilderness either makes you bitter or better. It's your choice. Write a brutally honest assessment of how you're handling your current delay. Are you complaining or worshiping? Drifting from God or drawing near? Isolating yourself or staying connected to community? Based on your assessment, identify one shift you need to make to navigate this wilderness well. Share that commitment with your group and ask them to hold you accountable.

Chapter 6:
Knocking/Crisis of Proximity

Question 1: Observation

The Canaanite woman faced rejection three times: the disciples wanted to send her away, Jesus initially didn't answer, and then He said His mission was to Israel, not her. How did she respond to each rejection? What kept her knocking when most people would have walked away?

Question 2: Interpretation

The Greek word krouo means to pound, not politely tap. Jesus told the story of the friend at midnight who knocked with "shameless audacity" until his friend gave him what he needed. Why does God respond to this kind of persistent, audacious pursuit? What does shameless audacity in prayer communicate about your faith?

Question 3: Personal Application

The chapter describes the crisis of proximity as being at the door but it's still closed. Have you experienced this? You've asked, you've sought, you've repositioned yourself, but the door remains closed. How do you typically respond to this crisis? Do you interpret the closed door as rejection, or do you recognize it as testing that requires sustained knocking?

Question 4: Theological Challenge

The chapter teaches that knocking is warfare, referencing Daniel 10:12-14 where spiritual resistance delayed the answer for 21 days. How does understanding the spiritual warfare dimension of unanswered prayer change your persistence? If the enemy is fighting to keep your door closed, what does that tell you about the breakthrough on the other side?

Question 5: Action Step

The chapter provides four principles for discernment (peace and promise, growth requirement, movement happening, counsel confirming) and five practical daily actions for knockers. Choose two of the five daily actions and commit to doing them every day this week: declare God's promises aloud, pray specifically with expectation, take one action toward breakthrough, document what you're seeing, worship before you see results. Track what happens when you move from asking to knocking.

Chapter 7:
Sound of Footsteps

Question 1: Observation

Elijah sent his servant seven times to look for the cloud. On the seventh look, the servant saw a cloud the size of a man's hand, and Elijah immediately prepared for rain. What does this story teach about recognizing signs of imminent breakthrough? Why does it matter that Elijah kept looking even when the first six times produced nothing?

Question 2: Interpretation

The chapter identifies seven signs of imminent breakthrough: increased resistance, unexpected peace, prophetic confirmation, divine appointments, strengthened faith, small movements, and clarity about next steps. Why would resistance increase right before breakthrough? What purpose does this serve in your spiritual development?

Question 3: Personal Application

Review the seven signs of imminent breakthrough. Are you currently experiencing any of these? Be specific. If you're seeing multiple signs, what does that tell you about your timing? If you're not seeing any signs yet, how should that inform your current posture (keep seeking, maintain position, increase knocking)?

Question 4: Group Discussion

The chapter includes the story of the skeptical officer in 2 Kings 7 who saw the promise but died before experiencing it because of his unbelief. Share honestly: Where are you skeptical about your breakthrough? What doubts do you need to confess and address before the door opens? How can your group help you maintain faith when circumstances haven't changed yet?

Question 5: Action Step

Based on the COVID-19 testimony in this chapter, the author experienced multiple signs before breakthrough came: unexpected peace during crisis, prophetic words, strengthened faith, and clarity about launching the ministry. Document what you're currently seeing in your pursuit using the Notes section at the back of this book. Create a "breakthrough journal" where you track resistance, peace, confirmations, appointments, faith shifts, small movements, and clarity. Review it weekly. Share patterns you notice with your group or accountability partner.

Chapter 8: Stewarding Breakthrough

Question 1: Observation

The chapter uses the Israelites entering the Promised Land and Joseph's stewardship story as examples. What did both stories teach about the responsibility that comes with breakthrough? What mistakes did the Israelites make that Joseph avoided?

Question 2: Interpretation

The first stewardship principle states: "You can't maintain breakthrough with less than what obtained it." Explain this principle in your own words. Why do people often relax immediately after breakthrough arrives? What's the danger in that?

Question 3: Personal Application

If you've experienced breakthrough recently, how are you stewarding it? Are you maintaining the prayer rhythms that accessed it? Are you staying positioned where breakthrough found you? Are you celebrating with gratitude? If you're still waiting for breakthrough, how is this chapter preparing you for what comes after the door opens?

Question 4: Responsibility and Growth

The chapter teaches that breakthrough increases responsibility and determines what comes next. How should this truth shape what you're pursuing? Are you ready for the responsibility your requested breakthrough will bring? What growth needs to happen in you before you're ready to steward it well?

Question 5: Action Step

The chapter ends with five action steps for stewardship. Even if you're still waiting for breakthrough, implement these now: Guard what God is building (protect the process), Celebrate the victory (gratitude for what He's doing), Consolidate the gain (don't move too fast to the next thing), Defend your territory (recognize the enemy will test), Help someone else (your testimony strengthens others). Choose two of these five and write out specifically how you'll implement them this week.

Chapter 9: Everyone Promise

Question 1: Observation

The chapter includes five testimonies: Sarah (single mom, financial breakthrough in 3 months), Marcus (unemployed 50-something, breakthrough in 6 months), Jennifer (mental health healing), Carlos (addiction recovery), and Linda (12 years barren, now has 3 children). What do all five stories have in common? What made these ordinary believers different from those who quit before breakthrough?

Question 2: Interpretation

The emphasis throughout this chapter is that breakthrough is for EVERYONE who knocks, not just spiritual elites. Why do we disqualify ourselves from this promise? What lies do we believe about who deserves breakthrough and who doesn't? How does 1 Corinthians 1:26-29 address this?

Question 3: Personal Application - Comparison Trap

The chapter addresses the comparison trap that makes us measure our progress against others' timelines. Are you currently stuck in comparison? Whose breakthrough are you watching with envy instead of celebration? How is comparison stealing your faith for your own breakthrough? What needs to shift?

Question 4: Personal Application - Self-Disqualification

Be brutally honest: Have you disqualified yourself from breakthrough? Do you believe God's promises apply to everyone except you? What's the root of that belief? Is it past failure, unworthiness, feeling ordinary, or something else? What truth from Scripture contradicts the lie you've been believing?

Question 5: Action Step

The chapter calls you to embrace your place in the "everyone promise." Write out Matthew 7:8 in your own handwriting in the Notes section at the back of this book. Circle the word "everyone." Write your name next to it. Declare out loud: "I am part of everyone. Breakthrough is for me." Now write down three reasons you've been disqualifying yourself. After each one, write the truth from Scripture that contradicts it. Share this exercise with your group and let them speak life over the lies you've been believing.

Chapter 10:
Father's Heart

Question 1: Observation

The chapter opens with "Your theology determines your tenacity" and then dismantles three distortions of God's character: reluctant giver, arbitrary ruler, harsh taskmaster. Which of these three distortions have you believed about God? How has this distortion affected your persistence in prayer?

Question 2: Interpretation

The parable of the prodigal son reveals a father who was watching for his son's return, ran to meet him, and celebrated his homecoming. How does this picture of God challenge your current view of how He responds to your requests? What does it mean that the father ran toward the son rather than waiting for the son to prove himself first?

Question 3: Theological Depth

The chapter builds three truths about God's character: He is good, He is generous, and He is perfect in His timing. Choose one of these three and defend it using specific Scripture. How does this truth reshape your prayers? How does it increase your tenacity when doors stay closed longer than expected?

Question 4: Personal Application

Romans 8:32 says, "He who did not spare his own Son but gave him up for us all, how will he not also with him graciously give us all things?" If God already gave you His best (Jesus), why would He withhold anything else that's good for you? How does this logic dismantle the lie that God is reluctant to give you breakthrough?

Question 5: Action Step

The chapter provides four practical disciplines to embed right theology: meditate on God's goodness, rehearse His faithfulness, study His promises, worship before you see results. Choose one discipline and commit to practicing it daily for the next week. For example, if you choose "rehearse His faithfulness," write down ten times God has provided, protected, or come through for you in the past. Read this list every morning before you pray for current breakthrough. Report to your group how this discipline affects your faith and persistence.

Chapter 11:
Life of the Knocker

Question 1: Observation

This chapter shifts from getting breakthrough to living as a knocker. What's the difference? Why does the book end with identity and lifestyle rather than just technique for opening doors?

Question 2: Interpretation

The chapter teaches five sustainability principles: build rhythms not regimens, celebrate progress not perfection, remember your why, surround yourself with knockers, and pass it on. Which principle addresses the biggest danger to long-term tenacity? Why do so many believers burn out after initial breakthrough?

Question 3: Personal Application - Identity

The chapter includes a spoken declaration: "I am a knocker." Say it out loud right now. How does it feel? Does claiming this identity feel presumptuous or empowering? What would change in your daily life if you truly embraced this as your core identity?

Question 4: Lifestyle Shift

The chapter describes what daily life looks like for a knocker: maintaining spiritual disciplines, acting on faith, worshiping before breakthrough, pursuing wisdom, and staying connected to community. Assess your current lifestyle. Which of these five elements is strongest? Which is weakest? What specific adjustment will you make this week?

Question 5: Action Step - Commissioning

The chapter ends with a commissioning tone, sending you out to live as a knocker. Write out your personal commissioning statement in the Notes section at the back of this book. Include: (1) What breakthrough you're currently pursuing, (2) How long you've been knocking, (3) Why you refuse to quit, (4) What you'll do when the door opens, (5) Who you'll help with your testimony. Share this statement with your group. Let them speak commissioning prayers over you. Then display your statement somewhere you'll see it daily as a reminder of your knocker identity and the breakthrough you're pursuing.

Final Reflection Questions
(For Completing the Entire Book)

Question 1: Transformation Assessment

You finished the book. How are you different now than when you started? Be specific about shifts in your theology, your prayer life, your actions, and your faith. What breakthrough has happened during your reading? What doors are you still knocking on?

Question 2: The Trilogy in Practice

You now understand the progression: ask, seek, knock. Where are you currently in this trilogy for each of your three specific requests from Chapter 2? Have any moved from asking to seeking? From seeking to knocking? Is there one you've been avoiding because moving to the next level requires more than you're ready to give?

Question 3: Your Wilderness

If you're currently in a wilderness season, how has this book reframed what God is doing? Can you now identify the purposes He has for this delay? How will you navigate the rest of this wilderness differently because of what you've learned?

Question 4: Knocker Community

Who are you walking with? Do you have knockers around you who refuse to let you quit? If yes, how can you strengthen that community? If no, what will you do this week to find or create it? Remember: you can't sustain this lifestyle alone.

Question 5: Passing It On

Your breakthrough, when it comes, isn't just for you. Who needs to hear your story? Who's standing at a closed door right now, wondering if they should quit? How will you use your testimony to strengthen their faith? Write down three names of people you'll share this message with once your door opens.

SCRIPTURE INDEX

THIS INDEX LISTS THE Scripture references used throughout *The Knock*, organized in biblical order from Genesis to Revelation. Each entry includes a brief note about how the passage is applied in the book.

The central text of this book is Matthew 7:7-8, which appears in every chapter and forms the foundation for the trilogy of tenacity: asking, seeking, and knocking. All other Scriptures support, illustrate, or expand on this core teaching about persistent pursuit of breakthrough.

How to Use This Scripture Index

This index serves multiple purposes for readers of *The Knock*. First, it allows you to quickly locate where specific Bible passages are discussed within the book, which is helpful when you want to revisit a particular teaching or return to a story that impacted you during your first reading.

Second, this index functions as a study tool for small groups or individuals who want to dig deeper into the biblical foundation of the trilogy of tenacity. You can take any Scripture listed here and study its full context in your Bible, then compare that with how it's applied in the book. This deepens your understanding of both the biblical text and the principles of asking, seeking, and knocking.

Third, this index makes it easy to find Scriptures for specific situations you're facing. If you're in a wilderness season and need encouragement, look up the passages from Chapter 5. If you're learning to steward a recent breakthrough, review the texts from Chapter 8. If you're struggling with wrong beliefs about God's character, study the passages from Chapter 10.

Finally, this index is designed to help you continue growing as a knocker long after you finish reading the book. The Scriptures listed here aren't just supporting texts for a message; they're the Word of God that will continue speaking to you in every season of pursuit. Return to this index regularly, meditate on these passages, and let them fuel your faith as you knock on doors that haven't opened yet.

Old Testament

Genesis 32:22-32 (Jacob wrestling with God) – Referenced in Chapter 6 to illustrate the kind of tenacious, refusing-to-let-go pursuit that characterizes true knocking. Jacob's wrestle demonstrates that God honors those who won't quit until they receive what He promised.

Deuteronomy 8:2 (God led you in the wilderness to humble and test you) – Central text in Chapter 5 for understanding the purposes of wilderness seasons. Used to reframe delay as purposeful rather than punitive, showing that wilderness isn't where you got lost but where God is doing something you can't yet see.

Deuteronomy 8:3 (Man does not live by bread alone) – Applied in Chapter 5 to explain how wilderness develops dependency on God. Illustrates why God sometimes lets us hunger so we learn to rely on His daily provision rather than our own sufficiency.

Ruth 2:3 (She happened to come to the part of the field belonging to Boaz) – Used in Chapter 4 to demonstrate physical geography and strategic positioning.

SCRIPTURE INDEX

Ruth's story shows how breakthrough often requires physical movement to a location where God has prepared opportunity.

Ruth 2-4 (Ruth's full story of gleaning and redemption) – Extended example in Chapter 4 of how all three geographies work together. Ruth repositioned physically by moving to Bethlehem, relationally by connecting with Boaz, and spiritually by maintaining faithfulness to God throughout.

1 Kings 18:41-46 (Elijah and the small cloud) – Primary story in Chapter 7 for recognizing the sound of footsteps before breakthrough arrives. Elijah sent his servant seven times to look for the cloud, illustrating persistence in watching for signs and refusing to quit before breakthrough manifests.

2 Kings 7:1-20 (Siege of Samaria and the skeptical officer) – Used in Chapter 7 to warn against unbelief that can cause you to see the promise but die before experiencing it. The officer's skepticism cost him his breakthrough even though deliverance came exactly as prophesied.

Psalm 37:4 (Delight yourself in the Lord) – Applied in Chapter 3 within the context of seeking alignment. Teaches that when your heart aligns with God's heart through delighting in Him, the desires you pursue become the desires He wants to give.

Psalm 84:11 (No good thing will He withhold from those who walk uprightly) – Referenced in Chapter 10 to establish God's generous character. Used to dismantle the lie that God is reluctant to give breakthrough to His children.

Psalm 139:23-24 (Search me, O God, and know my heart) – Applied in Chapter 3 as a prayer for seeking wisdom and examining motives. Encourages readers to invite God to reveal what needs to change before breakthrough can come.

Proverbs 13:20 (Walk with the wise and become wise) – Used in Chapter 4 to explain relational geography. Emphasizes that who you're connected to determines which doors you can access and whether your faith strengthens or weakens during the wait.

Isaiah 53:5 (By His stripes we are healed) – Referenced in Chapter 2 when teaching about asking with confidence based on what Christ accomplished. Used alongside 1 Peter 2:24 to establish biblical foundation for healing prayers.

Lamentations 3:22-23 (His mercies are new every morning) – Applied in Chapter 5 as a survival strategy for wilderness seasons. Teaches that celebrating God's daily faithfulness keeps your heart soft during prolonged delay.

Daniel 10:12-14 (Your words were heard from the first day, but the prince of Persia resisted) – Critical passage used in Chapters 1 and 6 to explain spiritual warfare as a reason for delayed answers. Daniel's experience proves that prayer can be heard immediately but delayed by spiritual resistance, which requires sustained knocking to break through.

New Testament

Matthew 6:8 (Your Father knows what you need before you ask) – Referenced in Chapter 2 to address the question of why we need to ask if God already knows. Explains that asking isn't about informing God but about aligning our hearts with His provision.

Matthew 7:7-8 (Ask, and it will be given to you; seek, and you will find; knock, and it will be opened to you. For everyone who asks receives...) – THE CENTRAL TEXT of the entire book. Appears in every chapter as the foundation for the trilogy of tenacity. This verse establishes the progression from asking to seeking to knocking and contains the promise that everyone who goes through the full progression will experience breakthrough.

Matthew 7:9-11 (What father would give his son a stone when he asks for bread?) – Primary text in Chapter 10 for revealing the Father's heart. Jesus uses this comparison to show that God is a better father than any earthly father, eager to give good gifts to His children.

Matthew 11:12 (The kingdom of heaven suffers violence, and the violent take it by force) – Referenced in Chapter 2 to establish that breakthrough requires aggressive faith, not passive hoping. Used to challenge believers to pursue God's promises with holy intensity.

Matthew 15:21-28 (The Canaanite woman's persistent pursuit) – Central story in Chapter 6 illustrating the crisis of proximity and shameless audacity. Despite three forms of rejection, she kept knocking until Jesus commended her faith and granted her request. Primary example of what knocking looks like in practice.

Matthew 25:14-30 (Parable of the talents) – Applied in Chapter 8 to teach stewardship principles. The master's response to his servants illustrates that faithfulness in stewarding what you're given determines what you're trusted with next.

Mark 5:25-34 (Woman with the issue of blood) – Major story in Chapter 3 demonstrating how faith gets feet. She didn't just pray for healing; she pressed through the crowd to touch Jesus's garment. Primary example of seeking in action.

Mark 10:46-52 (Blind Bartimaeus crying out to Jesus) – Referenced in Chapter 6 as an example of refusing to be silenced when pursuing breakthrough. Despite the crowd telling him to be quiet, he cried out louder until Jesus responded.

Mark 10:51 (What do you want me to do for you?) – Used in Chapter 2 to teach specificity in asking. Jesus knew Bartimaeus was blind but still asked him to articulate his need, showing that God wants us to be specific in our requests.

Mark 11:22-24 (Have faith in God... whatever you ask in prayer, believe that you have received it) – Applied in Chapter 2 when teaching about asking with expectation. Faith requires believing you have received before you see the manifestation.

Luke 11:5-10 (Friend at midnight parable) – Major teaching text in Chapter 6 for understanding shameless audacity. The man knocked persistently at an inconvenient hour until his friend gave him what he needed, illustrating the kind of bold, relentless pursuit that moves God.

Luke 11:8 (Because of his impudence/shameless audacity he will give him what he needs) – Key verse in Chapter 6 defining the Greek word for shameless audacity and applying it to how believers should approach God with their requests.

Luke 15:11-32 (Prodigal son and the father's response) – Primary parable in Chapter 10 for revealing God's heart toward His children. The father running to meet the returning son dismantles the lie that God is reluctant, arbitrary, or harsh.

Luke 16:10 (Faithful in little, faithful in much) – Applied in Chapter 8 to teach that how you steward small breakthroughs determines whether God trusts you with larger ones.

Luke 18:1 (Men ought always to pray and not lose heart) – Referenced throughout the book, particularly in Chapter 6, to establish that Jesus specifically taught persistence in prayer. The context is the persistent widow parable.

Luke 18:1-8 (Persistent widow) – Used in Chapter 6 alongside other persistence parables to show that Jesus repeatedly taught His disciples not to give up in prayer.

The unjust judge eventually responded to persistence; how much more will a loving Father respond?

Luke 22:42 (Not my will, but yours, be done) – Applied in Chapter 2 to teach surrender within asking. Jesus modeled how to ask specifically while remaining surrendered to the Father's better plan.

John 5:1-15 (Man at Bethesda pool for 38 years) – Central story in Chapter 4 illustrating the geography of breakthrough. The man waited 38 years in the same location and never experienced healing until Jesus showed up and asked, "Do you want to be healed?" Demonstrates that sometimes breakthrough requires repositioning.

John 14:13-14 (Whatever you ask in My name, I will do it) – Key text in Chapter 2 for teaching what it means to ask in Jesus's name. Explains that this isn't a magic formula but asking according to His character, will, and authority.

John 16:24 (Ask, and you will receive, that your joy may be full) – Referenced in Chapter 2 to establish that God wants to answer prayer so that believers experience complete joy.

Romans 4:18-21 (Abraham's faith against hope) – Used in Chapter 2 as an example of asking with expectation even when circumstances contradict the promise. Abraham believed God's word over physical impossibility.

Romans 8:28 (All things work together for good) – Applied in Chapter 10 when teaching about God's perfect timing. Even delays and disappointments are working toward your ultimate good when you trust His heart.

Romans 8:32 (He who did not spare His own Son, how will He not also give us all things?) – Critical verse in Chapter 10 for dismantling the lie that God is reluctant to give. If He already gave His best, why would He withhold anything else that's good for you?

1 Corinthians 1:26-29 (God chooses the foolish and weak things) – Used in Chapter 9 to establish that breakthrough is for ordinary believers, not just spiritual elites. God intentionally chooses those the world overlooks to prove that power comes from Him, not from human ability.

2 Corinthians 1:4 (God comforts us so we may comfort others) – Applied in Chapter 5 when teaching that wilderness prepares your testimony. Your breakthrough isn't just for you; it's for everyone who will need your story when they want to quit.

2 Corinthians 12:7-10 (Paul's thorn in the flesh, grace is sufficient) – Referenced in Chapter 1 as an example of when God's answer is different than our request. Sometimes God's "no" to our specific request is because He has something better, like demonstrating His strength through our weakness.

Galatians 6:9 (Do not grow weary in doing good, for in due season you will reap) – Applied in Chapter 7 to encourage endurance when breakthrough delays. The harvest is coming; you just can't quit before due season arrives.

Ephesians 2:8-9 (Saved by grace through faith, not of works) – Referenced in Chapter 3 to clarify that seeking isn't about earning breakthrough through works but about faith expressing itself through action.

Ephesians 3:20 (God is able to do exceedingly abundantly above all we ask or think) – Used in Chapter 10 to establish God's generous character. He doesn't just meet your needs minimally; He exceeds your expectations.

Philippians 4:6 (Be anxious for nothing, but in everything by prayer) – Applied in Chapter 2 as the proper response to need. Rather than anxiety, God invites specific, faith-filled asking.

Philippians 4:19 (My God shall supply all your needs according to His riches) – Referenced in Chapter 2 to build confidence in asking. God's resources are unlimited, so you can ask boldly without fear that you're depleting His supply.

Colossians 4:3 (Pray that God may open a door for the word) – Used in Chapter 3 when teaching about seeking opportunity. Even Paul asked others to pray for doors to open, showing that watching for and walking through divine opportunities is part of the seeking process.

Hebrews 4:16 (Come boldly to the throne of grace) – Applied in Chapter 2 to establish that believers have permission to approach God with confidence, not timidity. Also used in devotional to teach spiritual geography and positioning yourself in God's presence.

Hebrews 10:35-36 (Do not throw away your confidence, for you have need of endurance) – Key verse in Chapter 7 for sustaining faith when breakthrough delays longer than expected. Endurance is required to outlast the wait and receive what's promised.

Hebrews 11:6 (Without faith it is impossible to please God, for he who comes must believe that He exists and that He rewards those who diligently seek Him) – Referenced in Chapters 2 and 11 to establish that faith, not passive hoping, is what moves God. He rewards those who diligently seek Him, which requires action and persistence.

James 1:2-4 (Count it all joy when you face trials, for the testing of your faith produces steadfastness) – Applied in Chapter 5 to reframe wilderness as purposeful. The testing isn't punishment; it's producing endurance that makes you complete and lacking nothing.

James 1:5 (If any lacks wisdom, let him ask God, who gives generously) – Primary text in Chapter 3 for the first dimension of seeking. God gives wisdom generously to all who ask, providing divine insight about how to navigate toward breakthrough.

James 2:17 (Faith without works is dead) – Central verse in Chapter 3 establishing that faith gets feet. Asking is important, but real faith always produces corresponding action. This is the theological foundation for moving from asking to seeking.

James 4:2-3 (You have not because you ask not, and when you ask, you ask with wrong motives) – Key text in Chapters 1 and 2. Establishes both that failure to ask prevents receiving and that wrong motives can block answers. Used diagnostically to help readers examine why prayers seem unanswered.

1 Peter 2:24 (By His stripes you were healed) – Used alongside Isaiah 53:5 in Chapter 2 to establish the finished work of Christ as foundation for confident asking.

NOTES

NOTES

NOTES

NOTES

THE KNOCK

NOTES

NOTES

NOTES

ABOUT THE AUTHOR

Apostle Dr. Ivon L. Valerie knows what it's like to stand at a closed door wondering if God hears you. Born in St. Joseph, Dominica, and now based in Sint Maarten, D.W.I, Ivon has spent more than two decades walking with believers through their darkest wilderness seasons and celebrating with them when breakthrough finally comes.

The message in this book didn't come from a classroom or a commentary. It came from lived experience. In 2002, Ivon left Dominica for Sint Maarten with only one US dollar in his pocket. Life was hard in those early years. Building from nothing and navigating challenges that tested everything he believed about God's faithfulness. That terrifying leap into the unknown, trusting God to make a way when circumstances looked impossible, that was Ivon learning to knock long before he had this revelation of what God was doing. God opened doors during that season that he couldn't have opened himself. It taught him early that breakthrough often requires stepping into uncertainty with nothing but faith and refusing to quit when life gets hard.

But the knocking didn't stop there. Over two decades of ministry, Ivon has faced setbacks, closed doors, financial pressure, relational strain, and seasons where what he was believing for seemed impossible. The 18-month wilderness during COVID-19, when he nearly walked away from everything he believed, became the crucible where all those previous lessons crystallized into the revelation you're reading in this book. During that particular season, when his own prayers seemed unanswered and every door stayed closed, God gave him the breakthrough understanding of Matthew 7:7-8 that became the foundation for this message. What you're reading isn't theory from someone who's had an easy journey. It's tested truth from someone who's knocked through multiple wildernesses and seen the door open every time he refused to quit.

Ivon is the co-founder and lead pastor of Faith & Works Ministries, which he launched with his wife Jeanetta in 2021, right in the middle of a global pandemic when starting anything seemed insane. That act of faith, stepping through a door that had been closed for more than 18 months, became the beginning of everything God had been preparing during the wait. Today, Faith & Works Ministries serves as a living testimony that the door really does open for those who refuse to quit knocking.

As a Bible teacher with degrees from Grace Hill Bible College, Dominion Bible Institute, and Valor Christian College, Ivon brings theological depth to the subject of breakthrough. But his real credibility comes from the hundreds of believers he's walked with through their own wilderness seasons as a certified life coach specializing in two critical areas: parenting teens and Christian mental health. His work in trauma healing has equipped him to help people navigate the deep pain that often accompanies prolonged delay, giving him unique insight into what happens in the human heart when breakthrough takes longer than expected.

Ivon is the author of multiple books, including the three-volume *Trauma Detox* series, *The Meaningful Life: Discovering God's Purpose for You*, *Commanding My Morning*, *Prayer Lifestyle*, and his most recent release, *The Unknown: What You Need to Know But Don't*. His writings consistently blend biblical wisdom with practical application, giving readers tools they can use immediately.

What sets Ivon apart is his gift for building faith in others. Whether teaching at conferences, speaking at churches, or coaching through crisis, his niche is helping believers develop the kind of tenacious faith that outlasts closed doors. He flows strongly in the grace and office of a teacher, with a unique ability to make complex theological concepts accessible and actionable. If you've ever felt like your faith

ABOUT THE AUTHOR

was too weak to sustain you through the wait, Ivon's teaching will strengthen what you thought was broken.

Ivon travels extensively as a guest preacher and conference speaker, focusing on two primary areas: trauma healing for those who've experienced deep wounding, and edifying the body of Christ through practical teaching that builds mature, resilient believers. His speaking is biblically grounded, practically applicable, and specifically designed to produce transformation. He and Jeanetta are the proud parents of two daughters, Rebecca and Ariella, who are learning what it means to grow up in a family of knockers.

If you're reading this book, you're standing at a door that hasn't opened yet. Maybe you've been there for months. Maybe years. Maybe you picked up this book because you're one prayer away from walking away, and something told you to give it one more try. Ivon wrote this for you. Not as someone who has all the answers, but as someone who's knocked through multiple wildernesses, faced setbacks that should have destroyed him, and watched God open doors every single time he refused to quit.

The principles in this book work because Ivon proved them over more than two decades of trusting God through impossible circumstances. From arriving in a foreign country with one dollar to launching a ministry during a pandemic, from personal setbacks to prolonged delays, he's lived the trilogy of tenacity in real time. The congregation of Faith & Works Ministries has tested these principles alongside him. And if they worked for a young man with nothing but a dollar and a dream, and later for that same man standing in an 18-month wilderness wondering if God had forgotten him, they'll work for you.

You're not reading the words of someone who's never struggled. You're reading the testimony of a knocker who's faced multiple closed doors, refused to quit at any of them, and came back to show you how to do the same.

Keep knocking. The door will open.

Connect with Apostle Dr. Ivon L. Valerie: For speaking engagements or ministry inquiries, visit ivonvalerie.com or contact Faith & Works Ministries in Sint Maarten, DWI.

www.ingramcontent.com/pod-product-compliance
Lightning Source LLC
Chambersburg PA
CBHW070634160426
43194CB00009B/1459